'or'

Crossing the Curriculum
Multilingual Learners in College Classrooms

D1642800

Crossing the Curriculum
Multilingual Learners in College Classrooms

Edited by

Vivian Zamel
University of Massachusetts Boston

Ruth Spack
Bentley College

IEA

2004

LAWRENCE ERLBAUM ASSOCIATES, PUBLISHERS

Mahwah, New Jersey   London

Lawrence Erlbaum Associates, Inc., Publishers
10 Industrial Avenue
Mahwah, New Jersey 07430

Cover design by Kathryn Houghtaling Lacey

Library of Congress Cataloging-in-Publication Data

Crossing the curriculum : Multilingual learners in college
    classrooms / edited by Vivian Zamel, Ruth Spack.
        p. cm.
    Includes bibliographical references and index.
ISBN 0-8058-4691-3 (cloth : alk. paper)
ISBN 0-8058-4692-1 (pbk. : alk. paper)
    1. English language—Study and teaching—Foreign
    speakers. 2. Interdisciplinary approach in education. 3.
    Multicultural education.   I. Zamel, Vivian.   II.
    Spack, Ruth.

PE1128.A2C7442003
428'.0071—dc21   2003054730
                                                 CIP

Books published by Lawrence Erlbaum Associates are
printed on acid-free paper, and their bindings are chosen for
strength and durability.

Printed in the United States of America
10 9 8 7 6 5 4 3 2

Contents

    and Writing About Literature
    Rajini Srikanth

12 "Still Cannot Solve It": Engaging ESOL Students   197
    in the Classroom Conversation
    Estelle Disch

13 Voicing Names and Naming Voices: 207
    Pedagogy and Persistence in an Asian American
    Studies Classroom
    Peter Nien-chu Kiang

    About the Contributors   221

    Author Index   223

    Subject Index   227

Preface

As college classrooms have become more linguistically diverse, our work as professionals in the field of English for Speakers of Other Languages (ESOL) has expanded. This work now involves research on the experiences of multilingual learners not only in ESOL courses but also in courses across the curriculum. It now includes faculty development not only for ESOL instructors but also for teachers in a wide variety of fields. ESOL professionals, for their part, are trying to understand the academic challenges that learners will face beyond ESOL courses. At the same time, faculty in writing programs and in the other disciplines are trying to meet the challenges presented by the growing number of undergraduate learners of differing linguistic backgrounds. The goal of *Crossing the Curriculum: Multilingual Learners in College Classrooms* is to respond to these issues and concerns.

Crossing the Curriculum explores teachers' and multilingual students' experiences in a variety of undergraduate college courses and examines these experiences over time. Capturing the complex and content-specific nature of students' and teachers' struggles and accomplishments, this volume provides a nuanced understanding of the challenges of teaching multilingual learners. It thus makes a significant contribution to the literature on teaching ESOL students in academic settings as well as to the literature on learning across the curriculum. In bringing together the perspectives of researchers, students, and faculty, *Crossing the Curriculum* presents a unique and richly layered picture of how students and teachers actually experience college classrooms.

- Part I, "Investigating Students' Experiences Across the Curriculum: Through the Eyes of the Classroom Researchers," consists of chapters written by ESOL and composition researchers who have investigated multilingual students' experiences in undergraduate courses across the curriculum.

- Part II, "Learning Across the Curriculum: Through Students' Eyes," consists of chapters written by two multilingual learners who chronicled their experiences as they crossed the curriculum over time.
- Part III, "Engaging Students in Learning: Through the Eyes of Faculty Across the Curriculum," consists of chapters written by faculty from several academic fields—Anthropology, Philosophy, Nursing, Literature, Sociology, and Asian American Studies— who discuss their own attempts to address the needs of multilingual learners in their classrooms.

Whereas each section is informed by the particular perspective of researcher, student, or teacher, it is important to note that common themes and pedagogical principles resonate across the three parts of the book and across disciplines. The discoveries, insights, and implications discussed by the different authors echo one another in critical ways and reveal a shared understanding of how multilingual students' learning can be fostered and sustained.

Multilingual learners share in common the experience of undertaking academic work in a second or additional language. However, these students are remarkably diverse, bringing with them a multiplicity of specific experiences that influence how they manage the work assigned in each of their classes. Of course, there are multilingual students who, precisely because of their translingual and transcultural resources, perform as well as or better than students who know only English. But the concern of this book is with those students who face difficulties stemming from the challenge of having to negotiate new literacy practices and social identities—and having to do this in a language they are still in the process of acquiring. Inevitably, students who have had limited academic experiences in their first language will have difficulty when they take on this kind of work in English. Even learners who have successfully completed courses in their first language may find the transition to doing this work in English disorienting. Students who have studied in educational contexts whose values and expectations are in conflict with those of U.S. college classrooms will struggle, and may even resist, as they attempt to make sense of unfamiliar approaches to academic study. Depending on their individual abilities and strengths, students may bring greater facility to writing than to speaking or, conversely, demonstrate a competence in speaking that is in sharp contrast with what they produce in writing. Furthermore, the nature of second language acquisition is such that they may continue to produce error even if they have extensively studied the English language. This range of factors, though hardly comprehensive, helps to explain why students perform as they do.

Given the complex nature of what students bring to the academy and what they are expected to do, faculty need to consider unexamined assumptions they may hold about students' abilities. As *Crossing the Curriculum* demonstrates, even if students' initial college experiences are marked by fear, frustration, or failure, students can achieve success and make significant contributions to the classroom. Furthermore, even when second language features persist, students can express ideas in thoughtful and sophisticated ways. Thus it is crucial to resist making easy predictions about students' potential and to be wary of conflating linguistic proficiency with intellectual ability. Instead, we should examine students' progress in actual courses, and over extended periods of time.

The researchers, students, and teachers who contributed chapters to this book examine and reflect on the teaching and learning of multilingual students over time in context-specific and in-depth ways, thus making it possible to appreciate these experiences in their full complexity. These authors detail what can happen when faculty adopt pedagogical approaches that promote the learning of multilingual students—without compromising faculty standards and expectations. Indeed, in some cases, these students actually drive the standards and expectations higher. The chapters compellingly demonstrate that when faculty create opportunities for learners to engage meaningfully in coursework, to draw on their own resources and knowledge, and to take risks with unfamiliar material and tasks, students are able to take on intellectually challenging work, achieve academically, and, important to note, continue to acquire language. Writing in particular, these chapters reveal, can enable such engagement, achievement, and language acquisition. But, as the authors make clear, this progress is not an even or straightforward process. Learning and language acquisition are contingent and ongoing, evolving (and sometimes regressing) in response to the nature of circumstances students face. Given the long-term and complicated nature of this process, it is clear that ESOL faculty cannot be expected to prepare students to undertake successfully all of the work they will be expected to do in their college courses. Because each classroom may be experienced by the learner as a new culture—with its own specific terms, conventions, and approaches to inquiry—the responsibility for the academic progress of multilingual learners needs to be shared by all faculty.

At the same time that we see fostering progress as a shared responsibility, we recognize that this is not an uncomplicated endeavor. Just as is true for student learning, teaching multilingual students is not an even or straightforward process. In fact, many faculty—as is evident in Part III—experience their own disorientation as their interactions with multilingual learners raise new issues and concerns. However, as the accounts in this book reveal, these challenges create opportunities for faculty to engage in a transformative process as they reconceptualize their teaching—much as they create opportunities for students to engage in their own transformative process as they reconceptualize their learning. Most important, when teachers examine and reflect on their teaching, crossing their own curriculum to make such conceptual and pedagogical change possible, they enhance the learning not only of multilingual learners but of all students in the classroom.

Acknowledgments

We deeply appreciate the work of the researchers, students, and teachers who contributed chapters to this book: Kristine Alster, Estelle Disch, Steve Fishman, Ellie Kutz, Motoko Kainose, Peter Kiang, Lucille McCarthy, Martha Muñoz, Tim Sieber, Trudy Smoke, Rajini Srikanth, and Marilyn Sternglass. Our multiple communications about their chapters, from inception to revision, enriched our understanding of the issues that challenge us all. Their ideas have also caused us to reflect more deeply on our own teaching. In short, the process of editing this book has been an exciting and transformative experience for us.

We are grateful to Hân Nguyen, whose work has been exhibited widely in California, for allowing us to reproduce the photograph that appears on the cover of the book.

We express our gratitude to the people who played a critical role in the production of this book. Our editor, Naomi Silverman, gave us ongoing encouragement and wise advice. Lori Hawver and Sara Scudder skillfully guided us through the various stages of production and editing. Our reviewers, Linda Lonon Blanton and Judith Rodby, provided thoughtful feedback that helped us strengthen the book. Cheryl Rendel and Diane Ridgley of Bentley College provided significant assistance in the preparation of the manuscript.

I

Investigating Students' Experiences Across the Curriculum: Through the Eyes of Classroom Researchers

The chapters in Part I are written by ESOL and composition researchers who have investigated multilingual students' experiences in undergraduate courses across the curriculum. These authors examine various ways individual students struggled but eventually achieved success in the process of acquiring multiple academic literacies. Together, these studies reveal that the acquisition of language and literacy is a long-term, evolving process. They demonstrate that language is situated in particular contexts and acquired while exploring and engaging with the subject matter within these contexts. They also show that students' achievements in college courses depend on the complex interplay between students' abilities and backgrounds and the expectations and tasks of specific courses. These investigations make clear that ESOL and composition courses cannot prepare students for all the discipline-specific demands they will face. Faculty across college courses inevitably play a crucial role in students' ongoing acquisition as learners, readers, writers, and language users.

Chapter 1

Strangers in Academia: The Experiences of Faculty and ESOL Students Across the Curriculum

Vivian Zamel

Noting that many faculty focus on multilingual students' linguistic errors rather than on their academic potential, conflating language use with intellectual ability, Vivian Zamel emphasizes that the process of language acquisition is slow-paced and that it continues to evolve with exposure, immersion, and engagement. Thus the promotion of language acquisition needs to be a shared responsibility across the curriculum. Vivian encourages ESOL and all other faculty to collaborate in order to discover ways to enhance the learning of all students.

When I go into a classroom these days, I look around and feel like I'm in a different country.

—*Professor of Management*

A few weeks ago a professor came by the reading, writing and study skills center where I tutor. He was with a young Asian woman, obviously one of his students. He "deposited" her in the center, claiming that she desperately needed help with her English. The woman stared into the distance with a frightened, nervous look on her face and tried to force a smile. She handed me a paper she had written on the labor union and asked if I could help her make corrections. After a short introductory discussion, we looked at the paper that we were about to revise—it was filled with red marks indicating spelling, punctuation and grammar errors; the only written response was something along the lines of "You need serious help with your English. Please see a tutor."

—A Tutor

Students in the lab speak to one another in their own language so that they make sure they know what they are doing. So they may look like they are not listening to the lab teacher. He feels so isolated from them. He feels he has no control, no power. So he may get angry.

—An ESOL Student

These comments show evidence of tensions and conflicts that are becoming prevalent in institutions of higher education as student populations become more diverse. In 1977, Mina Shaughnessy referred to the students who entered the City University of New York system through open admissions as "strangers in academia" to give us a sense of the cultural and linguistic alienation they were experiencing. In listening to the comments of faculty (note, e.g., the comment of the professor of management), it occurs to me that they too are feeling like "strangers in academia," that they no longer understand the world in which they work. Neuleib (1992) similarly points out that although it is common to view students as "other," as alienated from the academic community, our differing cultural perspectives result in our own confusion and alienation.

One clear indication that faculty across the disciplines are concerned about the extent to which diverse student populations, particularly students whose native language is not English, constrain their work is the number of workshops and seminars that have been organized, and at which I have participated, in order to address what these faculty view as the "ESL Problem."[1] In the course of preparing to work with faculty, and in order to get a sense of their issues and concerns, I surveyed faculty across the curriculum about their experiences working with non-native speakers of English. Some faculty saw this invitation to provide feedback as an opportunity to discuss the strengths and resources these students brought with them. They indicated that ESOL students, because of their experience and motivation, were a positive presence, and noted the contributions these students made in discussions that invited cross-cultural perspectives. One professor took issue with the very idea of making generalizations about ESOL students. But this pattern of response did not represent the attitudes and perspectives revealed by other faculty responses. One professor, for example, referred to both silent students, on the one hand, and "vocal but incomprehensible students" on the other. But, by far, the greatest concern had to do with students' writing and language, which faculty saw as deficient and inadequate for undertaking the work in their courses. I got the clear sense from these responses that language use was confounded with intellectual ability, that, as Villanueva (1993), re-

BOOK ORDER

YORK ST JOHN UNIVERSITY 104950.00

Supplier	Dawson Books (UK)	Order R	
Order Date	05/06/2009	Item Re	
Quantity	1	ISBN	
Unit Price	22.99	Currency	
Instructions	*428.0071 ZAM*		

Author
Title   CROSSING THE CURRICULUM : MULTILINGUAL
                EDITED BY VIVIAN ZAMEL, RUTH SPACK.

Volume   Edition
Format   Publish
Shelf Mark   428.0071 ZAM
Site   YORKSJ
Fund   BB 5
Sequence   SHELVES-SJ
Loan Type   NORMAL
Quantity   1

-001

f

PO-39236
PO-39236/1
9780805846928
GRP

EARNERS IN COLLEGE CLASSROOMS/

r MAHWAH, N.J. , LONDON , LAWRENC

counting his schooling experiences, put it, "bad language" and "insufficient cognitive development" were being conflated (p. 11).

In order to demonstrate the range of faculty commentary, I've selected two faculty responses, not because they are necessarily representative, but because they reveal such divergent views on language, language development, and the role that faculty see themselves as playing in this development. I've also chosen these responses because they may serve as mirrors for our own perspectives and belief systems and thus help us examine more critically what we ourselves think and do, both within our own classrooms and with respect to the larger institutional contexts in which we teach. In other words, although these responses came from two different disciplines, it is critical for each of us to examine the extent to which we catch glimpses of our own practices and assumptions in these texts. The first response was written by an English Department instructor:

> One of my graduate school professors once told me that he knew within the first two weeks of the semester what his students' final grades would be. Recently I had a Burmese-born Chinese student who proved my professor wrong. After the first two essays, there was certainly no reason to be optimistic about this student's performance. The essays were very short, filled with second language errors, thesaurus words, and sweeping generalizations. In the first essay, it was obvious he had been taught to make outlines because that's all the paper was, really—a list. In the second essay, instead of dealing directly with the assigned text, the student directed most of his energy to form and structure. He had an introduction even though he had nothing to introduce. In his conclusion, he was making wild assertions (even though he had nothing to base them on) because he knew conclusions were supposed to make a point. By the fourth essay, he started to catch on to the fact that my comments were directed toward the content of his essays, not the form. Once he stopped worrying about thesis sentences, vocabulary, and the like, he became a different writer. His papers were long, thoughtful, and engaging. He was able to interpret and respond to texts and to make connections that I term "double face" as a way to comment on the ways in which different cultures define such terms as "respect." Instead of 1 1/4 pages, this essay was seven pages, and it made several references to the text while synthesizing it with his experience as someone who is a product of three cultures. This change not only affected the content of his writing, but also his mechanics. Though there were still errors, there were far fewer of them, and he was writing well enough where I felt it was safe to raise questions about structure and correctness.

This response begins with the recognition that we need to be wary of self-fulfilling prophecies about the potential of students, and indeed this instructor's narrative demonstrates compellingly the dangers of such prophecies. This instructor goes on to cite problems with the student's performance, but he speculates that these problems may have to do with previous instruction, thus reflecting a stance that counteracts the tendency to blame students. Despite the student's ongoing difficulties, the instructor does not despair over the presence of second language errors, over the short essays, the "sweeping generalizations," the empty introduction, the "wild assertions." Instead, this instructor seems to persist in his attempts to focus the student on content issues, to respond to the student seriously, to push him to consider the connections between what he was saying and the assigned reading, to take greater risks, which he succeeds in doing "by the fourth essay." In this, I believe, we see the instructor's understanding that it takes multiple opportunities for students to trust that he is inviting them into serious engagement with the course material, that it takes time to acquire new approaches to written work. What seems to be revealed in this response is the instructor's belief in the student's potential, his appreciation for how language and learning are promoted, his refusal to draw conclusions about intellectual ability on the basis of surface features of language—all of which, in turn, helped the student become a "different writer," a change that affected the content of his writing, that had an impact on the very errors that filled his first papers, that even illuminated the instructor's reading of the assigned texts. This response suggests a rich and complicated notion of language, one that recognizes that language evolves and is acquired in the context of saying something meaningful, that language and meaning are reciprocal and give rise to one another.

The other faculty response, written by an art history instructor, reveals a very different set of assumptions and expectations:

> My experience with teaching ESL students is that they have often not received adequate English instruction to complete the required essay texts and papers in my classes. I have been particularly dismayed when I find that they have already completed 2 ESL courses and have no knowledge of the parts of speech or the terminology that is used in correcting English grammar on papers. I am certainly not in a position to teach English in my classes. (The problem has been particularly acute with Chinese/S.E. Asian students.) These students may have adequate intelligence to do well in the courses, but their language skills result in low grades. (I cannot give a good grade to a student who can only generate one or two broken sentences during a ten-minute slide comparison.)

The first assumption I see in this response is the belief that language and knowledge are separate entities, that language must be in place and fixed in order to do the work in the course. This static notion of language is further revealed by the instructor's assumption that language use is determined by a knowledge of parts of speech or grammatical terminology. Given this belief, it is understandable why she is dismayed by what she characterizes as students' lack of knowledge of grammar, a conclusion she has seemingly reached because her corrective feedback, presumably making use of grammatical terms, has not proven successful. This practice itself is not questioned, however; instead, students and/or their inadequate English language instruction are held accountable. If students had been prepared appropriately, if the gatekeeping efforts had kept students out of her course until they were more like their native language counterparts, her commentary suggests, students would be able to do the required work. There is little sense of how the unfamiliar terms, concepts, and ways of seeing that are particular to this course can be acquired. Nor is there an appreciation for how this very unfamiliarity with the course content may be constraining students' linguistic processes. She does not see, focusing as she does on difference, how she can contribute to students' language and written development, how she can build on what they know. Despite indicating that students may have "adequate intelligence to do well in the course," she doesn't seem to be able to get past their language problems when it comes to evaluating their work, thus missing the irony of grading on the basis of that which she acknowledges she is not "in a position to teach." The final parenthetical statement reveals further expectations about student work, raising questions about the extent to which her very expectations, rather than linguistic difficulties alone, contribute to the "broken sentences" to which she refers.

What we see at work here is in marked contrast to the model of possibility revealed in the first response. What seems to inform this second response is a deficit model of language and learning whereby students' deficiencies are foregrounded. This response is shaped by an essentialist view of language in which language is understood to be a decontextualized skill that can be taught in isolation from the production of meaning and that must be in place in order to undertake intellectual work. What we see here is an illustration of "the myth of transience," a belief that permeates institutions of higher education and perpetuates the notion that these students' problems are temporary and can be remediated—so long as some isolated set of courses or program of instruction, but not the real courses in the academy, takes on the responsibility of doing so (Rose, 1985). Such a belief supports the illusion that permanent solutions are possible, which releases faculty from the ongoing struggle and questioning that the teaching–learning process inevitably involves.

In these two faculty responses, we see the ways in which different sets of expectations and attitudes get played out. In the one classroom, we get some sense of what can happen when opportunities for learning are created, when students are invited into a thoughtful process of engaging texts, when students' writing is read and responded to in meaningful and supportive ways. In the other classroom, although we have little information about the conditions for learning, we are told that one way that learning is measured is by technically correct writing done during a 10-minute slide presentation, and this, I believe, is telling. For students who are not adequately prepared to do this work, there is little, the instructor tells us, she can do. Given this deterministic stance, students are closed off from participating in intellectual work.

At the same time that I was soliciting faculty responses to get a sense of their perceptions and assumptions, I began to survey ESOL students about what they wanted faculty to know about their experiences and needs in classrooms across the curriculum. I felt that the work I was engaging in with faculty could not take place without an exploration of students' views, especially because, although faculty have little reservation discussing what they want and expect from students, the students' perspective is one that faculty hear little about.

Over a number of years, I collected more than 325 responses from first- and second-year ESOL students enrolled in courses across a range of disciplines.[2] I discovered from looking at these responses a number of predominant and recurring themes. Students spoke of patience, tolerance, and encouragement as key factors that affected their learning:

> Teachers need to be more sensitive to ESL students needs of education. Since ESL students are face with the demands of culture ajustment, especially in the classroom, teaches must be patients and give flexible consideration.... For example—if a teacher get a paper that isn't clear or didn't follow the assignment correctly, teacher must talk and communicate with the students.

Students articulated the kinds of assistance they needed, pointing, for example, to clearer and more explicitly detailed assignments and more accessible classroom talk:

> In the classes, most teachers go over material without explaining any words that seems hard to understand for us.... I want college teachers should describe more clearly on questions in the exams, so we can understand clearly. Also, I think the teachers should write any important information or announcement on the board rather than just speaking in front of class, because sometimes we understand in different way when we hear it than when we read it.

Students spoke with pride about how much they knew and how much they had accomplished, working, they felt, more than their native English-speaking counterparts, and they wanted faculty to credit and acknowledge them for this:

> I would like them to know that we are very responsible and we know why we come to college: to learn. We are learning English as well as the major of our choice. It is very hard sometimes and we don't need professors who claimed that they don't understand us. The effort is double. We are very intelligent people. We deserve better consideration.... ESL students are very competent

and deserve to be in college. We made the step to college. Please make the other step to meet us.

At the same time, an overwhelming number of students wanted faculty to know that they were well aware they were having language difficulties and appreciated responses that would help them. But they also expressed their wish that their work not be discounted and viewed as limited. They seemed to have a very strong sense that because of difficulties that were reflected in their attempts at classroom participation and in their written work, their struggles with learning were misperceived and underestimated:

> The academic skills of students who are not native speakers of English are not worse than academic skills of American students, in some areas it can be much better. Just because we have problems with language ... that some professors hate because they don't want to spend a minute to listen a student, doesn't mean that we don't understand at all.

Students referred to professors who showed concern and seemed to appreciate students' contributions. But the majority of students' responses described classrooms that silenced them, that made them feel fearful and inadequate, that limited possibilities for engagement, involvement, inclusion.

Although these students acknowledge that they continue to experience difficulties, they also voice their concern that these struggles not be viewed as deficiencies, that their efforts be understood as serious attempts to grapple with these difficulties. Though faculty may feel overwhelmed by and even resentful of working with such students, these students indicate that they expect and need their instructors to assist them in this undertaking, even making suggestions as to how this can be done. Indeed, the very kind of clarity, accessible language, careful explanation, and effort that faculty want students to demonstrate are the kinds of assistance students are asking of faculty. Without dismissing the concerns of the art instructor, these students nevertheless believe, as does the English instructor, that teaching ought to be responsive to their concerns.

Yet another source of information about students' classroom experiences came from my longitudinal case study of two students who attended my first-year composition course and who met with me regularly every semester until they graduated. At these meetings, they discussed the work they were assigned, their teachers' responses to and evaluation of their work, the classroom dynamics of their courses, the roles they and their teachers played, and the kinds of learning that were expected in their classes. These students also wrote accounts about their course experiences, documenting and reflecting on these experiences from their own perspectives and in their own voices.[3]

One of the students who participated in this longitudinal investigation was Motoko, a student from Japan who took a range of courses and majored in sociology. She described the occasional course in which lively interaction was generated, in which students were expected to participate, to write reaction papers and to undertake projects based on firsthand research, to challenge textbook material and to connect this material to their own lived experiences. But in most of her courses the picture was quite different. Lectures were pervasive, classes were so large that attendance wasn't even taken, and short-answer tests were often the predominant means of evaluating student work. With respect to one class, for example, Motoko discussed the problematic nature of multiple-choice exams, which, she believed, distorted the information being tested and deliberately misled students. In regard to another course, she described what she viewed as boring, even confusing lectures, but she persevered: "Because I don't like the professor, I work even harder. I don't want him to laugh at me. I don't want to be dehumanized. I came here to learn something, to gain something." In yet another course in which only the professor talked, she indicated that she was "drowning in his words." Even a class that Motoko completed successfully disappointed her because she had such difficulty understanding the assignments and because her writing was not responded to in what she perceived as a thoughtful, "respectful" way. Motoko confided that despite her success in this course, she had lost interest in working on her papers.

The other student whose classroom experiences I followed was Martha, a student from Colombia who, like Motoko, took a range of courses, and whose major was biology. Unlike Motoko, who had managed to negotiate "drowning words" and problematic assignments, Martha's sense of discouragement about the purposelessness of much of her work was far more pervasive. With respect to many of her courses, she complained about the absence of writing, which she viewed as essential for learning course content as well as for her own growth as an English-language learner. Commenting on one course in which little writing was required, she said, "I have no new words in my lexicon.... I was moving forward and now I'm stagnant." She referred to the passive nature of class discussions, contrived assignments that "don't help me think about anything," and the lifeless comments she received. It was in her science courses, however, that she felt the greatest dissatisfaction and frustration. About one chemistry course, she spoke of "just trying to follow the lectures and get a grade in a huge class" that she characterized as a "disaster." She talked of the sense of superiority her professors projected, of her inability to learn anything meaningful from assignments that required everyone "to come up with the same information." Her growing sense of despair provoked her to write a piece in which she questioned the purpose of schooling, assignments, and written work: "Each teacher should ask her or himself the next question: Why do I assign a writing paper on this class? Do you want to see creativity and reflection of students or do you want a reproduction of the same book concept?" She was frustrated by the "lack of connections with the material we listen on lectures," the "limited style of questions," and what she saw as the "barriers" to learning.

What Martha shared with me demonstrated her commitment to learning. It further revealed her insightful understanding of how learning is both promoted and undermined, how writing in particular plays an essential role in this learning, and how critical it is for teachers to contribute to and encourage learning. She, like Motoko and the other students surveyed, has much to tell us about the barriers that prevent learning and how these barriers can be broken. And lest we conclude that what these students perceived about their experiences is specific to ESOL learners, studies of teaching and learning in higher education indicate that this is not the case. For example, Chiseri-Strater's (1991) ethnography of university classrooms reveals the authoritarian and limited ways that subject matter is often approached, the ways in which students, even those who are successful, are left silent and empty by the contrived and inconsequential work of many classrooms.

This ongoing exploration of the expectations, perceptions, and experiences of both faculty and students has clarified much for me about the academic life of ESOL students and what we ought to be doing both within our classrooms and beyond. Given the hierarchical arrangement of coursework within postsecondary schools, given the primacy accorded to traditional discipline-specific courses, it is not surprising that ESOL and other writing-based courses have a marginalized position, that these courses are thought to have no authentic content, that the work that goes on in these courses is not considered to be the "real" work of the academy.

This view typically gets played out through coursework that is determined by what students are assumed to need in courses across the curriculum, coursework whose function it is to "guard the tower," to use Shaughnessy's term, and keep the gates closed in the case of students who are not deemed ready to enter (Shaughnessy, 1976). This often implies instruction that focuses on grammar, decontextualized language skills, and surface features of language. And we know from what faculty continue to say about these issues that this is precisely what is expected of English and ESOL instruction—and, unfortunately, many of us have been all too ready to comply. Rose (1985) speaks to the profoundly exclusionary nature of such a pedagogy and argues that a focus on mechanical skills and grammatical features reduces the complexity of language to simple and discrete problems, keeps teachers from exploring students' knowledge and potential, and contributes to the "second-class intellectual status" to which the teaching of writing has been assigned (p. 348). Furthermore, the problematic assumption that writing or ESOL programs are in place to serve the academy, that their function is to benefit other academic studies, prevents us from questioning our situation within the larger institution. "Service course ideology," Fox (1990) points out, "often leaves the curricular decisions in the hands of those who are not especially knowledgeable about writing instruction," which ultimately means that "political questions—in fact, any questions that challenge existing definitions of basic writing—become irrelevant to the bureaucratic task of reproducing the program" (p. 67).

Whereas skills-based models of instruction bring these kinds of pressures to bear on our work with students, our teaching has further been constrained by composition specialists who make claims about the need for students to adopt the language and discourse conventions of the academy if they are to succeed. Bartholomae's (1986) article, "Inventing the University," is often cited and called upon to argue that students need to approximate and adopt the "specialized discourse of the university" (p. 17). In the ESOL literature, a reductive version of this position has been embraced by professionals who maintain that the role that ESOL coursework ought to play is one of preparing students for the expectations and demands of discipline-specific communities across the curriculum. Such an approach, however, misrepresents and oversimplifies academic discourse and reduces it to some stable and autonomous phenomenon that does not reflect reality. Such an approach implies that the language of the academy is a monolithic discourse that can be packaged and transmitted to students *before* they enter the classroom contexts in which this language is used.

Those of us who have tried to accommodate institutional demands have, no doubt, found this to be a troubling and tension-filled undertaking, because even when we focus on standards of language use or conventions of academic discourse, students, especially those who are still acquiring English, are not necessarily more successful in meeting the expectations of other faculty. There seems to be little carryover from such instructional efforts to subsequent work because it is the very nature of such narrowly conceptualized instruction that undercuts genuine learning. Those of us who have resisted and questioned such a pedagogy, embracing a richer and more complicated understanding of how language, discourse, and context are intertwined, may be able to trace the strides students make and to appreciate the intelligence their language and writing reveal, and yet find that this is not extended by other faculty who cannot imagine taking on this kind of responsibility.

We need to recognize that in the same way that faculty establish what Martha calls "barriers" between themselves and students, ESOL faculty, too, are perceived as "outsiders." And as long as these boundaries continue to delineate and separate what we and other faculty do, as long as we are expected to fix students' problems, then misunderstandings, unfulfilled expectations, frustration, and even resentment will continue to mark our experiences. But this need not be the case. We are beginning to see changes in institutions in response to the growing recognition that faculty across the disciplines must take responsibility for working with all students. Studies, such as the ethnography undertaken by Walvoord and McCarthy (1990), have documented the transformation of faculty from a range of disciplines who became more responsive to the needs of their students as they undertook their own classroom research and examined their own assumptions and expectations.

In my own work with faculty at a number of different institutions, including my own, what first began with a concern about "underprepared" or "deficient" ESOL students has led to a consideration of the same kinds of pedagogical issues that are at the heart of writing-across-the-curriculum initiatives. But these issues are reconsidered with specific reference to working with ESOL students. Together, we have explored our instructional goals, the purposes for assigned work, the means for reading and evaluating this work, the roles that engagement, context, and classroom dynamics play in promoting learning. Through this collaboration faculty have begun to understand that it is unrealistic and ultimately counterproductive to expect writing and ESOL programs to be responsible for providing students with the language, discourse, and multiple ways of seeing required across courses. They are recognizing that the process of acquisition is slow-paced and continues to evolve with exposure, immersion, and involvement, that learning is responsive to situations in which students are invited to participate in the construction of meaning and knowledge. They have come to realize that every discipline, indeed every classroom, may represent a distinct culture and thus needs to make it possible for those new to the context to practice and approximate its "ways with words." Along with acknowledging the implications of an essentialist view of language and of the myth of transience, we have considered the myth of coverage, the belief that covering course content necessarily means that it has been learned. Hull and Rose (1990) critique "the desire of efficiency and coverage," noting how this focus limits rather than promotes students' "participation in intellectual work" (p. 296). With this in mind, we have raised questions about what we do in order to cover material, why we do what we do, what we expect from students, and how coverage is evaluated. And if the "cover-the-material" model doesn't seem to be working in the ways we expected, we ask, what alternatives are there?

We have also examined the ways in which deficit thinking blinds us to the logic, intelligence, and richness of students' processes and knowledge. In *Lives on the Boundary,* Mike Rose (1989) cites numerous cases of learners (including himself) whose success was undercut because of the tendency to emphasize difference. Studies undertaken by Glynda Hull and her colleagues further attest to how such belief systems about students can lead to inaccurate judgments about learners' abilities, and how practices based on such beliefs perpetuate and "virtually assure failure" (Hull, Rose, Fraser, & Castellano, 1991, p. 325).

Thus, we try to read students' texts to see what is there rather than what isn't, resisting generalizations about literacy and intelligence that are made on the basis of judgments about standards of correctness and form, and suspending our judgments about the alternative rhetorical approaches our students adopt.

In addition to working with faculty to shape the curriculum so that it is responsive to students' needs and to generate instructional approaches that build on students' competence, we address other institutional practices that affect our students. At the University of Massachusetts at Boston, for example, the Writing Proficiency Exam, which all students must pass by the time they are juniors, continues to evolve as faculty across the curriculum work together, implementing and modifying it over time to create a tool that immerses students in rich, intellectual, and thematically integrated material to read, think about, and respond to. As part of this work, we have tried to ensure that faculty understand how to look below the surface of students' texts for evidence of proficiency, promoting a kind of reading that benefits not just ESOL students, but all students. The portfolio option, which requires students to submit papers written in courses as well as to write an essay in response to a set of readings, has proven a good alternative for ESOL students to demonstrate writing proficiency. The portfolio allows students to demonstrate what they are capable of achieving when writing is imbedded within and an outgrowth of their courses.

Throughout this work, one of the most critical notions that I try to bring home is the idea that what faculty ought to be doing to enhance the learning of ESOL students is not a concession, a capitulation, a giving up of standards, for the approaches that faculty continue to put into effect may not and may never have been beneficial for any students. What ESOL students need—multiple opportunities to use language and write-to-learn, course work that draws on and values what students already know, classroom exchanges and assignments that promote the acquisition of unfamiliar language, concepts, and approaches to inquiry, evaluation that allows students to demonstrate genuine understanding—is good pedagogy for everyone. Learning how to better address the needs of ESOL students, because it involves becoming more reflective about teaching, because it involves carefully thinking through the expectations, values, and assumptions underlying the work we assign, helps faculty teach everyone better. In other words, rather than seeing the implications of inclusion and diversity in opposition to excellence and academic standards (as they often are at meetings convened to discuss these issues), learning to teach ESOL students challenges us to reconceptualize teaching and thus contributes to and enhances learning for all students.

Needless to say, given the complexity of this enterprise, these efforts have not transformed classrooms on an institution-wide basis. As is obvious from the surveys and case studies I have undertaken, change is slow, much like the process of learning itself. As we grapple with the kinds of issues and concerns raised by the clash of cultures in academia, we continue to make adjustments that, in turn, generate new questions about our practices. This ongoing dialogue is both necessary and beneficial. Like other prominent debates in higher education on reforming the canon and the implications of diversity, this attempt to explore and interrogate what we do is slowly reconfiguring the landscape and blurring the borders within what was once a fairly well-defined and stable academic community. According to Gerald Graff (1992), this is all to the good because this kind of transformation can revitalize higher education and its isolated departments and fragmentary curricula. Within composition, the conflicts and struggles that inevitably mark the teaching of writing are viewed as instructive because they allow students and teachers to "reposition" themselves, because they raise questions about conventional thinking about instruction and challenge us to imagine alternative pedagogies (Horner, 1994; Lu, 1992). Pratt's (1991) notion of a "contact zone," which designates a site of contestation, is embraced because it enables us to redraw disciplinary boundaries, to reexamine composition instruction, and to revise our assumptions about language and difference.

When faculty see this kind of redefinition as a crisis, I invite them to reconsider their work in light of the way the word *crisis* is translated into Chinese. In Chinese, the word is symbolized by two ideographs, one meaning danger, the other meaning opportunity. Because the challenges that students bring with them may make us feel confused, uncertain, like strangers in our own community even, as if our work and professional identities are being threatened, there will be dissonance, jarring questions, ongoing dilemmas, unfulfilled expectations. We can see this reflected in the second faculty response, a response that insists that there are students who don't belong, that the doors be kept closed. But, as we saw in the first response, perplexities and tensions can be generative, can create possibilities for new insights, alternative interpretations, and an appreciation for the ways in which these enrich our understanding. Seen from the fresh perspective that another language can provide, the Chinese translation of *crisis* captures the very nature of learning, a process involving both risk and opportunity, the very process that ideally students ought to engage in, but that we ourselves may resist when it comes to looking at our own practices. But as Giroux (1991) urges, teachers must "cross over borders that are culturally strange and alien to them" so that they can "analyze their own values and voices as viewed from different ideological and cultural spaces" (pp. 254–255). When we take risks of this sort—when we take this step into the unknown, by looking for evidence of students' intelligence, by rereading their attempts as coherent efforts, by valuing, not just evaluating, their work, and by reflecting on the critical relationship between our work and theirs—opportunities are created not only for students but for teachers to learn in new ways.

ACKNOWLEDGMENTS

An earlier version of this chapter appears in *College Composition and Communication*, 1995, vol. 46, pp. 506–521.

REFERENCES

Bartholomae, D. (1986). Inventing the university. *Journal of Basic Writing, 5*, 4–23.
Chiseri-Strater, E. (1991). *Academic literacies: The public and private discourse of university students*. Portsmouth, NH: Boynton/Cook.
Fox, T. (1990). Basic writing as cultural conflict. *Journal of Education, 172*, 65–83.
Giroux, H. (1991). Postmodernism as border pedagogy: Redefining the boundaries of race and ethnicity. In H. Giroux (Ed.), *Postmodernism, feminism, and cultural politics: Redrawing educational boundaries* (pp. 217–256). Albany: State University of New York Press.
Graff, G. (1992). *Beyond the culture wars*. New York: Norton.
Horner, B. (1994). Mapping errors and expectations for basic writing: From "frontier field" to "border country." *English Education, 26*, 29–51.
Hull, G., & Rose, M. (1990). "This wooden shack place": The logic of an unconventional reading. *College Composition and Communication, 41*, 287–298.
Hull, G., Rose, M., Losey Fraser, K., & Castellano, M. (1991). Remediation as social construct: Perspectives from an analysis of classroom discourse. *College Composition and Communication, 42*, 299–329.
Lu, M.-Z. (1992). Conflict and struggle in basic writing. *College English, 54*, 887–913.
Neuleib, J. (1992). The friendly stranger: Twenty-five years as "other." *College Composition and Communication, 43*, 231–243.
Pratt, M. L. (1991). Arts of the contact zone. In P. Franklin (Ed.), *Profession '91* (pp. 33–40). New York: Modern Language Association.
Rose, M. (1985). The Language of exclusion: Writing instruction at the university. *College English, 47*, 341–359.
Rose, M. (1989). *Lives on the boundary: The struggles and achievements of America's underprepared*. New York: The Free Press.
Shaughnessy, M. (1976). Diving in: An introduction to basic writing. *College Composition and Communication, 27*, 234–239.
Shaughnessy, M. (1977). *Errors and expectations*. New York: Oxford University Press.
Spack, R. (1994). *English as a second language*. Blair Resources for Teaching Writing. New York: Prentice-Hall.
Villanueva, V. (1993). *Bootstraps: From an American academic of color*. Urbana, IL: National Council of Teachers of English.
Walvoord, B. E., & McCarthy, L. B. (1990). *Thinking and writing in college: A naturalistic study of students in four disciplines*. Urbana, IL: National Council of Teachers of English.

NOTES

[1]The acronym ESL (English as a Second Language) is the commonly used term to refer to students whose native language is not English. At urban institutions, such as the University of Massachusetts at Boston, most of these students are residents of the United States. Furthermore, in the case of a number of these students, English may be a third or fourth language. Given this complexity, the editors of this volume have adopted the acronym ESOL (English for Speakers of Other Languages) to refer to students with multilingual backgrounds.

[2]This investigation of student responses was first initiated by Ruth Spack, whose findings were published in *English as a Second Language* (Spack, 1994). My ongoing survey built on her work.

[3]A number of these accounts appear in Part II of this volume.

Chapter 2

The Acquisition of Academic Literacy in a Second Language: A Longitudinal Case Study, Updated

Ruth Spack

Ruth Spack reports on her longitudinal case study of a student from Japan who experienced so much frustration in her first-year social science courses that she considered transferring to a university in Japan. Ruth focuses on how Yuko developed strategies to succeed as a reader and writer in several disciplines, including her chosen field, and reveals how Yuko's understanding of language and literacy acquisition changed over time as she reflected on her own learning process. In the Appendix, Yuko reflects back on the study 3 years after her graduation.

This study began informally at the beginning of a fall semester at a private 4-year liberal arts university. I had a 9 a.m. meeting with a first-year student from Japan who had requested a space in the ESOL composition program, which I directed. Yuko (a pseudonym) had not been invited to enroll in the program primarily because she had achieved a high TOEFL (Test of English as a Foreign Language) score—640—which indicated that she could do work at the same level as U.S.-born speakers of English. Yet nothing I said in the meeting could convince her that this was true; she gave no explanation other than "I can't." Partly because she was having difficulty expressing herself, I decided to allow her to enroll in ESOL composition. As she chose the time block in which I was teaching, I realized I had a unique opportunity to look beyond her TOEFL score to gain a fuller understanding of her acquisition of academic literacy before she entered the university and to determine if her assessment of her ability to do the work of the English composition program was valid.

The focus of my research began to shift when, in the third week of the semester, Yuko came to me for help with an introductory International Relations course that she could not manage. As International Relations was her intended major, this was a particularly disturbing circumstance for her. I decided then to investigate that experience in order to learn which factors constrained her ability to complete the reading and writing assignments for this course. Eventually, the study extended over 3 years during which time I gathered information through numerous interviews with Yuko, supplemented by interviews with two of her professors, observations of two classes, and the collection of texts from 10 courses in three disciplines— including course materials and Yuko's writing, with instructors' comments.

The purpose of the inquiry was not to trace the development of reading and writing ability per se but rather to understand how this individual student would draw on multiple resources as she gradually developed strategies to succeed as a reader and writer in a university setting. Throughout the study, I endeavored to contextualize Yuko's acquisition of academic literacy, to examine what Casanave (1995) calls the "local, historical, and interactive aspects of the contexts that writers [and readers] in academic settings construct for themselves" (p. 88). These factors include linguistic and cognitive development, previous educational experiences, and cultural background, as well as interactions with instructors and course-related texts. Though proficiency in English is undoubtedly a prerequisite for success in an academic institution that uses English as its primary medium of instruction, Yuko's case reveals that other factors must also be taken into account.

THE FIRST YEAR: "IT'S KIND OF SCARY"

Yuko: I wasn't ready to take English with American students.
Ruth: Why not?
Yuko: 'Cause I don't know how to write essays and I can't read that fast.
Ruth: Okay.
[long pause]
Yuko: It's kind of scary too.
Ruth: Why?
Yuko: Because of the American students.
Ruth: But you were taking other courses with Americans.
Yuko: Yes.

> Ruth: Why is it "scary" to do English?
>
> Yuko: 'Cause they know something that I don't know [pause] about English. So, like, the starting point is totally different.

Despite several years of English language instruction in Japan, a year as an exchange student at a U.S. public high school, 10 weeks at a summer intensive English program in England just prior to matriculation, and a high TOEFL score, Yuko was not confident about her English as she started her life as a college student in the United States. Not only did Yuko feel that the TOEFL misrepresented her communicative ability, but she emphasized that it did not measure the cultural factors that impacted her language learning and interactions. In a journal entry, written for her ESOL composition class in response to course readings on the subject of cross-cultural communication, Yuko discussed the issues that are key to understanding what it means for her to communicate across cultures as a speaker, reader, and writer:

> I had difficulty in making myself understood here because I didn't/don't speak up. There is a big cultural difference between the U.S. and Japan, in the way of communication: in Japan you don't have to say everything you think or feel because certain things are "understood" or even "to be observed." If you express your thoughts all the time, it could be seen as selfish or insistent. But then here in the States no thoughts or feelings exist unless you express them. Being reserved is not something respectable. And I had hard time (and still have) making myself speak up, and sometimes I feel that I'm being too superficial to say everything I feel or think.

Because she felt that she had not acquired American culture, assuming an American way of expression, Yuko did not believe that she had truly acquired English.

In addition to perceived language and cultural barriers, Yuko believed that issues related to her educational background in Japan made it difficult for her to achieve even in the areas of her greatest interest. In Japan (in Japanese), Yuko said, she had had little experience doing the kind of independent and creative learning that she believed characterizes much of American education. Yuko was attracted to what she perceived to be the "American" style because, in the American way, "I can have my own point of view." Still, according to Yuko, she had what she called a "Japanese style" in her background that was so ingrained that she could not cross over comfortably to the American style (partly because she was not convinced the American way was superior). This inability to make the crossover, she believed, affected her integration into the culture of the American classroom. But, in Yuko's view at that time, an even more significant barrier was her lack of background knowledge.

Year 1, Semester 1. International Relations

During the first semester of her first year, Yuko was unable to complete an introductory course in her intended major, International Relations (PS 51), which she had thought was a safe choice because, she said, it was an "introduction course" and therefore would put her on "the same level" with "native speakers." Although the course was "introductory" (according to the catalog) and the professor claimed students needed "no previous knowledge" (according to his course guidelines), in fact, its underlying assumption, as Yuko experienced it, was that students had a broad knowledge of U.S. and European history as well as an understanding of the relationship of the West to underdeveloped countries—neither of which Yuko had. Yuko was unable to understand the lectures because of what she perceived to be the professor's "really sophisticated vocabulary" and "random" presentation and, most important, because—at least as far as she could determine— he did not explain the course readings. Yuko was unable to contribute to the required debate-style discussions in the recitation section led by the teaching assistant (TA) because the discussions were based on the lectures or the readings, which were "so hard" and "so long" and "more argumentative" than she was used to. She often looked up words in a dictionary—in one case, seven words from just one paragraph in an article from the journal *Foreign Affairs: shrug off, recurrent, jittery, credence, imagery, pervaded,* and *adversary*. Nevertheless, she said, she still "didn't have a clue" because she "had no background" in what the author was discussing.

Yuko was also apprehensive about the six- to seven-page critical essay assignment, handed out on the first day of class, which was worth 30% of the grade. She had never written an essay longer than one or two pages, handwritten—in either Japanese or English. Furthermore, the essay was unlike any she had previously written: The instructions stated in capital letters that "IT IS NOT A TRADITIONAL TERM PAPER OR RESEARCH PAPER" and emphasized that it was to be an "original, aggressive analysis." Not knowing even what a "traditional" term paper was, Yuko had no idea how to deviate from tradition to be "original." Finally, she had not yet written a complete essay for her English class and so had no idea what her capabilities were at the college level.

In spite of the relative flexibility of the assignment (any topic related to course themes), some writing guidelines (e.g., "Organize! Introduce and summarize your focus...." "Be original! Be aggressive"), and samples of good writing on reserve at the library, Yuko was unable to tackle this assignment. She could not understand the course materials well enough to generate ideas. She tried to get tutorial assistance but no tutor was available for the International Relations course. At that point, she dropped the course.[1]

Year 1, Semesters 1 & 2. Composition

English 3 (Reading, Writing, Research) and English 4 (Writing Seminar), designed for students who identify themselves as second language learners, together fulfilled the college's two-semester writing requirement. Yuko's English 3 and 4 courses, which I taught, focused on a cross-cultural theme. The readings consisted of essays, research articles, short stories, and poetry, as well as a book that each student selected from a list of autobiographies and novels. Yuko did not have difficulty with the reading, she said, largely because the cross-cultural theme helped her "understand" her own experience.

Several weeks into the English 3 course, Yuko began to give up the word-by-word, dictionary-dependent approach that had characterized her reading in International Relations. Fascinated by the various interpretations presented by her classmates during class discussions of short stories, Yuko developed a new reading procedure: She read through a complete story first, just to get the general idea, and then read a second time for details. This new strategy would mark a dramatic change in her approach to reading nonfiction as well.

Yuko wrote five papers for English 3 and four papers for English 4. In addition, she wrote numerous brief in-class pieces and handed in a journal entry on each reading assignment, all of which I responded to in writing. The journal assignments asked students to share their reactions to what they had read and called for analysis and interpretation. With the exception of one personal essay in English 3, each of the essay assignments called for critical analysis of the course readings. Her writing, in my view, revealed that she was able to analyze and write about texts in English in sophisticated ways and had the added dimension of bringing her rich and unique cross-cultural perspective to bear on what she read.

Reflections on the First Year

Although she had developed successful reading strategies for her English courses, Yuko's perceived lack of background knowledge for the International Relations course heightened her fear of reading. Deliberately "avoiding reading courses" even though she expressed interest in them, she preregistered for three economics courses, a math course, and a computer science course for the fall semester of her sophomore year. Having taken Micro and Macro Economics, she found that Economics was "more concrete [pause], more structured [pause], more logical [pause], straightforward" than Political Science. She even decided to change her intended major from International Relations to Economics. Yet, despite the fact that she found Economics "attractive," she was ambivalent about her decision, as she revealed in a written response to my manuscript report about her first year:

My brother (he graduated from [a U.S. college] last December) told me, when we were talking about majors, not to fall into the trap of science/math major. Some Japanese students come here intending to do Liberal Arts but end up doing computer science, etc., because they cannot keep up with the readings and the course. For me, too, just like for other Japanese students, math is easier than social science/humanities courses because math is logic and calculation and involves almost no language. Yet it is very sad if I have to major in science, something I don't like, just because I don't understand the language. Then it loses the entire point of studying abroad. I came here for better education in my field, not to major in something that I can pass that I don't really care. I could have stayed home and done my intended major then.

Yuko's experience with writing differed from her experience with reading. By the end of her first year, she was "not afraid" of writing in general because she had done "so much" writing, mostly in English but also in her Freshman Exploration course and in Micro Economics. Yuko "really liked" doing a research paper in Micro Economics, in which she was required to research sources and to give her own "opinion." She called it a "really American" assignment. But the critical literacy Yuko developed for these courses had come too late to prepare her for International Relations in her first semester.

THE SECOND YEAR: "I HAD TO GET OVER IT"

Yuko came to my office at the beginning of her sophomore year and told me that she had decided to take "reading courses" after all: two courses in the Political Science Department. After reading and responding to my research report on her experiences at the end of her first year, and after discussing her experiences with friends in Japan over the summer, she decided that she did not want to view herself as a "quitter" and was determined to challenge herself and to follow her real interests. Of her previous reluctance to take courses requiring a heavy reading load, Yuko said, "I had to get over it. I'm interested in political science. If I didn't do it this semester, I'd be too afraid."

Yuko explained that she had overcome her fear of what she called "reading courses" during the summer, when she had read three books by a popular Japanese novelist (one in Japanese and two translated into English) and three suspense novels by U.S. authors (in English). To get through these long books, she said she "just read for the story, the suspense. I didn't use a dictionary because I wasn't paying attention to details." Yuko offered that she had developed this reading-first-to-get-the-gist strategy "from English class." This experience made her "not afraid of reading books [pause] anything [pause] thick books," and so she enrolled in courses requiring a lot of reading. When I questioned the logic of making the leap from reading fiction to the kind of reading she would have to do in political science, she answered, "It gave me confidence to read nonfiction too. It's totally different, but I thought I could."

My fascination with her decision to take political science courses—coupled with a sense of responsibility linked to having done a research project that influenced that decision—sparked my interest in continuing the study with Yuko. I wanted to learn how she would fare in the political science classes and what adaptations she and the instructors might make to ensure success.

Year 2, Semester 1. Political Science: Southeast Asia's International Relations

At the beginning of the semester, Yuko had no trouble understanding the lectures for Southeast Asia's International Relations (PS 160), especially because the focus was Southeast Asia, a region she felt knowledgeable about, and no trouble keeping up with the reading because, she said, the books "are not argumentative [pause] they're more informative [pause] mostly numbers, data," or "geographical." Nevertheless, Yuko found the reading "boring [pause] no entertainment, too much information." She figured out which reading had to be done and which did not, noting that there was "obvious overlapping" in the two required books and that material not covered in the lectures would not be on the tests.

Writing assignments for PS 160 consisted of two quizzes and two papers. In class Professor A had handed out bibliographies of works that might be useful for the first paper and told students how to do footnotes and use citations. But as to the writing of the paper itself, Yuko offered that he did not explain "how to; he just gave topics." Despite a brief meeting in Professor A's office during which he helped her narrow her topic (on Japan's economic aid to other nations), Yuko was confused about how to proceed: "I don't know if he wants just research or analytical/critical."

Later that semester, Yuko showed me the first paper for PS 160, on which she had received a B+. She thought my talking with Professor A about the research study I was conducting with her "made a real difference. 'Cause I don't see how I got B+ on the paper. My paper was really bad." By "bad," she first said she meant that it was ungrammatical. But Yuko's concern about the paper went beyond grammar. She felt she "didn't really analyze anything. It was a research paper and I [pause] basically I summarized both books [pause]; so it sounds really technical [pause], sounds like a big quote. That's why it was really bad." Despite the fact that she did well on the paper, the idea of not developing ideas to her own way of thinking bothered her greatly because "that's the way I always did it in Japan." She desperately wanted to write "like an American." However, it turned out that this was more than a cross-cultural issue. When Yuko said she "didn't have time to develop it to my own words [pause]," she meant it literally, for she had copied many phrases and sentences from the original texts, without using quotation marks, a circumstance that Professor B did not address.[2]

In the 14th week of PS 160, Yuko was working on the final take-home exam for the course, which, as she understood the assignment, was "interpretation of what was learned." She expressed no concern about her ability to fulfill this assignment, but she did not quite satisfy the requirements. She was criticized—ironically, I couldn't help thinking—for analyzing "from a U.S. perspective." She ultimately received a B in the course.

**Year 2, Semester 1. Political Science:
Politics of Developing Countries**

According to Yuko, the reading for PS 21, Politics of Developing Countries, was much more challenging than the reading for PS 160. Nevertheless, she said, "I can do it [pause] I have to concentrate." She developed a strategy of skipping sections that she could not understand, so that she could keep moving forward in the text. She compared this with her past strategy of giving up when she reached seemingly impenetrable passages. By the end of the semester, Yuko reported, she was using the strategy she had developed while reading short stories for English class to deal with the "difficult" readings in PS 21. She attributed much of her reading success to Professor B, who "talks about the reading [pause] so you are really interested in it." Professor B "does not summarize" the readings; rather, he "refers to them [pause]—he asks *why*." He "makes you think."

The writing requirements for PS 21 were a midterm examination and two papers. After a conference with Professor B, Yuko felt she had received enough information to give her confidence to approach the topic for the first paper: "I knew the answer right away and just looked for proof." She received an A– on the essay from the TA (Professor B told me he himself had never read it).

As she had in PS 160, Yuko was struggling to differentiate summary from argument. For the midterm take-home paper, worth 60% of the grade, the TA had advised that students "'make points' [pause] 'don't describe.'" Yuko thought that she had "messed up" because she just summarized the readings, as she had "nothing to say." Because Yuko got an A– on the midterm, she was "really surprised" because, she said, "it was not clear in my mind that I was making a point" (again, only the TA had commented on the paper). Yuko thought she had simply summarized because she was so dependent on source materials, was unable to put these ideas into her own words, and did not provide her "opinion."

For the final paper, Yuko gathered material from the library with five other students working on the same topic, each of whom wrote an individual essay. She was never worried about this paper: "[Professor B] tells us the points to think about; we choose the relevant ones." She felt she was able to present her view forcefully. As it turned out, Yuko was more successful in the course that had provided the greatest challenge. She received an A– on the paper and an A– in the course.

Year 2, Semester 2. Political Science: American National Government

Yuko entered American National Government (PS 11) 4 weeks late, having dropped out of Economics 18 (Intermediate Quantitative Macro) because she "didn't like the professor" and had "no idea what they were doing." PS 11, in contrast, had a "nice" professor whose class was "relaxing" because he related the course material to his own experiences in the Washington, DC, political world. She characterized the three books—on political campaigns and civil rights—as "easy to read" because they were "not heavy reading about theory, philosophy" but rather "biography and history." On the other hand, some of the material in the photocopied essay packet was a challenge.

In addition to a midterm and a final examination, the writing for PS 11 consisted of two short research papers. The instructions for both papers were to "*analyze* the material you have found—in other words, you should have a point to make." Yuko said she felt comfortable with the papers, largely because they fit with her sense that writing academic discourse entails forming one's own "opinion." Although she did well on the papers for this course, Yuko got a 72 on the midterm exam, largely because she didn't have enough time to write. After much debate with a friend from Japan who argued that she should not take advantage of her second-language status by requesting additional time, she did so, arranging to start the final exam 20 minutes early.

Year 2, Semester 2. Political Science: Western Political Thought II

Because they were not "written in current English," as she put it, the readings for Western Political Thought II (PS 46) were "very difficult," including as they did philosophical works of Descartes, Hobbes, and Hume. Nevertheless, with one exception, Yuko was able to follow the readings because Professor C was "great, amazing … lively": "he reads aloud in class … goes over the readings.... That's the purpose of the lectures: what the philosophers mean." Yuko focused on the importance of the lecturer's explaining the "why" of the readings, emphasizing how useful it was when lecturers "analyze" the readings, just as she did when she discussed the PS 21 lectures. What was new to her and most significant was the way Professor C "updated" the material by relating it to real life: "We're reading masterpieces and he gives examples that connect to our daily lives."

The writing for PS 46 consisted of two take-home examinations. Yuko said that the questions on the midterm were "so difficult" that "I didn't even know what I was supposed to write on." She had no choice but to write in the style that she abhorred: total dependence on the sources with none of her perspective. She received a C+ on the first of two essay questions and was criticized for relying heavily on quotation. She was therefore surprised when she received a B+ on her answer to the other exam question, written in what Yuko perceived to be a similar style. Yuko changed her approach to exam writing after this experience because she was dissatisfied with her performance. She started preparing early so that she could meet with both the professor and the TA to make sure she was on "the right track." She ultimately achieved a grade of B+ for the entire course.

Reflections on the Second Year

Yuko's successful experiences in political science courses in her second year convinced her to make Political Science a double major with Economics. Furthermore, she ended the thoughts she had had of transferring to a university in Japan.

At this stage, Yuko had gained confidence in her ability to devise strategies to cope with difficult readings. I asked if her reading in English had improved just because she was living in the United States, as she had predicted in the first year. She felt strongly that she had been wrong about that: "No, it's not the time [pause], no. It's the fact that you are forced to read something, you're reading something. I mean, I'm getting *practice*." She said that if she had not taken any political science course this year and wanted to take one next year, "I would have the same problem."

Yuko's writing experience in the second year was so complex that it defies neat analysis; writing was different for each course, each assignment, and even within each exam. Her understanding of her struggle with writing was tied to her theory concerning the nature of informative prose (dependent on sources) versus critical prose (dependent on the writer's own views). Framing the perceived problem in cross-cultural terms, Yuko claimed that there was a "Japanese" way of writing and an "American" way of writing, the former being a repetition of the ideas contained in a reading and the latter being an original opinion provided by the (student) writer. I did not challenge Yuko's view. Yet I recognized that a repetition-of-ideas mode is not specific to Japan but is common to U.S. academic writing, the proof of which lay in the fact that Yuko was rewarded for producing it in more than one course. To a great extent, she was experiencing an academic dilemma that most students confront when asked to include ideas from sources that are phrased in ways distant from their own (first or second) language. (See also Appendix for her own re-vision of this viewpoint.)

Determining exactly what Yuko was doing in each writing assignment and why instructors responded and graded as they did is difficult. Based on the data I collected and analyzed, I would tentatively offer the theory that (a) Yuko's writing reflected whether or not she understood the readings and the assignment and that (b) the instructors' comments and grades reflected their assessment of how well Yuko had demonstrated knowledge of the subject matter and fulfilled their expectations. At times, there was a discrepancy between Yuko's assessment of her own work and her instructors' assessment. She was not necessarily pleased by high grades. But she was always pleased when her theory about what constitutes "American" writing was matched by her perception of what an assignment called for and by her instructor's positive evaluation of what she had written.

After the first year, Yuko never mentioned the "lack of background knowledge" that had so haunted her earlier. Toward the end of the first semester of the second year, I "tested" her on background knowledge, asking her about some terms Professor A had used during class. She responded "yes" when I mentioned the *Berlin Wall* and *Cuban Missile Crisis* and "Nixon" when I mentioned *Watergate;* but she had no idea about the *Bay of Pigs, Khrushchev,* or *détente.* Yet she was no longer troubled by this lack of knowledge; she said she had learned to "ignore" the things she did not know.

THE THIRD YEAR: "I HAVE THE BIG PICTURE"

I was tempted to end the study at the end of Yuko's second year, as she had achieved success in reading and writing for political science. But because she reenrolled in PS 51, International Relations (IR), the course she had failed to complete the first year, I wanted to learn whether she could apply the productive strategies she had developed in the second-year political science courses to IR. Then, because she registered for a sociology course for the first time, I continued the study for another semester to see if she would apply the strategies she had used successfully for political science to another academic discipline.

Year 3, Semester 1. International Relations (Again)

Yuko waited to reenroll in IR (PS 51) until she was certain that she would not have the same professor who had taught the course her first year. But even with a different professor, she still found the course "difficult." Nevertheless, although she was behind in the reading halfway through the semester, Yuko said she was reading at a steady rate, and felt confident that she could do what had to be done. She ignored "unimportant" readings and focused on "the ones the professor has been talking about in the lectures." As she described how she was getting through the material, she referred to a strategy called "branching" that she had just learned in a speed-reading course: "first theme, main ideas, sub-ideas, branches out to the bottom. You must read the entire thing to be able to do the tree." The important thing, she said, is that "I have the big picture."

Having the big picture enabled Yuko to write the "contention card" for each recitation section, which required students to formulate a question or statement about the reading or lecture. When Yuko had "no time" to write, she would simply agree with whatever she had read or heard. But when she had "time to think," she would "criticize something." She was no longer afraid of being critical of texts or lectures, she said, because she had come to understand that "with any kind of theories there should be some fault." As to the critical paper, she indicated that she had control over the project, having figured out what was expected: "I got used to the concept. I like writing like that; it gives more space to put my opinion, even if it's more difficult than just putting facts…. You can choose any IR topic you want; it makes more sense to refer to readings. That's how to write a good essay: One is to refer to authority." Yuko added that writing a critical paper was not difficult for her if she picked "the right topic," if she started early enough, and if she consulted the TA during the process to see "if I'm on the right track." Even the length of 8–10 pages was not daunting: "eight is not bad."

Year 3, Semester 2. Sociology: Remaking the Welfare State

Yuko noticed that when she "didn't get" the difficult readings in Sociology 189, Remaking the Welfare State: Social Policy in the United States and the New Europe, neither did the other students. She quickly came to realize that the professor didn't expect them to understand everything ahead of time; the purpose of this "informal" seminar was to discuss the readings. For the first time, Yuko noted that she had an advantage having studied and traveled in more than one country because these experiences had given her a "real, accessible" perspective.

The writing assignments for Sociology 189 consisted of two papers and weekly journal entries on the readings assignments; in addition, six to seven proposals leading to the final 25-page research paper were required. The professor responded to all of the writing. At first, Yuko was confused about what to write in the journal entries. Early in the semester, Yuko produced a journal entry that did not demonstrate a grasp of the author's argument. The professor asked Yuko to revise her entry, giving her specific guidelines about how to address the assignment. Yuko followed the advice and produced an entry that met with the professor's approval. Within 3 weeks of the beginning of the course, Yuko had grasped the idea that the purpose was not to summarize—nor just to react—but to answer, "what does the author think? what's important?" Yuko said that this journal writing made her a "better reader."

Yuko said that having so many regular assignments helped her to improve her writing "a lot." With only 12 students in the class, there was close collaboration, with frequent trips to the library to do research and follow-up discussions of what they had found. The professor helped them throughout the process of researching. Yuko's only disappointment was that she did not get help with her writing "style," by which she meant the way she expressed herself rather than what she said. She attributed this to the fact that the sociology course was not an English course.

Reflections on the Third Year

By the spring of her junior year, Yuko had come full circle, having changed her major back to IR, as she had originally intended when she came to college, doubled with a major in Economics. She was able to say that she had truly overcome her fear of reading. The great difference between reading in English in her first year and now was that "I used to open some reading and the printed words used to scare me and that doesn't happen anymore."

Reflecting on her reading experiences in the first-year IR course she had failed to complete, she said she simply "wasn't ready" then. But, after some hesitation, she put some blame on the professor. According to her, she *"couldn't"* read in IR because the IR professor "didn't talk about" the reading: "I had no idea what the essay was talking about; he doesn't say anything about it. I have no clue it's about [pause] there's, like, no help [pause], no hope. And it doesn't make sense to read anyways 'cause he doesn't talk anything about it."

As to the critical paper for IR, which had so frightened her during her first year, Yuko said she now knew "how to do it" as a result of having written papers for other political science courses, particularly PS 21, where she had collaborated with other students. In the first year, she now realized, she had been paralyzed partly by the notion that what she was reading was "so perfect"; and she felt she had nothing to say. Now she knew how to challenge theories and analyze arguments, and she understood the convention of referring to authorities to make a point.

In the sociology course, for the first time since her first-year English courses, Yuko was given specific guidance in the classroom about writing. Her previous experiences in the social sciences were such that she could get advice about writing assignments if she sought out the instructors. Here, writing instruction was built into the course, as was the practice of writing papers in stages, of keeping a journal on the readings, and of revising work. By Yuko's own testimony, this process helped to improve her reading. It also gave her the opportunity to break her habit of summarizing a reading by repeating an author's words and instead to express someone else's complex ideas in her own words. She had now come to a genuine understanding.

At the end of the 3 years, Yuko discussed her newly evolved theory of learning. She had discovered that she could learn a lot in any class in which an instructor made knowledge accessible, but that that was not enough. To explain this, she referred to a team-taught World Civilization course in which no "connection" was ever made between one subject and the next. Yuko concluded that the professors were providing information but "not *constructing*" knowledge, which she had come to understand was the real purpose of teaching and learning.

DISCUSSION

The longitudinal nature of this project raises questions about the theoretical validity of short-term literacy acquisition studies. At the end of her first year, Yuko had drawn the major conclusion—and had convinced me—that her lack of historical background knowledge (especially of Western countries) was the key to her failure to manage two first-year courses. Toward the end of the first semester of her sophomore year, however, that idea had given way to a theory about the importance of practice in certain academic ways of reading and writing. That Yuko had not gained much more background knowledge in that one semester, yet achieved success, suggests that the first-year conclusion was premature. Furthermore, her second-year theory about acquiring academic literacy simply through repeated practice was not static. This theory was supplemented in the third year by a recognition that literacy acquisition involves being engaged in a process of constructing knowledge.

Qualitative research such as this investigation also raises ethical issues, for in pursuing this study, I involved not only a student but also two teachers in the process of reflecting on their own learning and teaching. To what extent the research itself, particularly as it relates to the professors, may have contributed to the outcome is unclear. To the extent that the research effected change in the student, there can be little doubt. Yuko changed her mind about taking courses with a heavy reading load partly as a result of the first-year study. Over the years, Yuko became more talkative and analytical and gained greater insight into her reading and writing processes. She came to the later interviews actively ready to interpret her experiences rather than to answer questions reactively as she had done in the beginning. The research itself, then, seems to have been an effective tool in helping her articulate and develop strategies for success. She may have become a better academic learner because she had the opportunity to reflect on her own learning.

As I examined Yuko's experience over 3 years, I was struck by significant changes in her approach to reading. At the beginning, she was constrained by a literal model of academic reading, believing that good students grasp meaning the first time they read, understand every word of every reading assignment, read everything assigned, and read everything on schedule. Slowly, over time, Yuko began to let go of these myths. First, she discovered that reading a piece more than once could enhance comprehension. She learned to read a first time just to get the gist and then to go back for the details. She resisted dependency on the dictionary, having discovered that reading fluently was often a more effective way of achieving meaning. She gave herself permission to eliminate some reading assignments or to skip some irrelevant or impossibly difficult sections. She learned to figure out what had to be read and what did not have to be read (as well as what was important in the lectures and what was not). She also learned to be flexible in her own reading schedule. Most important, she developed different strategies for different reading purposes.

It became clear over time what kind of reading posed difficulty for Yuko. She repeatedly emphasized that there was an enormous difference for her in reading informative versus argumentative pieces, or biographical/historical/factual writings versus theoretical/philosophical writings. She was undaunted by textbooks and other sources that functioned primarily to inform. She found such reading easy but often boring. Over time, the kind of reading that gave her difficulty—argumentative/theoretical/critical discourse—did not get any easier. What did change, though, was her confidence in herself as a reader, which was directly related to her ability to develop and adjust reading strategies in order to achieve comprehension of a variety of texts, as she herself realized long after this study was completed (see Appendix for Yuko's later recognition of the role confidence plays in generating—and being generated by—literacy acquisition). Furthermore, she came to appreciate the wealth of knowledge she brought to the reading.

In writing, too, she was conscious of a difference between informative and analytical discourse. She struggled to differentiate summary from argument, expressing surprise in her sophomore year that she had received credit for analyzing or making points when she thought she was just repeating information from sources. By her junior year, she had modified her view that "really American" writing emphasizes sources less and "opinions" more. She now understood that referring to published authorities was tied to critical thinking; for in selecting key points, she realized, she could analyze an author's stance toward a subject. The experience of writing journal entries in her sociology class showed her a way to use writing to clarify reading and to put other writers' ideas into her own words. An examination of her writing reveals that she could write at least two kinds of argumentative discourse: (a) using sources to support her own views and (b) shaping others' ideas into a coherent argument. Her ability to fulfill writing assignments was closely tied to her comprehending the readings on which the assignments were based, to her developing productive strategies to fulfill the assignments, and to her having access to instructors outside of class to discuss the assignments.

was immediately faced with lengthy reading and writing assignments that required analytical and critical skills and behaviors. Certainly, ESOL programs can find ways to provide lengthier and more complex reading and writing tasks. But that is not enough. To develop meaningful programs, we need to espouse an educational philosophy that recognizes that language and literacy acquisition takes place not only through the formal study of language, reading, and writing but also when language and literacy are viewed as a means for understanding and constructing knowledge.

We should also question the feasibility of designing ESOL composition programs for the purpose of preparing students for the other disciplines. This investigation into social science courses, like similar qualitative studies, reveals that particular tasks are tied to particular settings and particular moments (see, e.g., Belcher & Braine, 1995; Chiseri-Strater, 1991; Herrington, 1985, 1988; Prior, 1995; Walvoord & McCarthy, 1990). Professor A's and Professor B's two political science courses, for example, reflected the individual professors' styles and goals. The lectures served different purposes: For Political Science 160, they primarily provided information that could be used in papers; for Political Science 21, they served to analyze the readings and to challenge students to think about the material. The readings differed, accordingly: For Political Science 160 they were primarily informative; for Political Science 21, argumentative. Even within the same course, the writing assignments differed. The first paper for Political Science 160 was primarily fact-gathering research; the second, interpretation of material learned. The two papers for Political Science 21 were a brief interpretation based on the lectures and a report requiring prediction based on researched sources. Given this complexity within a single discipline, given that students move through several disciplines as they fulfill graduation requirements, and given that ESOL faculty cannot have expertise in all of the disciplines, we need to be realistic in our expectations of what can be accomplished in ESOL programs. Furthermore, there is no guarantee that skills and strategies learned in an ESOL program actually will be applied in new situations. Although Yuko benefited significantly from the English courses she took in the first year, for a variety of reasons what she accomplished in English did not always transfer to other courses.

Thus ESOL programs cannot be viewed only as providing a "service" to the university in preparing students for other instructors' courses (Zamel, 1995). The service orientation suggests that ESOL programs can furnish all the tools students need to succeed and thus misrepresents what the acquisition of academic literacy actually entails. It also ignores the fact that ESOL courses have their own content and provide a rich environment for learning. Academic literacy cannot be acquired within the context of a one-way-street, accommodationist approach to learning. Success can be measured not by whether students adopt particular discourse practices but rather by how productively they can negotiate their way through diverse discourses (Canagarajah, 1993). To fulfill that aim, higher education needs a pedagogical model that enables faculty to transform and enrich the culture of the academy.

We can begin by reflecting on the tendency to judge students' cognitive and intellectual development from the stance of a monolingual culture. As Kutz, Groden, and Zamel (1993) point out, much of the early work of cognitive psychology fail to account for the experience of bi/multilingual, bi/multicultural students. Second language students do not fit into a simple stage model of development: They vary in age and background, speak different languages, and may communicate in ways that do not follow recognizable conventions. A clearer picture may be provided by the more contextualized and culture-based approach of constructive-developmental theorists (e.g., Belenky, Clinchy, Goldberger, & Tarule, 1986; Kegan, 1982) who take into consideration diverse ways of communicating and of valuing knowledge.

We can also examine the way past teaching approaches affect student learning. Students may have strong first-language and second-language literacy experiences to draw on, but, as is often the case, they may have gaps in their educational backgrounds. The kind of literacy instruction they received prior to entering college may be inadequate to satisfy the demands they now face. It makes sense not to expect students to have English-language, college-level academic literacy already in place. Too often, academic discourse serves a gatekeeping role, preventing students from progressing educationally (Farr, 1993). It certainly stood in Yuko's way during her first year, when the lecturer did not help her make sense of the discourse of International Relations. That Yuko ultimately did succeed does not absolve faculty of responsibility. We need to ask ourselves questions such as these: If such a privileged, accomplished student could have such a difficult first-year experience, what must it be like for students with fewer advantages? Are we providing the kind of education that can give them access to what Belcher and Braine (1995) call "the mystifying labyrinth of academic discourse" (p. xv)? Kegan's (1982) notion of a "bridging environment," which offers a safe place from which students can move from a familiar world into an unfamiliar one, is relevant in this context (p. 186). But the bridging environment should not be limited to ESOL classrooms. Faculty across the curriculum can adopt responsive teaching strategies that support learning across languages and cultures. Based on her numerous interactions with effective teachers, Yuko identified several such strategies, which other studies indicate are effective for all students (e.g., Rosenthal, 1992; Walvoord & McCarthy, 1990): (a) build on the foundation of students' background knowledge and experience, (b) make connections between course content and real life, relating course material to multiple social and cultural situations, (c) provide handouts to help students follow what is being presented in a lecture, (d) read aloud in class, especially from complex texts,

(e) analyze and critique the assigned readings in class, (f) encourage student–teacher and student–student interaction in class, (g) be accessible outside of class, (h) arrange student groups for study or research, (i) assign informal writing tasks that help students make sense of the reading, (j) allow for writing tasks that tap into students' multicultural knowledge, (k) provide ongoing feedback on writing in progress, and (l) provide written comments that discuss content and style.[3]

It is important to develop strategies to facilitate students' acquisition of academic literacy because it can give them access to power in the larger society. However, we should examine what it is we are asking students to acquire. We can begin by considering the cross-cultural implications of expecting students to produce a certain kind of discourse. As Farr (1993) points out, a text that might appear logical through the lens of the essayist literacy that dominates the U.S. academy may be illogical from the perspective of a different culture; what U.S. academics call "rhetoric" is really only "Western rhetoric" (Matalene, 1985, p. 790). When instructors direct students to explain ideas with explicitness and precision, for example—rather than to communicate through subtle implication (as Yuko put it)—we may be asking them to embrace a certain stance toward knowledge that is not shared universally. Because discourse practices are "integrally connected" with a person's "sense of self," asking students to adopt new literacy practices is, in effect, asking them to change their social and cultural identity (Gee, 1986, p. 720). Because this identity shift is an understandably slow and difficult (and perhaps an undesired) process, we should give ourselves permission to accept wider varieties of expression and be careful not to insist on students' conforming to one way of communicating.

Embracing multiple ways of writing is not a revolutionary idea. It is already taking place within and across different disciplines and within many classes, as this and other studies show. What may take a revolution, however, is to challenge the very nature of U.S./Western academic discourse by examining the "assumptions about what it includes and what it doesn't" (Zamel, 1993, p. 37). Most definitions of this discourse appear to be self-contradictory. Matalene (1985) claims that Western rhetoric is a way of structuring thought that values "originality and individuality" but at the same time requires that "premises and conclusions [be] connected by inductive or deductive reasoning" (p. 790). According to Farr (1993), essayist literacy calls for "a rationalization of one's own position" but at the same time is characterized by a "depersonalization of language" (pp. 10–11). Given these seeming inconsistencies, it is no wonder that a student like Yuko can spend years trying to figure out just what it is U.S. academics are up to. Pennycook's (1996) analysis of textual ownership helps to explain Yuko's early confusion about what she calls "American" writing, for he exposes a system that first seduces students through a Western "cult of originality" and then forces them to adopt a Western tradition that demands a "wholesale borrowing of language and ideas" (p. 212). Faculty need to reflect on our own role and responsibility in asking students to fulfill the seemingly conflicting goals of both borrowing ideas and being original, especially when the students have not spent a lifetime immersed in a Western academic system.

Finally, faculty can reconsider the way we construct second language learners' identities. Although a large body of research in contrastive rhetoric provides information about rhetorical traditions across cultures (Connor, 1996), longitudinal studies such as this warn us not to predict what a writer is likely to do as a result of first language and culture. Many studies in contrastive rhetoric are based on a definition of culture as "a set of rules and patterns shared by a given community" (Connor, 1996, p. 101), but this older definition ignores what cultural anthropologists now recognize as "the blurred zones in between" (Rosaldo, 1993, p. 209). Rosaldo's definition of culture takes into account the crisscrossing of distinct processes and recognizes that cultural identities are constantly "in motion, not frozen for inspection" (pp. 20, 217). This definition makes sense in the context of students studying across cultures. When they literally and figuratively cross borders, as Tucker (1995) argues, "it is difficult to discern precisely where one collection of customs and assumptions leaves off and another begins" (p. 57). Students like Yuko thus need to be viewed not as products of culture but as creators of culture. What I hope readers will take away from this study, then, is not how "a Japanese student" reads or writes, for there is no such essence as "a Japanese student." In fact, any survey of studies in contrastive rhetoric will reveal contradictory findings about "Japanese students" (e.g., Connor, 1996). Rather, what is important to focus on is the finding that a student's acquisition of academic literacy in a second language may be shaped by a theory of what is appropriate for a particular academic audience, by an acceptance of or resistance to certain discourse practices, and by a unique perspective on culture—all of which are always undergoing change.

ACKNOWLEDGMENTS

This chapter is a shortened and revised version of "The Acquisition of Academic Literacy in a Second Language: A Longitudinal Case Study," which appears in *Written Communication,* 1997, vol. 14, pp. 3–62. The Appendix, "Yuko's Response to the Study," is published here for the first time.

REFERENCES

Belcher, D., & Braine, G. (Eds.). (1995). *Academic writing in a second language: Essays on research and pedagogy.* Norwood, NJ: Ablex.

Belenky, M. F., Clinchy, B. M., Goldberger, N. R., & Tarule, J. M. (1986). *Women's ways of knowing: The development of self, voice, and mind.* New York: Basic Books.

Canagarajah, A. S. (1993). Up the garden path: Second language writing approaches, local knowledge, and pluralism. *TESOL Quarterly, 27,* 301–306.

Casanave, C. P. (1995). Local interactions: Constructing contexts for composing in a graduate sociology program. In D. Belcher & G. Braine (Eds.), *Academic writing in a second language: Essays on research and pedagogy* (pp. 83–110). Norwood, NJ: Ablex.

Chiseri-Strater, E. (1991). *Academic literacies: The public and private discourse of university students.* Portsmouth, NH: Boynton/Cook.

Connor, U. (1996). *Contrastive rhetoric: Cross-cultural aspects of second-language writing.* New York: Cambridge University Press.

Farr, M. (1993). Essayist literacy and other verbal performances. *Written Communication, 10,* 4–38.

Gee, J. P. (1986). Orality and literacy: From *The Savage Mind* to *Ways With Words. TESOL Quarterly, 20,* 719–746.

Herrington, A. J. (1985). Classrooms as forums for reasoning and writing. *College Composition and Communication, 36,* 404–413.

Herrington, A. J. (1988). Teaching, writing, and learning: A naturalistic study of writing in an undergraduate literature course. In D. A. Jolliffe (Ed.), *Advances in writing research: Vol. 2. Writing in academic disciplines* (pp. 133–166). Norwood, NJ: Ablex.

Kegan, R. (1982). *The evolving self: Problem and process in human development.* Cambridge, MA: Harvard University Press.

Kutz, E., Groden, S. Q., & Zamel, V. (1993). *The discovery of competence: Teaching and learning with diverse student writers.* Portsmouth, NH: Boynton/Cook, Heinemann.

Matalene, C. (1985). Contrastive rhetoric: An American writing teacher in China. *College English, 47,* 789–808.

Pennycook, A. (1996). Borrowing others' words: Text, ownership, memory, and plagiarism. *TESOL Quarterly, 30,* 201–230.

Prior, P. (1995). Tracing authoritative and internally persuasive discourses: A case study of response, revision, and disciplinary enculturation. *Research in the Teaching of English, 29,* 288–325.

Rosaldo, R. (1993). *Culture & truth: The remaking of social analysis* (2nd ed.). Boston: Beacon Press.

Rosenthal, J. W. (1992). A successful transition: A bridge program between ESL and the mainstream classroom. *College Teaching, 40,* 63–66.

Tucker, A. (1995). *Decoding ESL: International students in the American college classroom.* Portsmouth, NH: Boynton/Cook.

Walvoord, B. E., & McCarthy, L. P. (1990). *Thinking and writing in college: A naturalistic study of students in four disciplines.* Urbana, IL: National Council of Teachers of English.

Zamel, V. (1993). Questioning academic discourse. *College ESL, 3,* 28–39.

Zamel, V. (1995). Strangers in academia: The experiences of faculty and ESL students across the curriculum. *Composition and Communication, 46,* 506–521.

NOTES

[1]During the second semester Yuko enrolled in Philosophy of Religion, but soon had to drop it because it was "too hard [pause], so hard [pause]—the reading." She thought this difficulty was more connected to the topic than to language: "Philosophy is hard in Japanese too." But vocabulary was a problem: "I didn't know what they were saying in class [pause]; I never heard of those words." The professor told her to come back in her junior year, when she would have "more background and language."

[2]It was not until I was preparing the manuscript for publication that I realized that Yuko had included language verbatim from the original sources. Although this was indeed problematic, I believe that her writing needs to be understood in the context in which it was produced. She did not really hide the fact that she had borrowed language so heavily. She used only sources that Professor A had listed on the assignment handout, and she cited those sources accurately. Furthermore, she had been given little guidance in PS 160 for how to work with this material. I do not condone what she did, but I do recognize that she was not deliberately cheating; she was simply overwhelmed.

[3]Two years after she graduated from college, Yuko again reflected on the kind of support instructors across the curriculum should provide. See Appendix: "Yuko's Response to the Study."

APPENDIX: YUKO'S RESPONSE TO THE STUDY

After a longer version of this study was published in Written Communication *in 1997, 3 years after Yuko's graduation, I sent a copy to Yuko, along with some questions about the study. Yuko later e-mailed me her response, which I have included here in its entirety, with her permission:*

Dear Professor Spack,

How are you? Here is my reaction to your article. (I am sorry it took a while.) I will first try to answer your questions, and then write other things that came to my mind (which may or may not be relevant).

How accurately does it capture my experience?
It is pretty accurate. The article nicely clarifies how I moved on in learning English. Every semester, I was so preoccupied with getting through the "writing" classes that I was doing whatever works for each class. I was not thinking about "how" (using a different approach for each class from a language point of view). Your observation well makes sense of my behavior.

Does anything surprise me?
A few things surprise me.

1. I was unaware of the fact that I had such a strong opinion about what a good "American" way of writing was until I read your article. I always thought that a good writing in English was the argumentative one, probably because my idea of Japanese writing was that it is non-fiction style, and I was categorizing the two by giving a "criticality" test. But now that I think about it, my theory about good "American" writing was wrong as you pointed out. There are different types of writing both in English and Japanese. The descriptive, report-like style that exists in Japanese also exists in English, a good example being the PS 160 class readings. It's only that I didn't accept it as a style of writing, but considered it more like numbers, an expression with no art or creativity. The critical writing style that I thought was very "American" also exists in Japanese. I was not yet exposed to it before I entered college. In fact a lot of the academic writing in Japanese follows the style. What I did not understand when I was in college was that different styles of writing exist for different purposes.

2. I was unaware of the fact that I was haunted by the idea that "lack of background knowledge" was the language barrier in the first years [of college]. Of course, having some knowledge about the topic you are reading/listening to makes it easier to understand the contents, but that is not the necessary condition. If you know the language, you will have no problem in understanding even unfamiliar topics. Or if you know the topic so well, even if you don't know the language, you can more or less understand what is being talked about. My problem was that I had neither. I think I wanted to blame something for my incapability to understand, so I blamed it on lack of background knowledge due to being raised in a different culture.

3. I should be ashamed to admit that of the seven words I looked up in the passage [from the journal *Foreign Affairs*], I only know the meaning of one for sure today, after seven years. (How little vocabulary I learned during all this time!!!) But I would read the passage differently. I would not check these words in a dictionary, and although I don't know exactly what the passage is saying, I can guess generally what it is saying (at least in relation to the structure of this article ... it is raising the topic for the article, isn't it?). I can surely guess that not knowing these words won't be very critical (at least in the first time I see it in the passage). I won't be bothered by the fact that the paragraph didn't ring a bell for me, and I will move on reading, and only after a while if it becomes very necessary to know the exact meanings will I check up the words. What I will do today is I will keep in mind where to come back to, to go over again/check up words while trying to go through the entire piece quickly. In other words, I won't read the passage word by word, but try to capture its writing structure/main flow of logic and once I have the big picture, I will go back to the details if necessary. So the difference between

the first time I took IR and now is not the improvement in the vocabulary (or background knowledge), but reading strategy and confidence/boldness not to be bothered by what I didn't understand. The importance of aiming for the "big picture" is already expressed in the article. I also think confidence plays a rather important role. The level of confidence people need to feel comfortable/capable in doing things is different for each person. It so happens that I am one of those who tend to lack confidence in what they do. I don't feel comfortable until I know the issue pretty well. And I think this personality was a language barrier in my case. If I were a more confident person, I would have been less intimidated by not understanding the first part of readings.

Does it give me any insight into my experience?
It sure does, as I have written already. The fact that it has been three years since I graduated from [college] helps me look back to my experience more impartially. It's nice to know that what I was blindly doing for survival turns out to be a coherent process of learning a new language.

Is there anything I would challenge?
I would say that my not speaking in class/discussion is not a language issue, but a personality issue. Even in the meetings held in Japanese I rarely speak up to ask questions or make comment in front of people. So I don't think that the fact I kept quiet in classes would have changed even if I were perfectly fluent in English.

Knowing what I know now, what would I have done differently?
Not much. I don't think there was an easier way out. I think I had to go though the steps I went though in learning the language. I am very glad that I kept taking "writing" classes after the freshman year (even though that could have meant lower GPA [grade point average]), because how I write today is directly the result of all the training I had at [our university]. While it is still far from native speakers' writing and much is left to improve, I feel comfortable about writing in English. After I graduated, I met some Japanese students who graduated from American universities. I have to say, with no intention to brag, that I and other Japanese graduates from [our university] have better command of English than others. I am very grateful to [the university] for giving me the training in English that I had.

Based on my experience, what advice do I have for ESL teachers?
I would like to say that the language barrier that may appear as cultural might in fact be personal, so it could be misleading to categorize ESL students by cultural background. (You might already know this well).

Based on my experience, what advice do I have for teachers across the curriculum?

1. I would like the professors to be very clear and direct about what they are looking for in the assignments. (It might be only me, but I was often confused about what the writing assignments were asking for, not in terms of what to do, but in terms of how to write up the answer.)

2. I would like the professors to talk about the readings they assign for classes, more so in the freshman/sophomore level classes. If there is not time to discuss the reading itself, even just talking about how the book relates to the course/lecture will help.

3. I would like the professors or TAs to be available outside of the class. Most of the time my experience at [the university] in this point was excellent.

4. It would be easier if there were more support given at the academic resources center for undergraduate students, especially at the beginning of freshman year. (I believe there is more support available for graduate ESL students at [the university]). I was devastated to find that they couldn't help me with IR in the first semester at [the university]. It was not so much the fact that I wouldn't get help academically that devastated me, but the fact that there was no way to get help to get out of the problem which I couldn't get out of on my own. They were indifferent to my problem. It is a very negative experience to feel the sense of failure just at the beginning of college. I did not go back to the resources center ever (even after you suggested) as I was not going to go through the experience again. Even if they could not give academic support, they could try to support students in other ways such as simply encouraging them.

5. I am lucky to have been able to enroll in English 3 and 4 which were particularly designed for ESL students. I cannot help thinking, however, that what if I were an American who had not much background in writing before I came to [college]. I would have had to be in English 1 and 2, and that would have been a very difficult situation. Because two freshman writing classes are required classes for all, I think it is important to recognize the different background in writing for native speakers and arrange accordingly.

Based on my experience, what advice do I have for other students?
My advice for students facing problems is not to keep them to themselves but ASK FOR HELP (despite my experience with the academic resources center). Usually they will receive help and at worst, they will receive no help. But if they don't ask, there is not even a chance.

Extra Comments (this may not be relevant):

1. What helped me significantly in terms of improving writing was seeing the process of others proofread my papers. I was able to see ex-

actly how a native speaker will follow (or not follow) my paper, and if a part was incoherent, how he/she will say it. Discussing the differences led to better understanding of the nuance of the words, expressions and writing style, as well as the actual contents of the paper.

    2. A while ago there was an interesting column in a newspaper here. A Japanese-American in Hawaii was asked in English what her future plan was. She answered that she would like to develop specific skills and pursue a career as a specialist. Later in the conversation when asked the same question in Japanese, she answered that she wants to be happily married and have a family (no mention of career). I think it is true that the language you speak affects the way you think and to some extent your personality. I think my personality changes when I speak in English and when I speak in Japanese. I have two identities, specified by the language used. So the process of acquiring a second language is not simply learning a way of communication, but forming who you are which might be different from your self in the native language. I think this contributes to some degree to the difficulty in learning a second language.

Finally, I learned a lot from your study. THANK YOU for giving me the opportunity to be a part.

Chapter 3

"It became easier over time": A Case Study of the Relationship Between Writing, Learning, and the Creation of Knowledge

Marilyn S. Sternglass

Marilyn Sternglass chronicles the journey of a student from the Dominican Republic who failed to pass a standardized writing assessment test but who moved on to major in psychology as well as to achieve a Master's degree in that field. Focusing on how writing functioned as a way for Delores to learn, Marilyn also highlights the critical role faculty played in initiating Delores into the demands of disciplinary work. These instructors encouraged her development as an independent researcher and acknowledged the value of her cultural background in the creation of new knowledge.

As early as their first year in college, students begin to establish important academic and social connections that provide continuity in their college experience. As I argued in *Time to Know Them,* my longitudinal study of students' experiences in college courses, writing can play a significant role in helping students make ongoing connections when it is reinforced in courses beyond first-year composition:

> Composition instruction is an important first step in assisting students to formulate their ideas and learn how to express them clearly. But composition instructors should not believe that they are the final influence, or perhaps even the most important influence, in the development of writing abilities. Their role is a crucial one, to get students started in understanding

what the goals of writing should be.... Once students can recognize these goals, they will understand that it will take time, effort, and commitment to be able to carry them out. But the period of a college education does provide the time to practice these activities and to master these processes. (Sternglass, 1997, p. 141)

The most important contribution that composition instruction can make to students' academic progress may be to demonstrate the role that writing plays in their thinking and learning. The very act of writing itself, whether in response to readings or lectures or visual materials, seems to activate a learning mechanism requiring students to engage in a deeper commitment to understanding theories and ideas. In addition, writers must put ideas into their own language, thus making them conscious of whether they have reached an appropriate level of comprehension of the materials and ideas they are interacting with. These were insights that all students in my longitudinal study came to, although at varying points in time (Sternglass, 1997). Writing, they discovered, helped them to recall facts they could use as evidence in exams and compositions. Writing helped them to focus more deeply on issues and thus to produce meaningful analyses and syntheses. And the relationship between writing and learning revealed another dimension: the capability to produce new knowledge. This capacity was acquired by the student I focus on in this chapter, who participated in a 6-year study I conducted with a group of students from 1989 to 1995 at City College of City University of New York (CUNY).

Delores emigrated from the Dominican Republic at age 14. Although she had studied some English in the Dominican Republic, Delores' first serious study of English began upon her arrival in New York City where she attended junior and senior high schools. At first she was placed into a bilingual program where, she said, she "was introduced to the English language, yet not losing track of other subjects." Most of the writing, though, was done in Spanish. Then she was moved into the regular program and had to write in English. "It was hard at first," she said, "but then it became easier over time."

Just before entering college, Delores took the timed Writing Assessment Test (WAT) required of all students. In fact, she took it twice, once in the summer of 1989 and then again just before the beginning of the fall semester. Failing both times, she was placed into the English 2 section (the second level of basic writing in the English department) that I taught in the fall of 1989. Because of the time constraints in taking this timed test, Delores was unable to use the benefit that writing could provide in less constrained circumstances, the possibility, as she said, "to look things over." Criticism of tests like the WAT is endemic, particularly in their emphasis on sentence-level features that may disadvantage second-language and second-dialect learners. Instead of seeing grammatical skill development as a gradually acquired skill, test evaluators tend to focus inordinately on grammar competence. Gleason (1997) has pointed out these and other features that reflect the inappropriateness of the WAT for second language learners:

> There are several criticisms of this test: the questions require cultural knowledge that students may not possess; the time limit restricts revision, a primary focus of writing classes; and the test discriminates unfairly against second-language speakers. Most problematic, the WAT screens for a number of variables, not all predictive of successful college writing: speed in producing a first draft, cultural knowledge, mastery of standardized forms of written English, test-taking ability, handwriting, spelling, and ultimately culture, class, and ethnicity. And many students who repeatedly fail the WAT fare well in their college courses.... (p. 311)

Two of Gleason's points resonate in Delores' experiences: the significant benefit that comes from opportunities to revise writing and the intellectual power that shines forth from students' writing even when second-language features continue to persist in their work. Zamel (1995) emphasizes that it is inappropriate "to draw conclusions about intellectual ability on the basis of surface features of language" (p. 509). This is an insight important not only for composition instructors but also for instructors of all disciplines. After initially failing the WAT, Delores succeeded exceptionally well in her college studies. She majored in psychology and continued at City College to obtain a Master's degree in that field. This chapter chronicles her long journey.

YEAR 1

Approximately two thirds of the English 2 course Delores enrolled in in her first semester of college were devoted to writing in response to readings and practice with analysis, with the balance filled by attention to sentence-level instruction and editing skills. While the papers Delores produced in English 2 exhibited unnecessary repetition of ideas and second language interference features, her writing simultaneously demonstrated the beginning of her ability to analyze and synthesize from materials she had read. In an essay reflecting on experiences with work based on interviews from a Studs Terkel book, Delores concluded by writing:

> In summary, we can visualize that as mentioned above, good opportunity for success and a reasonable degree of satisfaction are the two most important elements some individual look at when selecting a job or career. The level of motivation can either make the person look for better opportunities for success or can make the person lose good opportunities that would lead him or her to a better position in life. Also, the degree of satisfaction that the

individual may dirive from a given type of work, can make the individual feel good about him or herself. We can also conclude that without profesional satisfaction the individual not only diminishes his/her productivity, but also his or her self-esteem as a person. A high level of satisfaction can make the person feel good and perform the best at his/her line of work as the case of Donna L. Murray [a bookbinder] in Studs Terkel's interview.[1]

Delores passed the WAT at the end of the semester and enrolled in a freshman composition course in the spring, a course that required frequent writing of formal essays based on readings.[2] Her tendency to repeat rather than develop ideas continued, but she later told me that her writing had improved as a result of her work in this course because it helped her to think through what she wanted to say: "When you write, you think more about what you're writing and you have to be more careful about how you say what you want to get across—more so than in speaking. In writing, you don't have body language, you have to make things clear."

Concurrently with her English courses, Delores enrolled in courses in psychology, her intended major. At the beginning of the second semester, she noted, she was already "using concepts from the introductory course" in her second psychology course. Taken immediately upon her admission to the college, these courses became the basis for her engagement in and commitment to her major field. In fact, at that early point in her academic career, she was already considering the possibility of going to graduate school to study neuropsychology. At the end of that semester, as a result of writing for psychology, Delores had a new observation about writing: It "makes me get more into the subject and then remember more about it."

YEAR 2

As she continued to take psychology courses, Delores became more fully aware of the demands of these courses and began to develop strategies to fulfill these expectations. In the fall of her second year, Delores reported that she had learned how to do research in her psychology courses and how to "put things in my own words." However, in one of her psychology courses, she was having problems with her writing because her instructor was placing a heavy emphasis on grammatical forms and was criticizing her for "restating ideas rather than developing them," the same problems she had had in the English 2 and freshman composition courses. She later told me that she had been disappointed by her poor grades, which had been caused by her "spelling and writing style." Because she was "penalized because of the writing errors," she said, "I am going to the Writing Center for help." She would continue to use this support network as well as help from her friends to improve her writing in other courses.

By the spring semester, Delores was seeing that research writing played a "very important" role in her learning of subject matter. "World

Civilization requires papers," she said. "I understand the material better—I'm more into it—experience it when I have to write…. When I write, I have to look for references (resources). I learned more than what was actually in the course…. The main idea is what interests me. I want to learn about it."

YEAR 3

Delores' teachers played a critical role in initiating her into the demands of the field of psychology. Delores' psychology professors became mentors outside of class as well as in class, and Delores frequently went to their offices for help. The assistance she received from her professors was important to her and encouraged her to join the department's peer support committee that helped students who were having problems. By the beginning of this third year, Delores had already taken many psychology courses and had familiarized herself both with the substance of the program and with the faculty of the department. By joining the support committee, she demonstrated her respect for and commitment to the department's program. Because she was already held in high esteem by the faculty, she felt comfortable asking for their assistance by requesting letters of recommendation.

In an Experimental Psychology course Delores took the second semester of her third year, she was required to run experiments on the computer and then write them up as if for publication. She anticipated receiving poor scores on the initial papers and then improving over time. In fact, that is what happened. In general, Delores saw writing as helping her "discover more things. It helps to read and then put ideas in my own words…. It makes me feel I'm pretty aware of what I'm talking about…. When I write something, it goes more into my brain."

It is important to note that Delores' commitment to her academic studies remained "strong" even though having to work at her outside job meant that she sometimes had to leave classes to "go directly to work without time to do schoolwork." Her commute from New York City to New Jersey, where she was living with her mother, took her an hour and 15 minutes. She said that she stayed in the library until 8 or 9 p.m. and was "so tired when I got home, I feel so exhausted." She stayed focused on her goal of becoming a psychologist.

In the spring semester of her third year, Delores applied to a special program at Lehman College of City University of New York in which students could earn six credits over the summer and begin to prepare a 30-page research paper. Designed for minority students, this program provides mentoring throughout the year with the aim of encouraging these students to go on to graduate study. With her admission into this program, Delores began a project that culminated in her first original work.

YEAR 4

By her fourth year, Delores viewed writing as integral to her work: "When you write, you become more aware of things. It forces you to do research, go more deeply into things. You have to know what you're writing, be aware of things—write facts, something true, back up a statement with facts. Writing makes you do that." More confident of her knowledge in the field of psychology, Delores had developed enough security to posit criticisms of the studies she was analyzing. She also was applying that knowledge to her own life: "Sometimes I try to put ideas together—like a diary—sometimes personal and how I see society and how it's related to me. In the last nine months, I want to consider myself an academic, a thinker. I know I'll be writing books and this will help prepare me to do that." Here is clearly the voice of an emerging professional person.

Having been admitted into the combined BA/MA in Psychology in the spring semester, Delores was now taking graduate courses at the same time that she was completing her undergraduate requirements. She said she had "no easy course" now. She was also working 36 hours per week in a doctor's office. This work load was "affecting the time" she could put into the Lehman project. Nevertheless, by the end of that semester, Delores had completed her paper for the Lehman project. The final title of the paper was "Skin Color and Its Impact on Self-Esteem of Latino College Students—Dominicans and Puerto Ricans." The introduction and conclusion reveal that she has become a competent researcher, able to analyze a number of variables and report on their impact on her hypothesis:

Excerpt From Delores' Introduction

Latinos are one of the largest ethnic groups in the United States. They are a rather diverse group, for example of the color their skin comes in all shades and tones. Throughout the years, a sense of identity and ethnic consciousness arose in the Latino community of the United States. Although Latinos in the United States share a strong sense of unified consciousness regarding their Latino ethnic identity, earlier studies have found that Latinos as minorities have significantly lower self-esteem than Anglo Americans (Shelibow, 1973), while more recent reports show Latinos are not significantly different from Anglos or African Americans (DeBlasie, 1969).

The study of ethnic identity has tried to answer one question, whether ethnic identity has a positive or rather a negative impact on the psychological adjustment of minority group members. The issue has been argued in two parts: first a strong sense of identification with one's ethnic culture usually acts as an extra incentive on the well being of the individual, by providing him/her with a sense of belonging; it serves as a protection against the negative prejudices and discrimination. The argument also goes on the opposite direction in that the sense of belonging and membership could promote the internalization of negative stereotypes and emphasize one's difference from the dominant culture....

Skin color is a critical variable that has been *under examined* by researchers in their study of acculturation and assimilation of Latinos in the United States. It has been *overlooked* by the mental health profession (e.g., clinical psychologists) in the evaluation of problems in the Latino community; it has been also *ignored* by basic institutions such as schools. There is *the necessity to acknowledge the problem of skin color* as a fact of our lives in the society in which we find ourselves [Emphasis added. This is the original aspect of the research.]

Latinos in the United States encounter themselves in a society in which the categories for defining race are either black or white. They are living in a society in which light skin and European features are more highly valued than black skin and African features. The color of skin of Latinos falls into a continuum which goes from black to white, and there are many shades and tones of color in between....

The interest is in whether the darker skin latino college student externalize to a greater extent than the lighter skin latino college student (the negative prejudices and stereotypes of this society against he/her color.)

I hypothesize that: Skin color is related to the level of self-esteem of these students. I further hypothesize that there will be a negative or inverse relationship between the level of self-esteem and the score on the color scale, that is, the lower the score on the color scale—or the lighter the color skin the higher their level of self-esteem. My second hypothesis is that Dominicans and Puerto Ricans will not differ significantly from each other in their evaluation of the self (self-esteem).

Excerpt From Delores' Conclusion

Although weak, there is a significant relationship between self-esteem and skin color of the sixty-four students. This finding gives some rationale to the my hypothesis that in the populations of Dominicans and Puerto Ricans, the relationship is probably not zero. This means that these two variables (self-esteem and skin color) are some what related.

One explanation for this significant relationship between self-esteem and skin color could lied in the fact that when I compared the two groups (Dominicans and Puerto Ricans) in how worthy they valued the perceived self, Puerto Rican seems to value themselves significantly higher than Dominicans.

The results could be explained in the sense that Puerto Ricans are, in the average, lighter-skinned than Dominicans and as such, when asked to rate themselves in a continuum of color from 1 to 10, they rated themselves significantly lighter than Dominicans. It gives rationale to the hypothesis that the lighter one is the better one feels about one self, the higher the self-esteem.

Another explanation for the finding that Puerto Ricans valued themselves higher than Dominicans, could be the fact that Puerto Ricans are lighter therefore, they feel more attached to the Anglo Americans for the virtue that they share a similar physical traits with the dominant group. It is important to notice that although the correlation between skin color and self-esteem was significant, I must say that it only accounts for 9% of the total variance. This is that the variable of skin color is only related to self-esteem, for this population, 9% of the time.

If we really want to make an assessment of the other 91% of the variable it is not accounting for one can say that time in the United states could also be a factor. Puerto Ricans have lived longer in the United States with a length of stay of 18.76 [years] in the average, while respondents from the Dominican Republic had average length of stay of 8.89. Perhaps the longer the stay the more one is acculturated to the customs and norms of the United States, the better English one knows, the better an economic position one has secured for oneself. The stronger an ethnic identity one has, and the better relation one has sustain with the dominant group.

It could be also explained in terms of the status that one's country of origin is held in relation to the United States. Puerto Ricans hold different position in relation the United States and therefore different attitudes than Dominicans. Puerto Ricans, by virtue of their country being a Commonwealth of the United States, have assess to certain services that Dominicans do not have (e.g., they are citizens of the United States, they could travel back and forth for Puerto Rico to the United States. They have little by little gained some positions in state and local government ...)

Dominicans, on the other hand are not citizen of the United States unless they go through the process of Naturalization, which sometimes can be painful if one does not know English. Dominicans tend to be darkerskinned, do not share as much in common with the dominant groups (Anglo-Americans), and have spent significantly less time in the United States....

Although second-language interference features are still visible in her writing, it is clear that Delores not only has become a competent researcher but also has initiated an examination of issues that have been neglected by others in her field of psychology. Here she has used writing to create new knowledge, an ability about which Delores derived great satisfaction. She said, "When I finish [a paper] and see the project, it's a nice feeling. Sometimes I create it—it's my paper, my ideas, like birth—there wasn't anything like that before."

At the end of that semester, Delores was planning to finish her BA in the summer and then enroll exclusively in graduate classes so that she could complete her MA within the next year. The Lehman project, she said, had taught her a great deal about doing research, enhancing her self-esteem. Her mentor had been too busy to provide her substantial help so, she said, "I did the research, me alone." She was beginning to formulate questions that she could address in her Master's thesis related to acculturation. Delores also had come to realize that writing was important to her professional development:

> I cannot transfer my ideas unless I use writing. It's crucial. My professor needs papers for grading. He needs to see that I can put something conceptually on paper. Writing in English is important for me—as a college student. When I'm not around, you can see what I'm up to. It's becoming more crucial. Sometimes I have something in my mind, but it doesn't come clear until I write it down. Then I can understand it better.

Her comments clearly reflect her awareness of the deeper commitment that writing entails, compelling the writer to engage in the intense reflection required to know whether true understanding has been achieved.

In reflecting on the development of her writing, from her first composition courses to courses near the completion of her undergraduate requirements, Delores said: "The process has changed. When you write in a 110 class [freshman composition], you write why I'm against abortion, three reasons and explanation. Now the issues have changed, not so dry; it flows more. Before I didn't have statistics and knowledge. For example, in the women's study class, I learned how environment has shaped women. I learned what social psychologists say. Now I have richer knowledge and fuller information. You know what you're talking about. Before I was 'more empty' in terms of knowledge. I'm more academic now."

In one of her first graduate courses, the comments made by one of her instructors on a paper she wrote on Maslow's theory of the "self-actualizing individual" reflect the dual aspects of Delores' experiences as a student: growing ability in her field and lingering features of second-language interference in her writing:

> B+ Very good—but could be even better. The basic content is very fine—you really went deeply into the primary sources in two of Maslow's major books and did a nice job of presenting some of his most significant ideas in a way that shows real understanding and appreciation. This paper had more depth and fullness than the previous one. However the writing was somewhat uneven: most of it was clear and well stated, but there were places where the statement of ideas was awkward, uneven or ungrammatical. But over all it was a very fine account. And you have been a fine contributor in class.

Delores was able to tolerate the comments about her writing style because they were presented in the context of a positive response to the research in the paper. She continued to take such comments seriously and continued to work on refining her writing. Despite the persistence of second-language interference features in Delores' writing, both the psychology faculty at City College and the administrators of the special program at Lehman College recognized, valued, and encouraged Delores' movement toward independent research based on her original ideas.

At this point in her college career, Delores said that she was "pretty satisfied" with how things were going for her academically, but personally, her life had suffered a serious setback. She had just ended a 3-year relationship with her boyfriend. Her mother had sold her business and everyone in the family was working. "Financially, not so easy for me," she said. But Delores had a resilient personality. She said, "I have an incentive. After all these problems, I keep hanging on. Problems get to me, but I have the ability to get around them. I can have problems, but still do decent work. It takes a lot of energy. I have lost weight." Delores would be working at a psychiatric center in a hospital with schizophrenic patients. She was considering preparing for work in clinical psychology or neuro-clinical psychology. "I want to get a perspective of what goes on in the brain," she said.

YEAR 5

As she progressed in her graduate studies, Delores became more and more aware of writing's importance in stimulating original thinking. She said, "In writing, you project your impact by yourself, your own ideas—you're the author. There's an opportunity to express views that are different than others in your class: Why I think this or that. I can criticize the work, the studies, that I've read about. The subject becomes alive. When you write, it stays with you. The subject becomes more concrete. At the end of papers, I can add criticism of the work, something new."

At the end of her fifth year, Delores told me that "writing about something helps me understand something else. I see overlaps or where differences are." Because she was becoming ever more knowledgeable in the field of psychology, writing was helping her see relationships and question relationships within her field. Writing was also helping her to remember facts and theories in her field. She said, "When I write—it's visual—information gets more to my brain. I'm able to comprehend more when I do research on a topic. Once I do a paper on a topic, the information is there forever. It helps my memory." So writing as a basis for recall remained important to her, just as it helped her in formulating analyses and creating new knowledge.

YEAR 6

By the fall of her sixth year, Delores was working on her master's thesis and completing her graduate courses. The following text shows how she represented herself at the beginning of this sixth year in a paper she wrote for a Social Psychology course, in the process integrating her personal characteristics with her newfound professional competence:

As I have mentioned before, one is affected by the environment in which one lives, I have felt that there have been other events in my life that were crucial in shaping my sense of a woman. The education I am getting has influence my sense of a woman. I feel that education has given me the self-esteem and the confidence that I need to go on in life. Education has open my mind to the world and made me want to explore about life issues concerning me and my place in society. Through education I have become to realize that I am an important part of the coming generation, the generation who will be making the policies, and the important decisions that will affect the lives of others. A college education has made me become more self-aware of my humanity, and of my womanhood. [The instructor wrote "good!" beside this paragraph.] ...

Finally, living in the United States not only has strengthen my sense of a woman, but also my sense of ethnicity and the color of my skin, so that I do not only see myself as a woman, I also see my self as a Latino black woman. Woman in the sense that it is my gender and I will do my best to enhance it and work for the advancement of other women. A Latino woman in the sense that I am a Hispanic person in this country and I would work for the advancement of the Latino woman which up to the present lacks recognition. A black woman because as the Latino, the black woman is lacking the recognition deserved.

The instructor's final comments both encouraged Delores and gently prodded her to monitor her writing more carefully.

Over the 6 years of her academic studies at City College, Delores had used writing as a means of learning in three important ways: to help her remember facts, to delve more deeply into ideas and theories from an analytical perspective so that she could apply these theories, and to develop new insights that led her to original research projects. Her growing sense of identity fostered her professionalism by leading her to construct proposals in areas underserved by others but seen as relevant to her background. Despite the persistence of second-language interference features in her writing throughout all her undergraduate and graduate years, it is clear that Delores had become a successful professional in the field of psychology. Delores was planning to study ethnic ambivalence in Latino students for her Master's thesis, undertaking in the process a complex statistical analysis of factors including skin color and a self-esteem inventory.

CONCLUSION

Just as students' knowledge base grows in a developmental way, so does their ability to express their ideas in English, both substantively and grammatically. Support for clearer expression is essential to students' growth, but this support must be offered simultaneously with support for greater knowledge and analysis. Both aspects of writing—content and form—develop over time for students, and both aspects need to be nurtured.

Delores received important and substantial support from her instructors throughout her college years. They valued her ideas and complimented her on her thoughtfulness; simultaneously they prodded her within a positive context to work harder on the expression of those ideas. That she was so energized by this encouragement argues well for this dual approach to responding to all student written work.

One important implication of this study is that composition classes are the sites where writing instruction *begins*. As the variety in the writing tasks assigned across courses reveals, it would be impossible to prepare students in their composition classes for all the discipline-specific demands that may be made on them. But composition instructors can provide students with opportunities to practice reading and writing activities that lead to conscious awareness of the deeper level of engagement and understanding that writing promotes. I have long argued that students should be practicing analysis and synthesis at all levels of composition just as they are simultaneously practicing writing skills (Sternglass, 1997). As students increase their knowledge base, they are better prepared to provide the evidence that will support their perspectives. Instructors of freshman and sophomore students can encourage them to go beyond factual presentations to provide reasons for how and why their evidence is valid for the arguments they want to make. Such instruction should be followed up in other settings where students can come to appreciate the significant role writing plays in their understanding of the complex materials and theories they are encountering in their academic studies.

Analysis of evidence is critical to learning, and as students become more knowledgeable, they will become more willing to question "accepted dogma" in their disciplines and become able to propose original studies that will lead to new understandings in their fields. Because of the particular backgrounds second language learners bring to higher education, they are distinctly qualified to question societal norms and practices. And writing fosters the comprehension that permits questioning and critiquing of "established" perspectives, especially valuable when these new perspectives represent views that have not been investigated by more mainstream researchers. When students like Delores identify areas that are not recognized by others as being significant, these students are able, through their writing, to add important dimensions to their professional fields and contribute seminal knowledge to the larger community.

EPILOGUE

Today, with CUNY's new standards, Delores would be denied admission to City College or any senior college in the CUNY system. Any student who fails the skills test is assigned to a 2-year community college or to an external language institute. Delores thus would have been deprived of the continuity of long-term instruction that developed over time and contributed to her success. The faculty, too, would have been deprived of Delores' contributions to their classroom and to their field.

REFERENCES

Gleason, B. (1997). When the writing test fails: Assessing assessment at an urban college. In C. Severino, J. C. Guerra, & J. E. E. Butler (Eds.), *Writing in multicultural settings* (pp. 307–324). New York: Modern Language Association.

Sternglass, M. S. (1997). *Time to know them: A longitudinal study of writing and learning at the college level*. Mahwah, NJ: Lawrence Erlbaum Associates.

Zamel, V. (1995). Strangers in academia: The experiences of faculty and ESL students across the curriculum. *College Composition and Communication, 46*(4), 506–521.

NOTES

[1]The writing samples that are included are presented exactly as Delores wrote them, without corrections of spelling or sentence-level features. I have not made any attempt to alter the punctuation from the original pieces.

[2]Not all of the students in my study passed the WAT test after taking English 2.

Chapter 4

Lessons From Ming: Helping Students Use Writing to Learn

Trudy Smoke

Trudy Smoke revisits a case study in which she investigated the experiences of a student from China as she progressed through college. Trudy presents parts of the study in the context of her work with Hunter College Writing Fellows, doctoral students who have a role in promoting writing in classes across the curriculum. Describing Ming's writing experiences in several disciplines, Trudy explains how an understanding of Ming's writing processes can provide Writing Fellows with useful strategies and insights as they consult and collaborate with their faculty partners.

As Writing Across the Curriculum (WAC) Coordinator at Hunter College, I have the opportunity to work with a group of six enthusiastic, bright, and dedicated graduate Writing Fellows who assist faculty in a variety of disciplines. The City University of New York (CUNY) Writing Fellows program is an initiative that is integrated with the WAC program as part of CUNY's commitment to improve writing and academic literacy by encouraging writing-to-learn pedagogy across all 17 of its colleges. The Writing Fellows are doctoral students at the CUNY Graduate Center, most of whom have completed their coursework and passed oral exams but have yet to write dissertations. The Writing Fellows program was conceived to enable these graduate students to have a role in introducing writing in classes across the curriculum at an assigned campus. Working with Writing Fellows gives instructors across the curriculum the opportunity to discuss how their classes are viewed with someone who will not be making a tenure or promotion decision and who is in the class not only to assist the faculty member and the students but also to learn more about good pedagogical strategies. As a result, the program has been highly successful at my campus and across CUNY.

61

As part of their responsibilities, the 100+ CUNY Writing Fellows attend all-day workshops for 4 days at the end of August, organized and taught by Sondra Perl and several other faculty knowledgeable in writing pedagogy. Whether their specialty is anthropology, environmental psychology, biology, English, or art history, the new Writing Fellows learn about the rationale and strategies for including writing in classes across the disciplines and at all levels. They are introduced to techniques for helping the faculty with whom they will work to include a variety of writing assignments, to respond to students' work, and to evaluate writing. They learn how critical writing is to the process of genuine learning. After completing the workshops, they go to their assigned campus and meet the Writing Fellows coordinators and the professors with whom they will partner and learn about the departments (not always their own specialty) in which they will be working. As part of the work they do over the academic year, they attend classes, tutor students, offer in-class and larger departmental workshops, and help teachers develop assignments, syllabi, surveys, citation materials, and trait-specific scoring sheets. Although they serve as consultants to faculty and departments, they neither teach classes nor grade papers. Once a week the Writing Center director, Dennis Paoli, and I meet with them for "training" sessions. During those sessions, we discuss articles we have assigned, specific issues related to writing, and specific classrooms situations they have encountered. They share materials they have created, and we become a learning community.

One issue that is especially challenging concerns helping ESOL students as they progress through a variety of courses throughout the college, an area of special interest to me as an ESOL professional. In our weekly meetings, the Writing Fellows readily admit that they often feel overwhelmed by ESOL issues. They report that they do not know how to address ESOL students' lack of class participation or their struggle to read in a second language. But, most important, the Writing Fellows say, they have difficulty talking to their partner teachers about how to respond to ESOL papers that have "errors all over the place." Although most of them have been teachers themselves, they are not trained in linguistics or language acquisition and thus feel ill equipped to deal with papers whose grammatical and organizational problems arise out of students' lack of familiarity with English and its corresponding academic discourse conventions. For Dennis and myself, this is an opportunity to discuss relevant theories of language acquisition and techniques for responding to writing.

As part of this work with the WAC program and the Writing Fellows, I decided to revisit a case study I conducted several years ago describing one ESOL student as she progressed through college (see Smoke, 1991, 1994) with the idea that a discussion of a student's writing process could provide Writing Fellows with some useful strategies and insights as they consult and collaborate with their faculty partners. I wanted the Writing Fellows and faculty across the curriculum to understand that even though an ESOL student's writing may not be error free, most certainly not in early drafts, writing can be an effective tool of learning. For ESOL students, as for most of us, language acquisition is a long slow process. Over time writing does improve grammatically, and when students feel they have something important to write about, the content and organization also get better. I also wanted the Writing Fellows and faculty across the curriculum to recognize the importance of getting to know students and of not judging them simply by the products they produce in a 15-week semester. It is rare that one is able to view a student's writing over many years and across different courses, but this kind of longitudinal research, I believe, can give depth to our understanding of what the word *process* means when we talk about writing and learning.

MING LIANG

The student with whom I conducted this research is Ming Liang.[1] The preposition *with* is carefully chosen because without her full cooperation and dedication to the research, it could not have taken place. Ming was as interested in exploring her own process as I was in understanding it. I first met Ming when she registered for my upper-level ESOL writing course, which was paired with a social science course offered in the Black and Puerto Rican Studies Department (for more information about these courses, see Haas, Smoke, & Hernández, 1991). Ming was in her sixth semester; she had had to repeat each of the first two levels of ESOL courses and was taking my class because she had to repeat the upper-level ESOL writing course as well. It was, however, the first time that she was in an ESOL class linked to a class in another academic discipline. At the end of this semester, Ming passed both the ESOL and the Black and Puerto Rican Studies courses as well as the required writing proficiency test. In the following semester, she took and passed the college expository writing course as well as other mainstream college courses. From the time she was in my class until she graduated, I collected all the writing Ming did in the college and discussed with her the feedback she received as well as the drafts she prepared for other writing assignments. We met regularly, and I taped my interviews with her. In those tapes, Ming told me about her background and how it had affected her motivation to succeed and had given her the confidence that she would be able to manage the work assigned.

At the age of 14, Ming moved from a southern province of China to the United States with her family of one brother, two sisters, one older and one younger, and two parents. She knew virtually no English when she arrived in New York, but she had the advantage of having a grandmother, an aunt, and an uncle in the United States. She moved to Queens, New York, where she attended high school, taking both ESOL and non-ESOL English classes. Despite having taken these courses, she was placed into the college's lowest-level ESOL class on the basis of the college entrance tests. Her explanation for this placement was that she had done little writing in her high school classes; because of shyness, she had sat in the back of the classroom and rarely participated.

On the basis of these early problems, when she started college she initially planned to major in accounting because she found English, and especially writing, so difficult. However, as a result of her positive experiences in college writing courses, she said, she discovered that writing could be a vehicle for synthesizing her ideas, analyzing what she was learning, and creating new knowledge. Having gained confidence in her abilities, she changed her career goal. She decided to become a teacher at the early childhood level and anticipated working with children who, perhaps like herself, needed to build their English-language skills, and she began taking education courses.

From an early age, Ming had been a successful student; at the age of 12 she received a scholarship requiring her to leave home to attend a special school in another part of China. She achieved this honor even though her parents could not afford the tutoring that most other students received to gain admission to these elite schools. Despite the loneliness and illness she experienced while living at the school and despite the long hours of classes and laborious community work, Ming succeeded. So it was clear that she had within her the skills to succeed in college as well. To ensure that success, she actively sought out teachers, counselors, tutors, and peers who were willing and able to work with her. She also challenged herself by choosing courses, both within and outside her major, that required substantial writing. Although she felt some trepidation about writing these papers, she welcomed the opportunity to improve her writing further through feedback from professors across the college curriculum. The feedback she would receive turned out to be not always as encouraging, nor even as helpful, as she had hoped it would be. Yet over time she developed her own strategies for getting the feedback and assistance that she needed in writing these papers.

The longitudinal study I conducted with Ming spanned more than 4 years. In this chapter I focus on five assignments written during the last 3 years of her college experience to illustrate how she turned the assignments, the feedback she received on them, and the problems she encountered with them into learning experiences. I reflect on what the WFs— and all of us in academia—can learn from her experiences.

ACQUIRING CLASSROOM-SPECIFIC CULTURE AND DISCOURSE: ART EDUCATION

Researchers of writing across the curriculum have shown that because discourse and expectations differ across disciplines, there is no monolithic way to approach academic writing (see, e.g., Bizzell, 1999, 2000; Chiseri-Strater, 1991; Walvoord & McCarthy, 1990; Zamel, 2000).

Zamel believes it is necessary to "view each classroom as a culture in its own right—a culture with its own norms, conventions, expectations—and to understand that it is the process of working within this classroom that makes it possible for participants to acquire its discourse" (p. 9). But how do students acquire this classroom culture if professors do not make expectations clear? Ming's experience in an arts education course demonstrates what can happen when courses fall short in this way.

In her seventh semester in college, Ming took "Art in the Elementary School," a two-credit class required for her major, for which she had to write three papers. Each assignment called for a description of a visit to a New York museum chosen from a list distributed by the professor. Ming's task was to write a response paper about three works of art that she "enjoyed the most" at each museum. (Ming visited El Museo del Barrio, The Studio Museum of Harlem, and the Whitney Museum of American Art.) Though the writing assignment seemed to be intended to provide future teachers with an introduction to New York museums, its vagueness created problems for Ming. She had limited experience with the cultural institutions of New York City and had never written a paper about a piece of art.

One factor that contributed to Ming's choice of El Museo del Barrio for her first visit was the course in the Black and Puerto Rican Studies Department she had taken the semester before. This course led her to develop an interest in Latino culture and provided her with a cultural context for interpreting the artwork on exhibit. Ming tried hard to make her first paper interesting and personal. She explained where the museum was located and how she had found it and then described the three works of art that she had chosen and made an effort to bring these works of art alive for the reader. She described the first painting, "One More Time Columbus" by Fernando Salicrup with great care, including such details as its size and the materials used in its construction. In her interpretation, she focused on eyes that were concealed throughout the work:[2]

> I think that the title and the picture did tell a story. The title "One More Time Columbus" referred to the history of the Tainos (Boricua) and their constant acculturization which was caused by the enslavement of these people, which started when Columbus came to their land. In this picture, the eyes were hiding in the dark and behind the trees. Next time, when Columbus comes back, he will never capture them again.

After describing the next two pieces of art, Ming added a personal conclusion:

> I was so pleased with the exquisite painting that I spent two hours there. In addition, I also enjoyed writing on the three pieces of work that I have chosen. This, not only gives me an opportunity to practice my writing, it also gives me a chance to interest and to express my feelings about the paintings. Next time when I have time I will visit the museum again.

Her teacher's comments at the end of this final paragraph said, "I hope so. In next paper try being clear in what you say." Despite the fact that the professor had written "Beautiful" next to her interpretation of the concealed ideas, Ming was devastated by this comment and felt too embarrassed to ask the professor for further clarification. The teacher feedback was inadequate, she said, for it offered no direction and no explanation of what was expected on the assignment.

Ming had already written the first draft of her second paper on the Studio Museum of Harlem when the first paper was returned, so there was little time to find out what she had done wrong, even if she had been able to muster the courage to speak to her professor. In the second essay, she used the same strategies for describing the art displayed in the Studio Museum of Harlem, although she was even less familiar with the cultural and historical context of this work. Once again her paper was an attempt to articulate an internal process: Ming used her close observations and careful notetaking to make sense of art that was at first puzzling. One of the artworks she wrote about was a collage entitled "Sauvage" that included an inverted photograph of a "black naked man who is standing on the chair [with] four white dressed ladies looking at him." She wrote that one woman was pointing at the man and seemed to be ordering him to stand on the chair. The other women were standing staring with their mouths agape. In her paper Ming admitted:

> I don't really know exactly what this picture means. But I guess that the artist is trying to show us that the man was being punished by these ladies. The title "SAUVAGE" might refer to the history of the colonial days and how the Blacks were treated by the Whites. During that time, the Whites considered Blacks were savage, not civilized and inferior because they were mistreated and looked down upon by the society. The photo could also mean that this was the way Whites punished the Blacks.

Ming concluded this paper in a slightly different way from the way she had concluded her first paper:

> In conclusion, The Studio Museum in Harlem is a very interesting place to visit. Comparing this museum to El Museum del Barrio, The Studio Museum is much more attractive. Perhaps the exhibitions in this Museum are different, especially the story quilts. The artists in The Studio Museum in Harlem not only emphasize the Black culture, they also talk about the history in the past. Some of these stories also make use of the stories from the Bible. I believe that the exhibitions are not only educational for the adults, they are also beneficial and significant for children as well because children can learn the history of the Black culture. Also, it is a great idea for teachers to bring their students to this museum because the story quilts are very interesting and very educational and they are also appropriate for children of all ages.

The professor made a few corrections and wrote "Very good paper" at the bottom of the essay. He also added an "E" in a circle, which Ming interpreted as meaning Excellent. Ming was quite satisfied with these results. When I asked her what she thought had improved the paper, she said that "perhaps" it had been her statement that teachers should take students to this museum because the exhibit was educational and appropriate for children of all ages, which was a reference to the course she was taking. However, Ming could have no way of knowing why she had received a higher grade on this paper because her professor did not explain how the paper met his expectations. Nevertheless, this was an important step in Ming's awareness that academic writing is to some degree course- and discipline-specific. She understood the need to shape an art response paper for an art education audience. This was a critical insight.

Ming's third paper described an exhibit entitled "Image World: Art and Media Culture," shown at the Whitney Museum of Art. The exhibit included William Wegman's photographs of his Weimeraner dogs dressed in human clothes and depicted in human situations. Ming struggled to make sense of the photographs. One of the photographs was especially problematic for her. She wrote: "'Dressed for Ball' is insulting women because a dog dresses in a fancy silk gown and imitates a woman. Moreover, the picture also represents romance, fantasy and exoticism because the dog in the picture dresses in an oriental gown and stands on top of the table." Ming told me that she was personally insulted by the attempt to make a dog play a role often assigned to Asian women, but she did not state this in her paper. Realizing that it was considered a work of art and that she was writing a paper for a class, she instead concentrated on describing the details of the photograph. Because Ming had been heartened by the professor's response to her conclusion to the second paper, she ended this third paper by discussing the appropriateness of the exhibit for teachers and students:

> I think that the exhibition of "Image World: Art and Media Culture" is inappropriate for children because some of the works are very sexually explicit and some are difficult for them to understand and interpret. However, it may be appropriate for high school seniors and college students, because they might be more mature and aware of what is going on in today's society.

Having no sense of how Ming made meaning of this photograph, the professor responded to one section of her paper with the comment, "I don't believe you get the point," a comment that Ming found upsetting. Above the sentence in the conclusion that ends, "difficult for them to understand and interpret," he asked, "Did you understand many of them?" At the end of the last line he wrote, "True." The final comment on the paper is "Very good paper. Keep on pressing."

Pressing is a curious word. Ming was certainly pressing ahead in her attempt to become a better student and a better writer. The three required art response papers were difficult for Ming, yet they provided important lessons for her. They are instructive for the Writing Fellows as well. These papers suggest what a student can accomplish over time even when the expectations of course assignments are vague or problematic. Ming gained experience traveling through New York to several locations she had never visited before. She developed tools for looking at and interpreting visual images. She discovered how to slant her writing to suit her target audience. Ming's experience also illustrates what happens when a professor loses an opportunity to get to know a struggling student and to make course assignments more accessible. Furthermore, it raises questions about how to address cross-cultural issues that students might confront in assignments that call for completely new cultural experiences and that might create a conflict in response to what is perceived as culturally offensive material.

FROM INSECURITY TO INDEPENDENCE: SOCIOLOGY

Ming's response to an assignment in a Sociology course she took the following semester illustrates her ability to understand "the difference between the consumption of knowledge and the construction of knowledge" (Zamel, 1993, p. 37), a step that I believe to be critical to becoming a successful learner. With a teacher and in an environment in which she knew she would be heard and respected, Ming was able to move beyond the constraints of a writing assignment and to create a meaningful research project.

Ming took "Social Inequality" with a professor with whom she had taken other sociology classes. One of the early assignments in the class was to write a two-page abstract of an article from a professional journal. Ming selected "The Rise of the Jewish Professional: Case Studies of Intergenerational Mobility" by Stephen Steinberg from the journal *Ethnic and Racial Studies* because the topic fit with her interest in learning more about unfamiliar cultures and ethnic groups. She was especially interested in the strategies used by various immigrant groups in their struggle for success in the United States.

During our interviews a month before the paper was due, Ming showed me her first draft of the abstract. In the first paragraph, Ming described what Steinberg had identified as a pattern contributing to the successful intergenerational mobility of Jewish immigrants. Ming noted that according to Steinberg, the pattern of success related to the fact that the immigrants he described had come to the United States with professions and skills at a time when those professions and skills were needed. Because she felt dissatisfied with Steinberg's conclusions, Ming met with her professor and discussed the idea of doing her own research on this subject. Her teacher gave her permission to go ahead with her project. Ming was beginning to test the waters. In addition to the required abstract, the draft of this paper contained findings from interviews Ming conducted with two people whose families had migrated from the Caribbean to the United States—a student in her class and one of her former math teachers—as well as data about her own family. She described the professions each had brought to this country.

Ming explained to me that she had decided to try using interviewing as a method of obtaining information, as a result of having worked with me for the past several semesters. She used this paper, written for a trusted professor, as a way of conducting personally relevant academic research. Ming pushed the limits and expanded what had originally been a two-page abstract assignment into an authentic research project. She conducted several interviews, transcribed them, made charts, and described and analyzed her findings. She not only included her ideas and personal opinions in this paper but also critiqued Steinberg's research. She identified three limitations of his study—the small number of families interviewed, the omission of data about education, and the omission of data about women, which in itself revealed her new awareness of gender issues. During one of our interviews, she said: "Steinberg only looks at the men. The males are the dominant ones who control or who are always in charge of the business. That's why he would, probably like it was like, like in *A Doll's House,* you know that one. It's like the men always are the breadwinners in the house. What about the women?" Ming also criticized Steinberg's study for the lack of data about the role of education in the lives of the immigrants. Growing up with the belief that education is the most critical tool for social mobility, what she referred to as a "major path to success," Ming could not accept Steinberg's stress on the professions and skills immigrants brought with them.

In her critique of the Steinberg study, Ming treated her own findings as equal to Steinberg's. When she wrote, "Based on this (my) data, I can not conclude that this pattern is similar to Steinberg's," the two researchers were on equal footing. As part of the process of writing this paper, Ming was able to "indwell," which Polyani (1962) describes as the process of learning academic discourse from the inside. First, she had carefully read the Steinberg article and identified its major assumptions. In her paper, she questioned those assumptions and the evidence presented in his research. She compared Steinberg's research with research described in other professional articles she had read on this subject. Next, she attempted to replicate the author's research methods to develop her own evidence. She charted this, experimenting with the new (to her) discourse convention of conducting and documenting primary research. She identified a problem and worked step-by-step to reach a conclusion. She was able to view intergenerational mobility from both the narrow viewpoint of a critic and the broader perspective of an immigrant in this country. She brought the strengths of her own experience and ideas into her academic research. Ming received a "99" for her paper along with the professor's comment, "Excellent job."

In completing this paper, Ming illustrated how "academic writing, reading, and inquiry are inseparably linked; and all three are learned not by doing any one alone, but by doing them all at the same time" (Reither, 1985, p. 625). What makes this especially critical is that Ming created this project and carried it to its conclusion. She wrote herself into that sociology class and found out how research in the field is conducted and written by doing it herself. Like the art education papers, this project is instructive for the Writing Fellows. Ming's experience shows how an insecure learner can progress to become a student who can rewrite assignments to make them more useful, and who understands the power of research and the value of "writing as a genuine source for learning" (Zamel, 2000, p. 18). Furthermore, this classroom experience illustrates the benefits that accrue when instructors support students' interest in exploring subject matter, allow students to create meaningful assignments for themselves, and let them know that the time and effort they put into their assignments is valued.

BRINGING IT ALL TOGETHER: THE INDEPENDENT STUDY COURSE

Ming's final project, an independent research project, was in a sense her personal capstone experience. During her last semester, she registered for the first time for an Independent Study course. In order to complete this kind of course, a student must meet with a professor before the semester begins and propose a project that convinces the professor to work with the student on that project for the semester. Together, the professor and student decide on the number of credits the project is worth. In this case, Ming met with a professor with whom she had taken "Social Welfare" and "Child Welfare" (receiving a "B" and an "A," respectively) and convinced that professor that her intended research project was worthy of a six-credit Independent Study. The project Ming designed was a *Resource and Service Guide for the Children From Pre-K to Sixth Grade in the Chinatown Area.*

Ming had identified an area where there was a real need. No guide such as this existed. The writing of this guide also bridged her two areas of interest—sociology and education—leading to a document that would be appropriate for both. To do the research Ming had to go outside the college and into the community. She had to use resources not always easily accessible. She had to make extensive use of the telephone to contact directors of after-school and nursery school programs in Chinatown, and she had to assess quickly what language to use as she made appointments to meet with the program directors. She decided in advance what information would be needed in the guide and developed questions accordingly. She collected whatever brochures or printed materials the programs had produced. She told me that she did most of the data collection in English because "I guess I feel comfortable now." However, she was able to speak in Cantonese, Mandarin, or Toishanese (she had spoken Toishanese and Cantonese when she arrived in the United States and studied Mandarin in college) when needed. She was also able to use Spanish to communicate with parents and students because she had studied Spanish in college. After her research was completed, Ming organized her data and began to write what would turn out to be a 117-page resource guide. She decided to write the guide in English because she felt it would be more useful to the community, and she had decided to give copies of the resource guide to the Chinatown Community Center so that it could be made available to parent groups and others needing these services.

Explaining to me how she found out about the existence of the large numbers of programs and centers, she said that she consulted the Agency for Child Development and used the *Yellow Pages* and "her feet." This was a project that involved legwork. Ming walked through the community, going into churches, centers, and stores and asking about programs. She asked directors of programs to tell her about other programs. She took detailed notes and followed up each lead with a visit or a telephone call. The project ended up taking so much time that she could not complete it by the end of the semester. For the first time in her academic career, Ming asked a professor for an "Incomplete." She was concerned that she would never finish the project and would not be able to graduate, yet she persisted. As she neared completion of the guide, one of the directors of a program that she had visited contacted Ming and asked if she wanted a job in that nursery school when she graduated. She received an "A" for her Independent Study, graduated from college, and accepted the teaching job at the nursery school. She had determined an authentic need, created a research project to respond to that need, used her recently acquired writing and interviewing skills, and brought the project to fruition. In the process, she acquired the self-confidence to meet with and communicate with professionals in English as well as in the other languages of the community.

What Ming received from her sponsoring professor was just what she needed—support and encouragement throughout the course of the project. Her teacher never stood in her way. The instructor had confidence that Ming could and would complete the project and was available whenever Ming had questions or felt concerned that she did not have the ability to complete the guide. As a result of this and other positive experiences, Ming was able to go beyond the setbacks she had experienced earlier in her academic career—the categorization of herself as a "remedial" student, the three failures in writing courses, the unhelpful comments on papers—and instead was able to find an inner strength.

Ming's experience provides a sense of how ESOL students can become active learners who trust their curiosity and the value of their questions and perspectives and highlights what is possible when students persist, resist, and find their own way. Her experience also provides insight into how students can engage with the writing process and come to see writing as a way of learning. Furthermore, Ming's experience points to the value of fostering a student's multilingual identity and of viewing emerging bilingualism as an asset rather than the deficit it is often perceived to be. Perhaps most important, Ming's experience shows how students can rediscover their own power, a power that is often silenced or challenged because of their initial insecurity with English.

ESOL STUDENTS, WRITING FELLOWS, AND FACULTY ACROSS THE CURRICULUM

Studies such as the one I conducted with Ming can motivate Writing Fellows to develop productive strategies for working with ESOL students (and, by extension, with all students) and their professors. Just last week during our training session, one of the WFs, who is working in the discipline of Film and Media Studies, said that she has been concerned that many of the ESOL students in the large media classes do not understand some of what is said during lectures. They may know the vocabulary (and sometimes of course they do not), but many are unfamiliar with the cultural knowledge professors expect students to know. This Writing Fellow now asks students to write down words, phrases, names, or events that they do not recognize, and then she meets with students to discuss unfamiliar terms or references. She is also trying to anticipate difficulties, so she writes down what she thinks may be problematic for them. She acts as an intermediary when she reminds the professors that more than 50% of the students in our college did not grow up in New York or the United States, did not grow up speaking English, and do not have knowledge of much that seems obvious to these teachers.

Another Writing Fellow developed a survey that helped the psychology professors get some sense of students' prior experiences with academic writing and their attitudes about using writing as a tool of learning. She has also helped the professors realize that students often do not hear or understand what is expected of them when an assignment is presented only orally, especially when it is given at the end of a long lecture class. Yet another Writing Fellow, who himself formerly taught Urban Studies, discovered that the very project he had developed and that is now required of new students by most members of the department, is very difficult for first-year students to comprehend and actually do. As a Writing Fellow consulting with the department, he developed explanatory materials that help break the project down step-by-step; he also put together a set of examples to assist students when he discusses this project with them.

Being a participant in weekly or monthly meetings with the Writing Fellows and having the opportunity to discuss writing and teaching pedagogy across disciplines has resulted in my own growth as well. My work with the Writing Fellows has given me a broader view of college classrooms across disciplines and a deeper understanding of the students I teach. It has been exciting to discover that many colleagues are attempting to make student writing and their responses to it an important part of their course work. The opportunity to examine a student's experiences in depth and breadth by undertaking a longitudinal case study and reflecting on its implications within a larger institutional context reaffirms my belief that learning to be a teacher, like learning to be a student in college, is a long-term learning process. No matter how experienced we are, we are all capable of reassessing, learning more about, and improving what we do.

REFERENCES

Bizzell, P. (1999). Hybrid academic discourses: What, why, how. *Composition Studies, 27,* 7–21.

Bizzell, P. (2000). Basic writing and the issue of correctness, or, what to do with "mixed" forms of academic discourse. *Journal of Basic Writing 19*(1), 4–12.

Chiseri-Strater, E. (1991). *Academic literacies: The public and private discourse of university students.* Portsmouth, NH: Boynton-Cook/Heinemann.

Haas, T., Smoke, T., & Hernández, J. (1991). A collaborative model for empowering students. In S. Benesch (Ed.), *ESL in America: Myths and possibilities* (pp. 112–129). Portsmouth, NH: Boynton-Cook/Heinemann.

Polyani, M. (1962). *Personal knowledge: Towards a post-critical philosophy.* Chicago: University of Chicago Press.

Reither, J. A. (1985). Writing and knowing: Toward redefining the writing process. *College English, 47*(6), 620–628.

Smoke, T. (1994). Writing as a means of learning. *College ESL, 4*(2), 1–11.

Smoke, T. (1991). *Becoming an academic insider: One student's experience of attaining success in college.* Unpublished doctoral dissertation, New York University, New York.

Walvoord, B. E., & McCarthy, L. B. (1990). *Thinking and writing in college: A naturalistic study of students in four disciplines.* Urbana, IL: National Council of Teachers of English.

Zamel, V. (1993). Questioning academic discourse. *College ESL, 3*(1), 28–39.

Zamel, V. (2000). Engaging students in writing-to-learn: Promoting language and literacy across the curriculum. *Journal of Basic Writing, 19*(2), 3–21.

NOTES

[1]Ming Liang is not the student's real name.
[2]No corrections have been made to the student's original text.

Chapter 5

From Outsider to Insider: Studying Academic Discourse Communities Across the Curriculum

Eleanor Kutz

Eleanor Kutz reports on a project she developed for her first-year composition course in which she asks students to become researchers in classes across disciplines. The students undertake an investigation of one of their college courses in order to gain an understanding of how best to participate in the work of that academic discourse community. In presenting the projects of four ESOL students, Ellie shows that students' insider or outsider status may be tied more closely to discourse learning than to language learning.

The freshman writing course I teach aims to help students draw on their prior knowledge and experience as language users in order to adapt to an academic discourse community in the college. The focus is on discovering the underlying discourse competence they have gained as insiders to a variety of discourse communities—communities where people share ways of talking or writing as well as interests, beliefs, and values. Through the coursework, students see how that competence and the strategies that underlie it can help them as they work toward functioning as members of the new academic discourse communities of their current courses. The curriculum calls for students to reflect on past experiences in discourse communities, to investigate familiar discourse communities in which they currently participate outside of the university, and to study, from the same discourse community perspective, their current academic courses and the disciplines these represent. Whereas most students choose to focus their academic discourse community studies not on their writing course but on other courses across the curriculum, one ESOL student, Quy Houang, decided to focus on the writing course itself, which allows us to see some elements of the course design through a student participant's eyes.

THE CHALLENGE

Like many ESOL students, Quy Houang has memories of difficult experiences in moving from one language community to another. In a memoir, he tells us of two quite different experiences of school after he came to the United States. In his first year, he was sent to a bilingual program where most of the subjects were taught in his native language, and where he "got along fine" with his American ESOL teacher, even if he didn't quite understand all that she said. "Because of the bilingual program, I was able to adapt to the new environment quite easily." The next year, however, he attended a school without bilingual or ESOL classes. There, not surprisingly, he found that "I had a hard time trying to make the teachers understand me. When I tried to say something and the teachers had no idea what I wanted to say, I usually got frustrated and gave up." Despite this frustration, Quy's English continued to improve, and with it his academic work, to the point where he was accepted for high school at the elite exam school in the public school system. There, however, he suffered academically because "my English wasn't even good and I had to deal with two other languages [French and Latin]," and he had to transfer out of the school. Now, as he starts college, Quy feels confident that he can use both English and Vietnamese well enough to communicate with others using either language without much difficulty. But he is still concerned that his English may not be adequate for undertaking demanding academic work.

Quy's account of his experience points to concerns many ESOL students have as they begin their college-level study. He has adapted well within a sheltered language environment but has not always had academic success without that support. Though he knows that he is now a fluent speaker of English who can communicate in the language, he continues to fear that his English, which he sees as "far from perfect," will hamper his academic performance. As a graduate of a non-ESOL curriculum in a U.S. public high school, Quy is not identified as an ESOL student for his college study, and yet as he begins his college work, he retains aspects of that identity in his own picture of how he is situated and what he faces. Like other students, Quy enters the university with an established social identity as a student: one that has been shaped by his prior school experiences. A central aspect of that identity comes from his experience as a speaker of English as a second language, and it is the first thing that he points to when he is asked to write about prior experiences with discourse communities at the beginning of his freshman writing class.

It is not uncommon for ESOL students to attribute difficulties with academic courses—both current problems and those that they anticipate having—to their level of mastery of English (Spack, 1997). They see their problems as unique—as unlike those that native speakers of English encounter—and they are most likely to attack those problems with discrete language-learning strategies. In writing, they may be particularly focused on grammatical concerns, word choice, and surface errors, especially if these are the kinds of issues teachers' responses emphasized. In reading, they may draw on single-word or sentence-level strategies—looking up unfamiliar words in a dictionary, translating sentences, and trying to work out sentence-level meanings (Auerbach & Paxton, 1997; Shih, 1992). Even very advanced students like Quy, whose writing displays few traces of their non-native status, may return to these familiar language-learning strategies when they encounter difficult texts and demanding writing assignments in unfamiliar disciplines. To the degree that they respond to their academic experience from the familiar social identity of ESOL student or English-language learner, they are more likely to apply those language-learning strategies for which they've proven their competence and to attribute ongoing problems to a need to learn more English vocabulary or to have their teachers mark for correction every nonstandard surface feature of their writing.

Within the designated ESOL writing courses at our institution, students are guided in moving beyond language-learning strategies to a broader conceptualization of what's involved in college-level reading and writing in a second language. But mainstream courses typically give little direct attention to the needs and concerns of ESOL students, and mainstream teachers frequently attribute any difficulties these students may face in courses almost entirely to the fact that English is their second language (Zamel, 1998). This attribution confirms students' own fear that it is their performance as users of a second language that is at issue, and that, as ESOL students, they are outsiders to a learning enterprise to which native speakers are insiders. The effect of approaching their work from within the identity of ESOL student may be to highlight the uniqueness of the problems they encounter in their academic courses, encourage their unconscious dependence on language learning versus more general academic learning strategies, and discourage alliances with other, non-ESOL, learners.

Yet the problems that Quy and other advanced ESOL learners face in their academic study are not unique. They are not so much language-learning problems as discourse-learning problems, and they are better approached with discourse understandings and strategies. It is those meta-level understandings, and the discourse strategies that go with them, that this curriculum is designed to address.

A DISCOURSE-BASED APPROACH TO WRITING
WITHIN THE COLLEGE CURRICULUM

What does Quy, like other freshmen, need to know in order to move effectively among his college courses? To put it most simply, he needs to
know how to meet the expectations of various faculty, from various disciplines, who will teach his courses. That means he must be able to make
sense of what he reads and hears and to respond to assignments in ways
that approximate the genres of student writing in the discipline. To accomplish these things within his introductory courses he will need to do
the following:

- Begin to build a relevant framework of content knowledge—key
  concepts, terms, figures, methods—that provide the underpinnings for each discipline.
- Learn something about the purposes of study in these disciplines and how the significant content knowledge relates to
  those purposes.
- Develop an awareness of the ways people typically talk and write
  in that discipline—of how ideas are introduced and organized and
  presented, for example—and an understanding of how to participate in the work of the classroom community.

In other words, he'll need to focus his attention, not on vocabulary or sentence and paragraph structures in isolation, but on how these are shaped,
in this context, by the nature and purposes of the conversations that go on
there. And in order to participate fully in those conversations, he'll need
to develop, like all other insider participants, a sense not only of *what* is
talked about in this context, but of *why* and *how*. As he participates, he'll
gradually come to develop, as well, new aspects of his social identity as a
student—and begin locating himself among college sophomores or sociology majors or creative writers.

In *Lives on the Boundary* (1989), Mike Rose recounts the experiences of
students at the University of California at Los Angeles who lack these
sorts of understandings and effective strategies for obtaining them. Their
problems—those for which they need "remediation"—are not problems
of intelligence or motivation, nor are they problems of language, even for
those whose first language is not English. In some sense they are problems
of successful students—students who have succeeded at defined academic
tasks in their prior education and who don't understand that their college
courses require a new relationship with what they learn: in a sense, a new
social identity as a learner. Whereas the old social identity of successful
high school student could be achieved largely by completing what was
asked at a competent level, the new identity of college student (at least as

it is seen by professors, and in retrospect by those who have been successful students) involves understanding the meanings behind the assigned tasks, being able to determine and take on their purposes, and becoming more of an active learner (in the sense of shaping one's own understanding of a field) than a student who waits to receive what has been shaped.

Studies of students' progress through their college years highlight these changes, which are often seen most clearly in the cases of nontraditional students who have had to cover the most distance in negotiating new identities and new discourses. Marilyn Sternglass, in *Time to Know Them* (1997), reports on a longitudinal study in which she followed students who had entered college through City College of New York's experiment with open admissions. Although the students she followed took longer than the traditional 4 years to complete their degrees, by the time they were involved in upper-division work in their majors, they were writing, reading, and participating in the work of their disciplines like any other student. Likewise, Ruth Spack, in "The Acquisition of Academic Literacy in a Second Language" (1997) shows, from following a hesitant EFL student through her college work at an elite university, that initial setbacks gave way over time to accomplishment in those very fields that had been most problematic to start with. Yuko's success was accompanied by her growing sense that she was getting "the big picture" of the field she was studying while developing her own effective strategies for getting that picture—for "constructing" knowledge (p. 44). At the same time, students must come to understand something of the social world they are entering and social functions that their writing serves as they move across academic settings, as Lucille McCarthy (1987) found in her study of a freshman student composing in three different courses.

One theme that emerges strongly from such studies, and that's named explicitly by Spack's student, Yuko, is that one of the things that makes the biggest difference for students who succeed in various areas of their academic study is their ability to see the big picture. They need to have a sense of what the terrain they are attempting to traverse is like, why it has the shape that it does (in relationship to the goals of the discipline and the purposes of sequenced courses within its typical course of study), and how those pursuing knowledge within the discipline write and think about their work. Unfortunately, introductory courses, despite their intention to provide an entry point to work in the discipline, are rarely explicit in laying out this terrain and in providing the interpretive context that will allow students to engage meaningfully with the information they find in their textbooks (Geisler, 1994). Most often, they simply identify students who are already partially able to perform in the ways in which past successful students have performed—who enact the identity of a successful student in Psychology 101, for example—and to weed out those who don't know how to perform in these ways. And this is a problem across the curriculum. As Sheila Tobias (1990) found in her study of successful students in other disciplines who had hesitated to venture into science courses, these introductory courses too often focus on the *what* without the *why*—on facts and algorithms and formulas without much sense of the purposes for which they would be used.

READING THE BIGGER PICTURE: SEEING WHAT'S SHARED AND VALUED WITHIN A DISCOURSE COMMUNITY

How can we help entering students to see the big picture that will let them make sense of their introductory courses and of their place within them and within the larger academic setting—that will help them negotiate and enact new social identities as successful students within these settings? One answer is to introduce them to a set of understandings about discourse and discourse communities, including academic ones, that will let them see that their work as writers and readers in the setting involves more than attending to surface forms and looking up new vocabulary. These understandings include the notion that particular discourses—ways of talking, thinking, valuing, and enacting a social identity—evolve in particular contexts (Gee, 1992; Heath, 1983; Kutz, 1997); that once they move out from the primary discourse of their homes, people are always in the process of acquiring new, secondary discourses (Gee, 1992); and that they acquire these discourses and the literacies associated with them through meaningful participation in the new settings (Kutz, Groden, & Zamel, 1993). Offering students the opportunity to explore their own experiences in different discourse communities, both familiar ones in which they are insider participants and the new ones that they are entering in their academic courses, allows them not only to participate in meaningful ways in the sort of inquiry that uses and creates academic knowledge, but also to gain meta-level understandings about how discourses work and about their own process of moving from "outsiderness" to "insiderness" as they begin to try on the discourse of a new setting.

One way of thinking about the discourse of an introductory course is to see it as an extended conversation about the underpinnings of the discipline—a multifaceted conversation that is carried on through reading and writing as well as speaking and listening, and that not only involves the participants in the classroom (the teacher and students) but links to prior/larger conversations (the big picture) in both the discipline and the broader academic context. Insiders to such a conversation know how to use language in ways that let them achieve three important functions of discourse simultaneously: naming and making propositions about the world in the ways that are typical in this setting; carrying out the intentions and purposes that are understood and shared in this setting; and doing both in the ways that are seen as appropriate to this setting. (See Halliday, 1978, on the ideational, interpersonal, and textual functions of language.) These functions can be represented, again as the *what, why,* and *how* of discourse in any given context, and they provide a useful tool of analysis for students who are studying how discourse works across settings.

Returning to Quy, let's see what he has to say about the study of discourse communities in freshman writing, as he looks at how the course works in relationship to these discourse functions. Here's some of what he tells us about *what* the course is about:

> English 101 composition revolves around the idea of discourse communities. They are communities that we are a part of. They are part of our everyday life, even if we are consider outsiders or not in those communities. Each discourse community has its own characteristics, values, and ways of communication. People moving from one discourse to the next all the time, and by looking at and understanding the values of those communities, we will know how to act appropriately and being consider as insiders to those discourses.

His naming of *why* the course has the focus it does appears in the paragraph that introduces his report: "The goal is to help develop your writing skills, to adapt to the new setting, an academic discourse community that is college." Quy then reflects on *how* the course works to achieve these goals:

> This class is not all what I expected. Instead of concentrating on grammar it focuses on how to write expressive papers using your background experiences as a tool and build on them. For example, we have to write an essay on our discourse community by first taping an everyday conversation and then transcribe it. After the conversation was transcribed, I was asked to analyze it to find out what was being talked about. Who are the people? Did they take turns? Why were they talking about it? I also have to look at what shared knowledge that an outsider would need to know in order to understand it.

After drawing from the example of a course assignment, he comments:

> As you can see, the professor is always concerning with the what, how, and why. She wants us to dig deep into the subject and not just looking at the surface. The teacher always asks for the students' opinions about some topic or another. When s/he gives his opinions, the professor encourages her/him to say more, to elaborate on it.

And he comes to see that, "How a class operates depends on what is value in that class."

To see more of how this curriculum works and what it values, I'm going to turn back to Quy's study of a familiar discourse community outside of the university. For that study, Quy had chosen to tape-record a conversation at the family dinner table, translating it from Vietnamese to English after he transcribed the tape. Guided by the now-shared concepts within this course, he analyzes the conversation to discover what is being talked about, why it is being talked about, and how it is being talked about—looking at how each of these elements is shaped both by the immediate context in which the conversation is taking place and by the larger cultural context. He looks for what the participants know, as insiders: for the shared knowledge, shared purposes, and shared ways of carrying out this sort of conversation that insiders have in common but that outsiders won't necessarily understand. He is helped in this enterprise by having members of his research group look at the transcribed text with him, asking questions, as outsiders, about whatever they don't fully understand.

Quy begins his analysis by circling repeated words in his transcription to discover what is talked about. Here the words fall into several sets: homework and home; class, classes, and school; study, dishes, allowance; and lazy, silly, crazy. Having read Spradley and Mann's (1978) study of speech acts in a college bar, he identifies common speech acts: "of these speech acts, *asking* probably is the most frequently being use at the dinner time. My parents are very concern with their children's progress in school, and these questions are routinely being asked to keep track of us." Questions are part of how this conversation is carried out, but who asks them and the pattern of turn taking and responding are significant as well, and Quy looks at each contribution to the conversation, considering why it appears. For example:

> From the beginning of the transcript, you might have notice that the question of "did you do your homework?" (ln. 1 & ln. 12) was asked twice. This might seem normal in most families, but in mine it is weighted a little bit heavier than most. My family considers very highly of education. We feel that a good solid education is the key to a successful future and so it is always being regarded with the highest priority. This topic, more or less, is always the first subject being discussed at the dinnertime, and sometimes it is the only one.

Here Quy links what happens in this conversation with a larger pattern for his family, one that represents both his family's beliefs and values and those of a larger home culture:

> In my family, like most Asian families, my father assumes to role of a leader, a person who is in charge of the family. He is dominant in terms of decision making: what he said goes. However, he does not like to talk much, he prefers quiet and reading. However, if you look at the transcript you would notice that my father seemed to be the one who did most of the talking. As I said before, he speaks mostly at the dinnertime because he wants to be up-to-date with our progress in school, otherwise he would rather stay quiet

so that we can study. Thus he always wants us stop talking to each other so much and spend more time on studying. Although we don't always agree with him, his words are usually final words.

Quy entitles his final essay for this unit "Family Values." And he situates his own family's exchanges within a larger sense of the nature of family conversations that he has gained from his classmates. He now sees those family values as common to all families, as well as to Asian families: "The 'what did you do today?' and 'did you do your homework?' are common topics that I think everyone can relate to. My family is no different, only that it is in another language and the expectations are higher."

This sort of work leads students to a clearer understanding of the complex nature of discourse competence—of the competence that allows them to function as participants in the spoken and written conversations of a variety of discourse communities. They can see the sorts of shared knowledge that come into play in familiar discourse communities where they function as insiders, and they perceive that similar elements are likely to be at work in other communities to which they are still outsiders, including academic ones. Although the close analysis of conversations directs their attention to words and sentences, it also guides them to look at how these connect to larger, more global patterns in any exchange. And it leads them to make a link between features of any particular text and the context that gives shape to it.

SEEING ACADEMIC COURSES AS DISCOURSE COMMUNITIES

Quy was able to apply some of these understandings in his study of the academic discourse community constituted by his 101 class. Other students, looking outward from that class to their experiences across the curriculum, draw on these newly shared understandings in similar ways to help them negotiate the terrain of their other courses. They too have looked to understand the shared knowledge, shared purposes, and shared ways of talking and writing within these introductory academic communities, and to see the ways in which their classes serve (or don't serve) to introduce students effectively to the knowledge, purposes, and ways of the larger academic discipline. In the process, they have seen themselves applying some of their discourse competence from other settings to their participation in this academic work, even as they come to understand that competence in new ways.

Situating New Vocabulary in the Shared Knowledge of the Classroom

Dorian, in writing about his earlier experiences in discourses communities, recalls his isolation as a young teenager speaking Albanian in a neighborhood where only English was spoken: "I didn't feel as part of that discourse community because I couldn't speak its language and didn't have the same tradition as the other people did. " He describes his strategies for moving into a new, English-speaking world:

> I remember seating down in my couch with the English book in my hands, trying to learn the words that I couldn't even pronounce. Often I would get mad and throw the book away and think about my own language. I remember asking my father, "Why doesn't everyone speak the same language?" and he would answer, "Because not everyone is the same."

As he begins to study his current experience in the academic setting of a freshman seminar on "The Mind-Body Connection," Dorian worries at first about the difficulty of the reading, that "these articles vocabulary was kind of hard to understand." But as he goes on to observe specific moments of classroom interaction and to see how shared knowledge, shared purposes, and shared ways are created there, he discovers that the patterns of classroom discourse and the shared understanding that's created within them makes the vocabulary-learning problem quite different from what it was in his earlier experience, because it is helped by "classroom interactions and participation." He goes on to describe how "the professor would go over the readings with the students to make sure we understood every key concept and theory," and how "the professor placed each one of us in different groups in which we were able to discuss the articles and express our thoughts." He describes the work that groups did in defining and presenting particular concepts to the class, and his own group's effort to define "excellence," and in the process he begins to move comfortably into the academic style of the texts he's been reading and writing: "According to Morgan, who was an illustrator, excellence occurs when you use your brain to illustrate reality."

In his final report on this classroom discourse community, Dorian focuses first on the "big picture":

> [The course] provides a shared knowledge that allows you to understand and read about a variety of topics. In terms of reading content, we traced some key theories of the mind through Western and Eastern literature, ancient and modern. The course content focused on a) how our physical being and our awareness of our physical being affect mental functions and also b) how directing the mind alters the body.

After reading an article by Chafe (1982) on some differences between spoken and written language, Dorian comes to realize that it's not only the classroom interaction patterns but specific features of the professor's discourse style that have contributed to making the difficult concepts of the readings part of the knowledge that students can share:

> The vocabulary of this course was kind of hard to understand in the beginning, specially reading Western and Eastern readings, but later on it got cas

ier as we went along. It got easier because of all the work that we did made me an insider. Being an insider of this community I could define key concepts such as excellence, intelligence, schizophrenia, etc. that an outsider would have a hard time with. The professor played an important role in explaining those key concepts by using his informal speech which is easier to understand. The informal speech that the professor used was similar to Chafe's spoken and written languages. As Chafe studied in his article he found out that spoken language was easier to understand but written is more formal. By studying Chafe's article I found out that the professor of my course used involvement features in talking to make the material of the reading accessible and make sure we understood the essential concept information. He did that by giving us examples and talking about the different tests that observers have done in his own words.

As an insider who has also become aware of what's involved in sharing one's insider knowledge with outsiders, Dorian also begins to reflect on his own goals and strategies as a writer. Having presented a detailed analysis of the ways in which elements of the course build on each other to create a larger framework of understanding, Dorian compares what he is trying to accomplish for his readers to what Rose has tried to do in his study:

> Just like Rose said, "Framing an argument or taking some else's argument apart, systematically inspecting a document, an issue, or an event, synthesizing different points of view, applying a theory to disparate phenomena." In this particular quote Rose names some elements of what he terms critical literacy. By doing this he wants to make sure the reader knows some background towards the literacy. He feels that by giving the readers some background they would feel as insiders. If the readers understand the purpose of study in a discipline it would be easier for them to see more clearly the conceptual framework that he has been applying. I was trying to do the same thing as Rose was, give readers some point of view in order for them to understand what this discourse community is about.

By studying the ways in which discourse communities create and maintain shared knowledge through the patterns of their discourse, Dorian has gained a richer understanding of what's involved in successful communication, not only among friends or between teacher and students, but between writer and reader. He now works consciously to create the shared knowledge for his own readers that he himself depends on, and he sees the ways in which others writers do the same. No longer isolated by language or discourse, he now places himself in a conversation that, like many academic conversations, takes place in writing as well as in speaking and that is shaped in interaction with other texts as well as with other people. Seeing how he has become an insider to some classroom discourse communities, he is ready to enter others.

Discovering the Relationship of Language and Discourse

Not all students find themselves to be insiders to their academic courses—sometimes for reasons that surprise them. Abby, whose first language is Spanish, focused her discourse community study on her family's use of Spanglish (a study that led her to appreciate the beauty of her family's "wild tongue"). As she turns her attention to her course on Hispanic Writers in the U.S., she describes own initial "naive concept of a Spanish class." As a Spanish speaker who had also studied Spanish throughout high school, Abby expected to fit easily into the class, but "I later realized I was somewhat more of an outsider than an actual insider." Abby finds that her fluent but nonacademic Spanish does not prepare her for the critical discussion of literature. Here she captures a bit of that class discussion:

> Class begins like every Monday, Wednesday and Friday at 1:30. As usual the professor arrives five minutes after. Puts her texts and notes in front of her as though her life depended on it for reference. The discussions about a text on immigration, exiles and memories within an author will take place as it has been for the entire semester. The professor begins her lecture with the eight students present. "Buenas tardes, como estan? Hoy empeamos con la lectura de tropicalizacion. Quiero saber cuales son sus comentarios o critica sobre el texto leido. Haber Abby que piensas?" That's Spanish for "Good afternoon, how is everyone doing? Today we will start by going over the text read: tropicalization. I would like to know what were your comments or even criticism about the text. Let's see, what did you think Abby?"

After reflecting on her own uncertainty in this moment and her own memories of immigration and exile when she came to the mainland United States from Puerto Rico as a young child, Abby goes on to recount more of the classroom discussion, translating the other students' comments into English for the readers in her writing class:

> "I think tropicalization is different—it's basically coming in terms with issues of Latin America." (Student 1) This is one of the answers the professor gets from the most outspoken person in the class. While the other immediately responds, "I thought with the title we were going to learn about the Caribbean—hoping something positive. After having read that I found it to be a way of boxing-out types of people." (Student 2). During the course of the discussion I noticed how both students tried being in control over the class by commenting, agreeing and disagreeing with the text, while the professor jumps to a passage of the text: "Drawing on the value of transculturation as the dynamic, mutual influence that a subordinate and a dominant culture effect upon each other in the contact zone ..." (Pratt), thereafter picking up a chalk and writing other concepts that connect one way or another with what this passage is emphasizing. While lost in the

term tropicalization, I am only left to somehow put all this information together to figure out what is talked about.

Abby too is discovering that moving from one setting to another involves
more than moving between languages. She is having difficulty with a style
of academic discourse that is syntactically dense, with specialized vocabulary that is not opened up and translated by the professor into the informal language that will make it accessible (as happened in Dorian's class).
She is also uncomfortable with a competitive style of class discussion,
rather than one that is collaborative and exploratory. Although Abby's
personal experience is much like those represented in the course readings,
there appears to be little space in this course for her to draw on that experience and make her own connections.
     Abby also turns to Rose to frame her own experience:

> My sentiment can also be compared to that of "Politics of Remediation"
> from *Lives on the Boundary* by Mike Rose. In it he talks about the inside/out-
> side knowledge in an academic discourse community and says "this sense
> of linguistic exclusion can be complicated by various cultural differences."
> (154) What I am emphasizing here is that I might dislike this class for its
> linguistic exclusion. Having been a student of the course, Hispanic Writers
> in the U.S., I realized the one place I really thought I was an insider I actu-
> ally turned out to be more of an outsider. The language of the course is not
> one I share with the rest of the class, although the issues are similar. I am
> not comfortable with the constant competition in order to have the last
> word or to be "politically correct." Perhaps Hispanic poet Sandra Maria
> Estevez said it best:

> > I am two parts/a person
> > Boricua/spic
> > Past and Present
> > Alive and oppressed
> > Given a cultural beauty
> > ... and robbed of cultural identity.

It is unfortunate that Abby's course has reinforced her sense of exclusion
and outsiderness. Yet her close attention to the discourse of the texts she
has been reading has given her a new discourse strategy for representing
that very confusion in ways appropriate to academic writing, drawing
another text into her own in order to represent what she would say.
Though she may feel ill at ease in the classroom conversation, she has begun to see how to craft a conversation of her own, one that brings together different texts, read in different classes, to create new
understandings of her own experience that she in turn will share with the
readers in her writing class—expanding their knowledge of some aspects
of the Latina experience.

ENTERING THE DISCOURSE OF A DISCIPLINE

Finally, Sophia, a young Korean woman who arrived in the United States 2 years ago after having lived with her family in Argentina, and who responded to Abby's studies of her family's Spanglish with accounts of her own family's typical blending of three languages—Korean, Spanish, and English—shows us the academic discourse community of a large introductory lecture course in Sociology. She too has taped moments of classroom discussion and she explores the ways in which these discussions work to bring students into not only the specific shared knowledge of the course but the larger frameworks of the discipline:

> The subject that we are covering at this moment is the religion. In our course book, religion is described as following: "Religion has been defined as any set of coherent answers to the dilemmas of human existence that makes the world meaningful. It has also been defined as a system of beliefs and rituals that serves to bind people together into a social group." (W. Kornblum, 288)

> For the introduction of this chapter, the professor asked a question to the class. The question was "How does sociology talk about the belief system?" Later, she mentioned two major sociological perspectives, functional theory and conflict theory, relating to this topic. Several hands went up rapidly and students were enthusiastic to answer that question. There were interesting but different answers.

> Student 1: "I think that religion supports the functional theory. It provides spiritual needs."

> Student 2: "Give hope to people. That might be good for society."

> Student 3: "The religion keeps the community tight."

> Student 4: "Marx is right. All contributions of churches go to pastors. They teach people to contribute because that is part of there reverence to God, but the church's pastors were the most rich in town.

> Student 5: "I don't like the statement that the religion makes people in peace because if we study history, many wards were caused by different religions.

Sophia not only captures the exchanges of students in her sociology class, she observes other aspects of the students' interaction and the professor's response:

> While students were doing comments, other students listened them carefully and they tried to look the face of students who are speaking. The professor also listened them carefully and she had an eye contact with the student who is doing comment. Then she repeated their main points and mentioned if she was agreed or disagreed. Later, she related student's thought to the different social perspectives.

Sophia discovers that this classroom, although large and without the opportunities for small-group work that Dorian's class offered, does provide an effective bridge between students' own understandings and the shared knowledge of the discipline, and moving from this typical moment in the classroom, she traces out what it contributes to an understanding of two larger sociological perspectives on the problems of human society, the functionalist perspective and conflict theory. She sees the purpose of the course as guiding students to an understanding of those perspectives as well as an understanding of how they can be applied to various social issues. And she finds that the patterns of classroom discourse, with engaged debate accompanied by polite and respectful responses from both teacher and students, encourage an exchange of ideas and a use of new terms that has allowed her to move from outsider to insider. She agrees with the comments of Eric (the humanities student whose experience in Physics 101 Tobias studied), quoting: "'The best classes I had were classes in which I was constantly engaged, constantly questioning and pushing the limits of the subject and myself' (S. Tobias, course book, p. 139)." And she concludes: "Students' experiences and opinions are extremely important in this course. I believe that students who participate in this 'debate' are the most insiders in this class. For them, this class is 'an exciting debate.'"

In studying her Sociology class, Sophia is very conscious of the extent to which she is getting the big picture of what work in this discipline is about—its purposes and theories and ways of thinking, learning, and talking/writing about the world. Her sense of her growing insiderness to this work is confirmed in an assignment for her writing class—to find an article in a sociology journal that interested her but that had not been assigned for her class, and to gloss it as a reader who had entered the discipline but who was not yet a full insider to the scholarly community represented in its academic journals. Reading an article on social stratification, she finds, "I was familiar with vocabularies, terms and expressions that were commonly used in sociology field and also able to recognize the definitions and its meanings." By the end of her study, she realizes that: "I have become extremely interested in this field because the study of sociology has improved my perspectives of human behavior in society by learning different points of view represented in the history of sociology."

Like Dorian and Abby, Sophia has also been learning a great deal about how academic conversations go on in writing, and about her own work as a writer in an academic setting. At the end of the semester, Sophia comments on the work she has done in this unit:

> By completing all the assignment for this unit, I found out that I, as a writer, had to analyze and be specific to write a presentation for the community that I'm belong to. I have the responsibility to the reader (the outsider) to give him/her understanding of what my ADC [academic discourse community] is like and what the reader should know to feel as an insider. Before

writing my final paper of my academic discourse community, I asked questions like, "What could be an typical behavior in my sociology class? What terms have to be explained for the outsider? Is there any connections with other essays on different ADC in the course packet?" and so forth. This type of work helped me to improve my writing skills because I learned how to use detailed examples, including explanations of typical moment in my ADC and to make connections with other information.

IMPLICATIONS

What can we learn from these students' studies of their classroom academic discourse communities that can help us, as their professors, to ease their entry as readers and writers into the varied discourse communities they will find across the disciplines?

From Dorian's study, we can see the importance of opening up the language of the texts we assign—of giving students the opportunity to work with the words and the concepts they find in them and to negotiate their meanings in discussion with each other as they come to use them and make them their own. We can also see something of the way a professor's discourse style can serve as a means of translation—not between languages (because for students in our college classrooms it's rarely language alone that's the problem) but between discourses—between the compressed, densely packed, and distant language of many academic readings and the broken-out style of ordinary conversation—full of involvement features like frequent rewordings and expressions like "you know" that serve as an ongoing audit of whether shared understanding is really being created.

From Abby's study, we can see what happens when we don't make space for students to negotiate the discourse of academic readings in their own terms, to make connections between the knowledge they bring to the classroom and the new knowledge that we're trying to create there, and when we don't make space somehow (through group work, through including lots of informal, reflective writing that allows students to express their understandings in their own words and to share them with others) for students to comfortably enter the conversation. Having called on Abby, the teacher would probably be surprised to learn of Abby's feeling of exclusion from the classroom conversation. Yet Abby has identified some of the elements—the assumption that everyone is ready to use terms like *tropicalization* comfortably, the sense of competition in students' contributions—that leave her unable to voice in the classroom the thoughts in her head. That the discussion takes place in Spanish, her native language, highlights the fact that it is discourse, not language per se, that most positions our students as outsiders or insiders.

Sophia's study affirms that making space for student voices, giving them a chance to test their words and experiences against the concepts we would have them learn, and working *with* them constantly to create a shared bigger picture can not only make them feel like insiders to a particular classroom community but can engage their long-term interest and excite their sense of possibilities that academic study offers. Sophia, like Dorian, also shows us that students can use their discourse experiences as both insiders and outsiders to different communities to become more aware, not only of how they are positioned as readers, but also of what they need to provide as writers, to create the background knowledge needed to bring readers into the conversation that any written text invites.

Though many of these understandings have emerged from other research on students' experiences across the curriculum (see Spack, 1997, for a summary), these studies were carried out by the students themselves. What they all show is that students will begin to become insiders to our academic discourse communities, to read and write and think in the ways that we value in those communities, when we invite them to join us in our inquiry—to read and write and think *with* us, not just *to* us about the things we would discover and understand. These students have shown how engagement in one area of inquiry—into the complex nature of discourse competence and the ways in which it is manifested in different discourse communities—can offer new understandings that can facilitate their movement into new ones. Comparable engagement in meaningful inquiry in other disciplines is likely to have the same effect of facilitating both their movement toward insiderness and their understanding of what insiderness means.

Finally, I would like to return to the question of what it means to be an ESOL student who is writing for courses across the curriculum. It is significant, I think, that, although all of these students highlighted their ESOL background at some moment in their early inquiry into their experience as insiders or outsiders to different discourse communities, background is not named in three of these four final studies of academic discourse communities. Quy, who began his semester worried about whether his English would be good enough for successful academic performance, no longer sees his work, even in a writing class, from this perspective. It is striking that nowhere in his account of his experience as a member of the academic discourse community of English 101 does he identify himself as a non-native speaker of English. Rather, he emphasizes commonalties:

> From the beginning of the class, all students are strangers to each other, so they are outsiders to the discourse.... I could tell that I was not the only one who was nervous and did not like the whole concept of speaking out to the rest of the class on the first day.... The semester is coming to an end, and I feel more like an insider now. I know almost all of my classmates and am not at all uncomfortable speaking to them.

Dorian sees himself as an insider to a particular classroom community. Sophia is beginning to identify herself as a potential sociology major.

Even Abby, who feels more sharply the ways in which she is situated between languages, now sees the relationship between language and her identity as a student as much more complex.

Each of these students has discovered not only the larger patterns that characterize the ways their courses work and the values they represent, but their own place within the academic discourse communities these courses represent. They have participated in spoken and written conversations with other students who have studied the discourse patterns and shared knowledge and values of their courses across a range of academic disciplines in similar ways. The shared framework provides a bridge that connects students' prior knowledge and experiences outside of academic settings to their experiences and developing knowledge within them, as they reframe those experiences in academic terms. And this helps students to see how their prior knowledge of how to function as an insider at a discourse level in nonacademic communities *in any language* builds underlying competence that provides a base for their participation in academic communities. In bringing together students' experiences of academic discourse communities across the curriculum, this inquiry allows students to perceive how much is common in all students' academic experiences, not unique to the experiences of ESOL students, as they move from outsider to insider in new classroom and disciplinary communities. And it lets them see that, like families, the academic discourse communities of introductory courses have both similar concerns and notable differences, that these can be shaped both by the immediate situation of a particular class and professor and by the larger beliefs, values, and shared purposes that arise within an academic disciplines. Finally this inquiry into discourse communities allows students to discover that they can become agents rather than passive receivers of their own education as they begin to look analytically and critically at what insiderness means in the different academic communities they explore in their own ongoing studies.

REFERENCES

Auerbach, E., & Paxton, D. (1997). "It's not the English thing": Bringing reading research into the ESOL classroom. *TESOL Quarterly, 31*(2), 237–261.

Chafe, W. L. (1982). Integration and involvement in speaking, writing, and oral literature. In D. Tannen (Ed.), *Spoken and written language: Exploring orality and literacy* (pp. 35–53). Norwood, NJ: Ablex.

Gee, J. P. (1992). *The social mind: Language, ideology, and social practice.* New York: Bergin & Garvey.

Geisler, C. (1994). *Academic literacy and the nature of expertise: Reading, writing, and knowing in academic philosophy.* Hillsdale, NJ: Lawrence Erlbaum Associates.

Halliday, M. A. K. (1978). *Language as social semiotic: The social interpretation of language.* London: Edward Arnold.

Heath, S. B. (1983). *Ways with words: Language, life, and work in communities and classrooms*. Cambridge, UK: Cambridge University Press.

Kutz, E. (1997). *Language and literacy: Studying discourse in communities and classrooms*. Portsmouth, NH: Boynton/Cook.

Kutz, E., Groden, S. Q, & Zamel, V. (1993). *The discovery of competence: Teaching and learning with diverse student writers*. Portsmouth, NH: Boynton/Cook.

Rose, M. (1989). *Lives on the boundary*. New York: Penguin.

McCarthy, L. (1987). A stranger in strange lands: A college student writing across the curriculum. *Research in the Teaching of English, 21*(3), 233–263.

Shih, M. (1992). Beyond comprehension exercises in the ESOL academic reading class. *TESOL Quarterly, 26*(2), 289–311.

Spack, R. (1997). The acquisition of academic literacy in a second language: A longitudinal case study. *Written Communication, 14*(1), 3–61.

Spradley, J., & Mann, B. (1978). *The cocktail waitress: Women's work in a man's world*. New York: Wiley.

Sternglass, M. (1997). *Time to know them: A longitudinal study of writing and learning at the college level*. Mahwah, NJ: Lawrence Erlbaum Associates.

Tobias, S. (1990). *They're not dumb, they're different: Stalking the second tier*. Tucson, AZ: Research Corporation.

Zamel, V. (1998). Strangers in academia: The experiences of faculty and ESL students across the curriculum. In V. Zamel & R. Spack (Eds.), *Negotiating academic literacies: Teaching and learning across languages and cultures* (pp. 249–264). Mahwah, NJ: Lawrence Erlbaum Associates. Originally published in *College Composition and Communication, 46* (1995), 506–521.

II

Learning Across the Curriculum: Through Students' Eyes

The chapters in Part II are written by two multilingual learners who chronicled what happened as they crossed the curriculum over a 6-year period and took courses in several disciplines. Both writers began their projects while they were students in Vivian Zamel's first-year ESOL composition course. Both recount their experiences in courses in their majors—biology and sociology—as well as in other courses that had an impact on them, sometimes in profoundly personal ways. Their reflections make clear that their sense of engagement or alienation had less to do with the content they were studying than with the pedagogical approaches and conditions of particular courses. Precisely because these compelling narratives give voice to perspectives and interpretations that are often unheard or unacknowledged, they serve as a unique resource for understanding the relationship between learning and teaching and offer a rare opportunity to see the classroom through students' eyes.

Chapter 6

Martha's Reflections on Learning Across the Curriculum

Martha Muñoz

Martha Muñoz, a student from Colombia who majored in biology, discusses her experiences in a freshman seminar and in chemistry, literature, and biology courses. As she reflects on her observations of and reactions to these courses, Martha points to course-specific factors and conditions, especially with respect to the professors' pedagogical approaches, that either promoted or undermined her learning.

DIVING IN

When I think about my Freshman Studies class, a sense of freshness such as the one in a summer morning or the breeze from the beach invades my memory, and the solid figure of my female Chinese professor appears in my mind's eye. I can describe this professor as a professor of deep and spiritual questions that invited you to dive in the darkness of yourself.

I was very curious about knowing how a Chinese-American person could teach since she was the first Asian professor in my student career. Our class was small, 25 students, compared to my science classes, and that was like a treat for me. Most of my classmates were Asian. For me it was very interesting that the professor asked us to sit in a circle because at the same time that I was taking this course, I was also taking Freshman English 101 E, and we also used to sit in a circle. I thought, maybe all the classes that are not science courses sit in a circle. And I liked that.

---

[1] My professor gave me the title, "Diving In," by Mina Shaughnessy because Shaughnessy has transformed the way people think about teaching and teaching writing.

I liked the circle's set up because it helps to hold in the middle the energy generated by each of the individuals there. It feels as if you are close to a fireplace that has been fed by different pieces of wood producing many flames but only one big pillar of smoke. And when you look at this fireplace your eyes never get tired because the flames are always changing. The circle creates a more challenging atmosphere for me because it represents an open opportunity to break the silence that sometimes is around. It also provides the space to meet everyone's eyes and the opportunity of learning how to be generous by sharing our company and thoughts. The circle demands your presence one hundred percent.

My professor used to give us long homework assignments that always included a piece of writing and a few chapters to read. We were also asked to write a weekly letter to exchange in class. That part of the homework was very intimidating to me because I used to find my mind's eye a blank! I used to feel short of words to write and share with my classmates and professor. I was just starting my connection with writing in a second language and the five hundred minimum length of words seemed overwhelming to me. Most of the time when I was trying to write the letters the only statement that came into my mind was "What am I going to write about?" Now when I look back at this required piece of the course, I say to myself "Five hundred words is not enough space for me to write about anything!" Everything that I write is a representation of who I am, of my mind's eye vision about life. I realized that my professor was always asking me to connect my writing with my culture and the textbook we were using, *Nisa*. And I found myself not only learning about a new culture, the Kung society, but also about my culture and how similar and interesting each one is. I realized cultural aspects that I never thought about before.

I usually felt nervous in this class because it was hard to keep up with the readings even though the textbook was easy and interesting to read. It was just a lot. One day my professor took her place in front of the blackboard and drew a line from one side to the other side and addressed a question to our class. She wanted from each of us a thoughtful answer. Our reflection needed to be done based on the chapters we were supposed to read for that day. We were supposed to say one activity that the Kung society used to practice.

I was almost the last person in the circle to speak and I could feel how my anxiety was building up while I was attentively listening to my classmates say what I had already thought seconds before! I was seeing how the line my professor drew at the beginning was getting full of small divisions, representations of the many activities that we had found through the reading. "What else, what else did they do?" I was echoing the question to myself desperately in my attempt to find one more answer. My turn was coming up and my mind was unable to see away from what was already said. All my classmates had given the answers and if someone needed a little extra time to think, my professor waited very calmly for one. I checked the book to see if there was something that was not written on the blackboard. Suddenly right before my turn, a flash of light illuminated my mind's eye! I had found something else about the Kung's activities. I had a picture in my mind about what I read before, but I did not really "see it" until that moment because

Too many words

Too many sounds

Too many attractions

Turned me around[2]

That exercise had helped me to become more aware of my quality as a reader and critical thinker. I had learned that even though I read something, I was not "reading" it mindfully and therefore I easily missed the gist and deeper meaning of the material. I also had learned that what I was considering trivial, my ideas, culture, and association with the Kung society, are powerful aspects of my own immigrant experience and history.

My professor had helped me to spend quality time learning how to read with others and from myself through the exercises and questions she gave us. There were many opportunities when I was feeling thwarted because I could not come up with a satisfactory answer for myself. I was afraid of putting my thoughts in words and on paper. And when I received back my assignments, a sense of willingness to explore deeply myself was generated. I could identify her interest about my written work by seeing my name at the beginning of her extensive commentary. I knew she was aware of the writer she was reading. I could sense her presence and support by her challenging questions that encouraged me to think more about what I wrote. My professor always included her thoughts and emphasized my ability to follow the details given for the assignments. I felt highly valued, respected and free to express myself. She challenged me to be myself more, and as a result I have gained strength to be active in the different "circles" I have joined since then. She had helped me to gain self-confidence and stronger voice.

My connection with writing was so amusing and strong because of the commitment of my professors and the dynamics used in this course and my ESOL first-year 101 E composition course. They were hand in hand supporting the voice of the writer within me and constantly invited me to explore my limits, my darkness, and the mythical and realistic world of a

---

[2]This is a segment from a poem by Fred Small that my Freshman Studies professor has shared with me at a later time.

foreigner. The second language that I was learning was providing me with more opportunities to develop my reading and writing skills, and I could use these skills to proclaim in depth what was not touched upon before. I always felt like I was being lifted up from darkness to the surface with such a tenderness that I was able to let go of my fear of reading and writing. I was then able to dive deep and explore my true self.

THE ABSENCE OF CHEMISTRY

The first time I walked into the auditorium for my first chemistry science class, I was very disoriented. I thought we would be divided in small class-rooms! That was an ominous starting point for me because before I came to UMass, I was used to small classrooms with only women. I found myself scared just looking for an empty chair. Some people were sitting on the floor and some were just standing in the back talking. I felt my English tongue was glued. There was no way for me to emit any words out of my mouth. Everyone's sounds, gestures, laughs seemed so strange to my ears, and created a barrier between them and me.

Something was separating us but I was not sure what. I thought the problem was only the language. I could see others; but I could not see myself. People hidden in their own conversations once in awhile checked their surroundings as if to search for or avoid something else. I was lost and desperate in the middle of nowhere. I needed some place to hold into. Women were talking to other women. Men were talking to men. I did not see anybody whom I had met days before at the short orientation given to us. And the lack of "chemistry" that I experienced since entering that classroom seemed to be increasing. My only companions were my big bag and coat that I held tight. I found myself counting my steps in my mind, but in Spanish. And somehow my glued English tongue came free but only temporarily when I asked a tall man "Is this chem 107?" He answered "yes." I continued to inspect the scenario full of strangers; but I only encountered their sharp cold eyes.

Around the entire room students were sitting in the aisles, leaving only one empty space in the upper row. That empty space seemed strange to me because nobody close by seemed to want it. I also hesitated to walk towards the space not knowing if I was allowed to occupy the seat. But I commanded my legs to move carefully around the "unfurnitured" students with their bags and books. Then I discovered the reason for that empty chair. It took me a minute to understood why I felt such a lack of chemistry around the room! The bitterness created by some part of the North American white society was there in my first Science course at UMass. The available space represented the absence of communication between a white North American woman and a young Black woman. Even though they were sitting in the same row, the Black student was facing the back of the white North American classmate.

I remember vividly how the young Black woman kept her eyes looking down to the floor. Although I wanted to talk with her, I felt myself stuck once again because of my glued English tongue. But I could sense from Lakezia, the young Black woman, some of her feelings which were also mine. I could identify in her the same awareness I felt about the lack of human chemistry in our classroom. When I looked at her, all I could find was a deep sad expression on her face. However, soft sounds came forward when I asked her what her name was! That was enough to change the expression of those sad eyes. We started to share our backgrounds and feelings about the classroom. We even agreed to share notes and save a place for each other to sit when one or the other came in the classroom earlier. And we helped each other to break the silence of that forsaken corner in the classroom.

Minutes later, the professor, a white man with blue eyes, came in carrying a big box. Suddenly for a moment everybody in the room seemed to be in the same position. We were silent. The professor started to talk with high speed for my ears. "Professor who?" Even his name was not clear to me. An avalanche of unclear information invaded the silent room. I felt intimidated by the amount of information about this course and the related laboratory. Most of the time, I was asking Lakezia "What? What?" She tried to explain to me what was going on and made me feel much better by responding to all my "What's." I found out the last name of the professor in the syllabus and in the first homework assignment he handed out. The homework was due in a week!

From the very beginning of that course, I was concerned about my English language disadvantage, especially because of the five-minute quizzes promised for each week. I was going to be tested in my second language in a short period of time about chemistry! "Five" minutes! It takes at least two minutes for me to read the question very fast and then some more minutes to really get what is asked! What time is left to write a good reasonable answer? I guess none!

Most of the time I was lost during what I learned is called "lecture." The lecture represented by one person's ideas about oxygen and salts. The lecture was one person who wrote something hard-to-read on the blackboard and who did not look at all at the students but only at the floor.

My effort to keep up with the class never seemed enough. I felt like I was climbing a muddy mountain! If I ascended five inches, I was soon down ten meters! I spent hours trying to read and understand the textbook's language. The lecture did not help me to clarify concepts. And the room never generated the right chemistry to bond with other people besides Lakezia. We were two alien oxygens.

Alien Oxygen

I was very frustrated looking at the blackboard totally covered by unfamiliar information. A board packed form corner to corner with thousands of invading alien oxygens! Weird shapes, long complex names, long chains of them with no ending! They appeared and disappeared from the blackboard with the movement of my professor's hand. "We take one from here and here" was his typical explanation. There was not a clear reason in my mind's eye for their fate. Many formulas were there too; but the invitation to understand them well was not offered, and memorization was the key to survive. My index cards were not a successful effort. My professor often made jokes about these alien oxygens and my disappointment grew even more. I had no idea what was his point or punch line. But people around me were laughing and I still wonder why. The same way the alien oxygens were playing on the blackboard, my classmates played with me keeping me isolated by the use of "their chemistry!" In my desperation to keep up with the class material, I asked my classmates several times for some words of sentences I had missed, but they always replied, "Don't you know how to take notes?"—just like the explanations and jokes given by the professor about the oxygens. I guess I was supposed to know how to take some notes, how to understand chemistry in English. And how to behave around North American white students' "chemistry."

I probably did not learn much school chemistry, but I did learn about human chemistry that first semester. After all, I did start my friendship with Lakezia. She was always willing to study with me. Soon it became normal that she and I would receive many reproachful "looks" whenever we walked around "our" campus, especially whenever we went to the cafeterias or the library. Some North American students used to ask me questions when they saw my homework sheets all answered. But I was never invited to join their study groups. I was like another alien oxygen in the room.

LITERARY METAMORPHOSIS

After I finished my English as a Second Language courses, I started to fulfill my core distribution. And the first class that I took was a humanities English Course. I heard a lot of positive observations about the professor for that course; but I was feeling very intimidated by the required readings: *Metamorphosis* by Kafka, *Inferno* by Dante, *Selected Poems* by Gwendolyn Brooks, *Kindred* by Octavia E. Butler, *Herland* by Charlotte Perkins Gilman, and *Ishi in Two Worlds* by Theodora Kroelier. I could not imagine how was I going to read all those books in a semester, not even as I thought about the package of reading from my last ESL class which was quite a substantial volume and the heavy portfolio that contained all the writing that I did in that class.

During the first day of class, and after my professor introduced himself, he handed out a questionnaire. He was interested in our expectations, goals, suggestions, and fears regarding our class. That was a very pleasant surprise for me. I generated a lengthy answer focused on my concern with English, the time I need for reading and writing in my foreign language. I was afraid of being lost by the readings, anxious about how my professor would treat my papers. I was afraid of being left out and not respected by my fellow students because of my accent and not yet rich enough vocabulary. I did not want to relive the sensation of being seen as different, the foreigner, among strangers, which was usual in my Science courses. And as I was letting my hand move freely on the paper, I realized that I was surrounded by predominantly white native English Speakers and I panicked! I was also very surprised because my professor provided us with a lot of time to write and that was very special to me because I understood that as his first invitation to create a source of communication with him. His politeness addressing his students and making sure that the pronunciation of our names was correct, set a tone of this nice man's classroom. Still, I remained there in the first row without saying a word.

From the beginning of our second day of class, it became clear to me that my professor has *read* carefully our answers to his questions. I was thrilled by his suggestion of having groups lead the discussion of the books throughout the semester. And he called on me and asked me to be in the first group to lead the discussion of *Metamorphosis*. I received the challenge because I realized that he wanted me to start having my own metamorphosis in class! I was supposed to concentrate on and represent Grete's, Gregor's sister, role in this literary work. I liked that my professor encouraged creativity. For me that represented a safe strategy to face my fears with my foreign language. This ignited my energy to be able to respond to that huge responsibility of teaching and creating a learning celebration!

I experienced daydreaming through Kafka's scenes, I felt the words, I felt disgusted by his invented "bug." However, I felt that it was crucial for me to get in touch with Grete's feelings, which for me, was the gist of my presentation. But how to do that? How am I going to experience what I felt about my "bug brother"? were the questions that assaulted me constantly during my days of reflection and preparation for my project. I found myself with no imagination to recreate Grete and her inner world. Suddenly it occurred to me to do some free writing to activate more thinking. EUREKA! It was not until I sat and wrote down, as I imagined Grete with her journal, feeling very frustrated, what it meant to have a "bug brother" with his messy room, that I was able to allow myself to convey all that gist that I was looking for. I was amused by how much I had discovered from that free entry. I allowed myself to read that revealing entry in class. And after that presentation I felt grounded in my class.

That feeling increased as my fellow students were calling me by my name, as we were able to have debates and different opinions and interpretations of poems, as my professor was aware of what we said, what we expressed with our faces and silence.

The creativity he encouraged us to use, was one of his powerful tools to display his love of teaching literature. What a great poignant lesson it was to be in class with this professor who showed so much passion for his teaching, so much respect for his students, so much commitment to help all of us to appreciate and enjoy literature, humanity, human kindness. We traveled together through *Inferno* with his exotic, detailed, and colorful drawings that covered the entire blackboard. It was as if the book had come to life, to meaning. It was as if Dante's phrases had acquired resonance in my ears, meaning in my heart, as if his words had suffered a metamorphosis! There were not only the drawings, the net to pull me and the rest of my classmates in, from the darkness of the language in *Inferno,* but the repetitive and provocative questions of my professor. His questions helped me to break up into small pieces the literature I once thought was impossible to read and write about. After this experience, who is to say that there is no space to make connections across disciplines such as Art and Literature in a classroom?

MORE THAN 6 AMERICAN WRITERS

"You must be crazy!," "Are you crazy teaching Hawthorne, Melville, Dickinson in college?" were the kind of reactions that my professor received from some of his friends when he referred to his next literature course to be taught at UMass. And what a great anecdote my professor told us about when he referred to this conversation about his desire to spend a semester teaching 6 American writers to a group of college students!

He certainly started to shape our classroom with the special gesture of learning everybody's names and something about each other. That was the "book" we wrote and read that first day.

Some of his initial suggestions to have in mind when we were doing our readings were to keep a journal about the readings and to practice what he referred to as "interactive notes." "Interactive notes" were encouraged and repeated throughout the semester. These kinds of suggestions and notes were first introduced to me during my ESL courses. And I was very surprised with my professor's suggestions because not many professors take advantage of these handy tools to support students' writing and learning. I was, in that sense, ahead of my classmates who looked confused by the idea of "interactive notes." I know how to work with them to start building up my ideas for my papers. Unfortunately, those journals and notes were only for ourselves. We were not asked to pass them in or share them in class.

One of my professor's closest friend in class, was the blackboard. We were able to see the transformation of an empty blackboard that got enriched with our spoken ideas written on it. We were able to see the transformation of difficult vocabulary from our books, into simplest forms of expression, and all that was done with our contributions during our dialogue in class. That encouraged me to continue with my participation and questioning things from the books in class.

When I felt that the reading was too hard to make sense of, I found a refuge in my journal where I wrote many questions that I was able to ask one of my classmates before or in class. I also visited my professor's office and told him my frustrations with a particular author's writing style, and he always made me aware that the material was difficult to read and that that was OK. I admired that every time I had my meetings with him, usually before class, he came to class and part of our discussion, part of his agenda was to acknowledge the difficulty of our assigned reading. He was very sensitive to our needs, my needs. He spend more time walking us through the story and had great ideas on how to start the discussion of a hard reading. He asked us to identify the characters, their meaning and roles in the story. Other times, he brought us back into history by encouraging our imagination to work. We were asked to place ourselves in a specific place, maybe a cemetery in front of one of the headstone at a certain time and then go from there. He could provoke a lot of thinking and analysis from us, from me. After that explosion of ideas, the blackboard came into play. One of the exercises he practiced with us, and that I found most fascinating, consisted on dividing the board into two columns. For each of the columns, he assigned a difficult word form one of our books. Then we were invited to say what we thought it meant and several minutes were dedicated to discuss our guesses. We were able to discover by ourselves the meaning of those words and the spaces in each of the columns shrank as they got filled with the synonyms we came up with for those previously unfamiliar and old English words.

When we were talking about writing our papers, he used to bring up the point that "[we] have been taught to generalize. What we're trying to do is to focus on details that at first seem irrelevant, and see how much [we] can see on details." Our first paper was dedicated to what the written story by a slave girl meant to us. We were asked to explore in depth that meaning and were encouraged to use as many examples as we needed to support our points. For me, this was again a very productive and familiar way of approaching writing that, to a great extent, brought me back to exercise the way I was taught to read and write during my ESL classes, using different threads and making connections with my readings. He also encouraged creativity and I took advantage of that. I wrote a letter addressed to Harriet Jacobs, the author of the book. When I read his response to my paper, it became clear to me that he read and noticed my ideas. He highlighted points that he found more interesting, asked me questions about other points he did not understand. I could feel that he had higher expectations for me. That represents, to me, one of the most powerful approaches to teaching in the academic world, one of the essential components of a professor in a classroom, in a course, in the way of reading and interpreting a comment from a paper. That assured me in my academic progress, in my strategies of reading and writing 6 American authors. Fortunately, this class was not only 6 required American Writers.

To add to our list of readings, my professor provided us with samples of students' papers. He did that in order to give us a taste of our own abilities of thinking and writing about the twentieth century. I also interpreted his commitment of teaching as a way to enrich our vision and understanding our points of view and curious minds.

When we were exposed to poetry, a part of literature that I used to feel not very interested in, he showed me a way to walk around a poem. He motivated the entire class by first reading one poem aloud to the class. His passionate reading and tone of voice made the words tangible, alive. After that, we started to play with the words. We chose only one aspect of the poem, maybe the kind of words in it. Then we looked at the same aspect in other poems from the same author in order to learn as much as we could from that specific aspect and author. And, as he sometimes asked, "What if you try to change the words to illustrate your point?" or rewrite "[my] own version of a poem and see what happened!" The kind of freedom that he provided us with to create or redo a homework assignment, or exercise, or a poem, or a sentence is usually out of the margins of academia, and that freedom is so needed when we are teaching and learning! In his agenda, it was more important to make meaning and to practice interactive literature than to cover a syllabus, than to cover a list of books by 6 American Writers.

"WHAT'S THAT?"

I used to feel unsure about what my professor for General Biology was talking about. Plants seemed very boring to study because we were only exposed to their many different parts and functions through a monotonous type of lecture where there was no interaction between student and student, or student and professor. We were totally deprived of the importance and connection of plants in our environment and our lives! There were no pictures shown in class to illustrate the point that my professor was trying to make. There was no motivation for me to immerse myself in the different biological kingdoms.

I always felt that the rhythm of the lecture made me feel like I was a prehistoric creature learning things that I never saw before, but that I was supposed to absorb and understand because I was present, there in the room! My professor assumed that by then, I knew about evolution in a lot of detail! My body also felt the impact of that expectation, the muscles of my hands felt tight after scribbling notes that made no sense. There was no time to really get a coherent idea. I felt out of control going from one theme to the next, having no transition between them nor an opportunity to appreciate their characteristics and meaning.

During the lectures, there was no other challenge but to be the passive and invisible student desperate trying to take some notes. The lectures were not interesting at all. My professor used to read straight from the book. He was not even regurgitating the material! These kinds of lectures left me with many confusing and unclear basic biological concepts. The lectures were leaving empty holes about knowledge which were never filled. Many students decided to stop by and leave their tape recorder with other students. Some others, like me, stayed there trying to educate my ears by listening to the reading-lecture. The only times when I remember seeing the classroom full of students were during the first day of class and during the hour long exams.

At the beginning of the semester, it was interesting to notice a sense of community in a Science course. And this was a community that formed within the larger course. And it was joined only by ESL students. We took over one of the corners of our classroom. We supported each other by sharing and exchanging our class notes and tapes. We also exchanged our common confusion and sense of being strangers in this classroom. We were an ESL community trying to get fluent in the language used in General Biology. This goal was very difficult to achieve because we were in the middle of an abstract and poorly elaborated course. And we were only required to do long readings and listen to a reading-lecture.

It was sad to see how this ESL community started to disintegrate gradually because the course was generating not only frustration and confusion, but also a feeling that Biology was not for undergraduate students. And the large community of about fifteen students was diminished to five! Why are there not many minority students in biological sciences? The way this course was taught helps to answer this question.

In this course I also experienced another very unusual thing. My professor's exams were photocopied from different textbooks! I could read in the upper margin "Chapter 8, p #1." I could interpret this situation in a classroom as a case of bored teaching, a gap of inspiration, a lack of responsibility. The class needed not only guidance and support, but also a teaching leader, someone with passion teaching and willing to create something positive in the classroom.

It seemed that the repeated attempts that I made, requesting that my professor write down on the blackboard biological terms or names, were not powerful enough to be attended to. I remember once when my professor was talking about some eukaryotic. He was going on and on about different species. And I could not tolerate or understand that lecture so I interrupted him. I angrily and impatiently mumbled "What's that?" when he mentioned the name of an animal. I did not know what he was referring to. His response was "Someone asked 'What's that?' We all know it's a name of a fish, it's a kind of fish right?" And he looked at this sleepy audience, searching for a reaction, but he did not get one. I felt lost in that classroom, seeking anonymity and wondering who else did not know that "that" was a kind of fish! And I finished my semester wondering if he understood my messages, if he listened to then, if he realized who was in his class, where not everybody knew the English name and pronunciation of a fish.

THE LANGUAGE OF IMMUNOLOGY

In the traditional setting of a classroom for my Science classes, the usual "box of sardines," I was sitting to learn Immunology. And I was feeling very intimidated by the material that I was going to learn since it was my first 300 level course. The word Immunology sounded very remote and at the same time advanced for my boundaries of knowledge. "This is introduction to Immunology," said my tall and serious professor. Then he introduced himself and passed to each of his new students a piece of paper with some of his former students' quotes describing their feelings about Immunology. "Oh, my God, Immunology, oh no!" "Are you crazy taking immunology?" He certainly broke the anxiety that I walked into this classroom with. And he added his personal jokes too, "Oh, you want to stay here?" I could perceive from his tone of voice and gestures that he was having fun mocking the students' quotes. What he did then was to express his expectations of the way the course would proceed, the kind of exams, and warned us about the heavy amount of reading required for the course. He seemed very organized and realistic about the initial difficulties of students.

According to him we were going to learn a new language, "the language of Immunology." A language that he recognized as challenging especially during the first couple of weeks because we were going to be learning a lot of new words that later on would build up into complex concepts. But he said that it was not impossible to learn if we kept up with the work. It was very encouraging to hear from him saying that "things would not look clear for awhile" but that eventually they would, as we got the vocabulary under our belt.

The Immunology lexicon was much easier to learn because of the simple and practical examples that he used to illustrate it with. We were exposed to daily situations to relate the meaning of the new words. Before he went into defining and introducing a concept or word, he played with it. He usually broke down words and did not assume that we knew what their roots were or meant. After he dissected the words, he presented the concepts and in that way it was more productive and easy to grasp the ideas. The concepts were perceived, received and learned. He kept on doing this during the entire semester and I kept on learning "the language of Immunology" too! He also loved to use the board and overhead to write huge words. On the overhead, we could see the notes from the lecture. These notes were available at the library every Friday, and that facilitated my concentration during the lectures because I was able to pay more attention to what he was explaining rather than to trying to take notes. And he constantly invited us to his office. We were encouraged to go as many times as we needed to, and if he was not in his office, we were also invited to his lab. "If I'm not in my office, go to the lab."

For me he was an artist, an "antibody" against the "antigen" of boredom and frustration, with a very simple style and ability to state and clarify his ideas and his position in a classroom. An artist who allowed himself to combine brushes and colors to teach something. Many times during the lectures, he did his drawings and made fun of them. "This is not the version of an artist, but …" And he made a good use of them when he needed to illustrate "a mouthful," a complicated or long concept. He made me laugh and learn in class!

Following his advice, I visited his office and lab many times. He not only kept his doors open, but maintained a sense of humor and made honest remarks to motivate students. During one of my visits, I was thwarted by some material that I could not understand at first. I told him "I don't get it." and his response was "I'm sure you know it." He did not mind doing his goofy figures and explaining them back to me. He allowed himself to use more than one way to teach Immunology. He even used to go further and challenged me with questions. And his closing remarks were always "Come any time and if I'm not here, I'm in the lab. Do you know where it is?" He constantly reminded me that I will get things clarified later on because I was learning a new language, "the language of Immunology."

I was thrilled when at the beginning of the semester he also announced that he expected each student to do a presentation as a requirement for the course. That I found very challenging, exciting and very uncommon among my Science courses. I was asked to run the show in a Science course! I felt very positive about my professor's teaching approach. He was leaving space for us, the students, to teach each other. He was open to subjects and encouraged creativity and most important a collective responsibility. We were put on the spot to teach each other. That experience gave me presence in this Science course, helped me to build up confidence, shaped my skills for putting together a presentation, and created communication with my classmates. This Science professor has written and marked a different history for me. He drew different figures about Science and teaching Science. He offered a different way to learn a different language with no fear of asking, conceptualing and breaking it into small pieces in order to see the whole picture later on, in order to be able to become a beginner undergraduate student and "teacher" in a Science course!

Before each exam, he used to make fun of the situation: "Oh, my God here is the exam" and that helped to break the anxiety among us. He never interrupted us during the exam.

I admire his ability of being realistic and sensitive about what he could teach during his class time. Several times he used to stop 3 or 4 minutes before the class was over and said "I prefer to stop here and continue next time because the next subject is very important and I do not want to rush. See you next time." It was a pleasure and deep incentive to see his commitment to and respect for students' learning in that way too. That was another of my Immunology professor's "antibiotics" during the semester to prevent boredom and lack of audience for class. He did not rush with the material and did not burn out our beginners Immunology minds. He prevented the disease of dropping out from the course and that makes me believe that he is aware of the high rate of that epidemic that invades classrooms very often. What a great amount of healthy learning did I share with my classmates taking this Immunology class! I feel that my knowledge about Immunology has been rooted within me because of the process of learning that took place in the classroom when learning a foreign language. Such language was not assumed to come all at once; but with time, patience, appreciation and most important with direct connection. My ability of getting the expected control with the subject had developed in me new ways, "antibodies" against the cancer that surrounds our classrooms. I had been provided with the challenge of discovering my own strength of learning a new language, "the language of Immunology."

Chapter 7

Motoko's Reflections on Learning Across the Curriculum

Motoko Kainose

Motoko Kainose, a student from Japan who majored in sociology, discusses her experiences in American studies, philosophy, sociology, and literature courses. Motoko's writing provides insight into the workings of her mind as she moved through each course and faced issues that evoked powerful memories and triggered strong emotional responses. Her reflections also reveal how her background affected her experiences in these courses.

BEST INTENTIONS: A SMALL STORM

There is a scene that keeps coming back to the surface of my consciousness. More than a half year has passed since then, but for some reason that scene remains clear in my memory, and it often leaves a bitter taste in my mouth. It grows more vivid every single time. So, I cannot erase it from my mind.

It happened in the beginning of last semester at the very end of one of my classes. Right after we students were given a writing assignment, the following words were uttered in a loud clear voice: "People where English is not your first language, you don't need to worry about your grammar!" said the professor. How was I supposed to feel at that moment? As an ESL student who is always troubled with the grammatical problems, perhaps I should have felt relieved at the thought of life without that burden on my shoulders. Yet, my reaction was completely different from what it ought to be or what the professor might expect. I neither felt relieved nor content; instead I was struck with a very uncomfortable feeling.

"Why did you say that? Why did you need to say that in front of everybody?" I wished I could express my uneasy feelings to the professor, not in

front of everybody, but after everybody left the classroom. Instead, I put
my stuff into my bag, swallowed my emotions or sentiments, and left the
classroom with haste to my home.

On my way home, I was bothered by what the professor said, but on
the other hand, I was also disturbed by the fact that I could not easily accept and appreciate those words; especially when I was pretty sure that
those words were uttered to take a little burden from us. I did not, however, know how to deal with that complex situation. By the time I arrived
at home, a collision of those two sentiments came to emerge a small
storm in my mind.

As soon as I recognized my partner Kevan, the feeling of chagrin overwhelmed my mind and the tears kept filling my eyes and would not stop.
By tapping my back softly, Kevan consoled my mind and cheered me up.
By the time my tears stopped, I was able to face that day's incident and explore the reasons why I was so upset.

One purpose of the course was to examine stereotypes—which we ordinary people innocently, unconsciously, or ignorantly have carried for
many years—and if we found those images did not reflect the reality, we
were ready to tear down and to banish them. Since the beginning of the
course, my chest heaved with anxiety when I thought about how meaningful the course was, and how seriously the professor took the subject. I
thought the professor might be one of those professors whom I secretly respected and looked up to.

Then that incident. I felt startled; I felt as if somebody poured cold water on my face. Those words were the last thing that I expected to hear
from the professor *in front of the class*. Yes. This is the key. I did not want
the professor to make such a statement before the class because I was
afraid of the professor's words. There was a strong chance that they would
perpetuate the stereotypes of the ESL student—neither writing nor
speaking as efficiently and effectively as other non ESL students. It is true
for many of us, at least for myself, cannot express myself effectively and
efficiently like I can do in my own language. But because of this fact—
knowing my own deficiency, I have been trying and working so hard, especially when it comes to writing.

I did not know and I still don't know what made the professor make
such statement. Did she make a judgment based on our spoken English in
the classroom? Or, based on the professor's past experience with other
ESL students? Or was it based on just the professor's general ideas about
us? I still believe that the professor did not need to say those words before
the entire class. The professor could have showed such gentle and
thoughtful consideration while grading our papers by using commentary.
I still believe that it was not too much trouble for the professor to wait until our first paper to see what kind of work we produced. Because of that
incident, to write the paper I worked three times as hard as I used to in order not to be harmed by the conventional idea of the stereotype of ESL

students. As a result, I received an excellent grade an A+. Yet, that grade could not help me forget the incident.

"[M]ost of what you know is a matter of believing what you've been told," states one of my sociology books. Moreover, most of the time, what we think we know is affected and depends on our authority figures. Therefore, I believe that people who are in charge, especially teachers, can never be too careful about what they say.

THE SOUNDS OF SILENCE

One early summer afternoon in the unpretentious Wheatley cafeteria, sitting by the windows I was agonizing over my course selection for the fall semester during which I was planning to take five courses. Four courses were smoothly written down on the form. The fifth course, however, since it would be counted as a part of my elective courses, and therefore not as demanding, was not chosen yet. I did not look for one that would really give me a headache. Quite, frankly, I was looking for one where I could relax and enjoy during the semester.

"You should take one of the philosophy courses, especially with these guys" pointing out several professor's name on the schedule book, suggested my friend sitting before me. He started to convince me how my thoughts were suitable for those philosophy courses. I made no reply. In fact, his words slightly massaged my ego, yet they were not enough to make me take next step. However, his words prompted past memories. I started to recall those boring school days when I involuntary took Western philosophy courses in Japan, and at the same time as a chain reaction those Great Greek philosopher's stuffy faces run across my mind. Compared to Eastern philosophy, those ancient philosopher's words and rational reasoning were to me, nothing but "quibble," and hardly touched to my heart. Though they really make sense, things that really make sense do not necessarily turn out to be the "truth." And if you do not explore the "truth," what is the significance of pursuing the subject? Since I was so sure that my mind would not fit and open toward the subject, there was no way for me to put myself in the situation where there would have a chance to give myself more frustrations.

It was as if my friend saw through my mind, he did not push his opinion further, yet instead by looking over the waveless ocean through the windows, he let drop the words with "archaic smile," (which means mysterious) "(This one is) easy and nice." Those words clearly reached both ears, and captured my mind. That commentary was exactly what I was looking for. Without asking him any further questions, I wrote down the name of the course and completed my form. At that time, I had no idea about what he meant by "easy and nice."

The class was held in a small room on the first floor of the McCORMACK building at 8:30 am every Monday, Wednesday, and Friday. The classroom was mostly occupied by white students and some minority faces. According to the syllabus, contrary to my initial impression or preconceived idea toward the philosophy courses, it seemed to me that the course materials were accessible. Especially, when I saw one of the textbook titles—*You Just Don't Understand,* the book's familiarity unintentionally made me smile. Since that course was Core-course, the grade would be dependent on our three assigned written works, though the class participation and attendance were still important. That information somehow eased my feelings because I was always worried more about my lack of class participation than writing papers. "Now I have only three papers to write, and since I decided to take 'pass and fail' for this course, all I need to do is to write passing papers," I chuckled to myself. (Note: Eventually, I did not take "pass and fail.")

The first day of the course, the professor gave us an ungraded paper assignment: The subject was about our image toward philosophy. On the second day, he posed the same question to the class, and started to call on the students from the first row. Since I was sitting in the left corner of the front row, he called on me by verifying my first name. I was nervous to speak up in front of everybody whom I had not yet known, but because I already organized my idea and image toward philosophy last night in my assignment, though it was far from the fluent English, I somehow managed to bring myself to the end.

After I finished, the professor briefly summarized what I just said by using more sophisticated and philosophical sounding words. Then he raised two important issues from my statement and wrote down on the blackboard. I felt so delighted. I felt I was included. I felt my existence was affirmed. The reason why I was and still am hesitated to raise my voice in the classroom is because I am always intimated by two big worries, which are "Will everybody be able to understand what I say?" and "Is my idea important enough to be raised?" Most of the time, these two questions envelop my mind so that I cannot release my words; especially when I sense that the class circumstance is neither comfortable nor worthy enough to take the risk.

But this time, the professor displayed very warm and sensitive conduct before me. Perhaps that was a really trivial matter for other people, but because I was always worried about my English deficiency, even such a small matter became a big deal in my mind. A kind of hope was gradually growing in my mind, and I sensed that something urged me to take future changes in the class. I felt fortunate to take his course. I thought I came to understand why my friend called him "nice."

I recall, in the beginning of the semester the students were actively participating in the classroom. After the professor posed a question, most of the time two elderly students made first discussion wave, and that would lead the following students to make more waves. At that time there was certain interaction between the professor and the students. I felt I could join those waves, yet by the time I finally got all my courage together to jump into the class discussion, the subject went on to the next one. I would miss my every single chance to participate in the classroom, yet I did not mind because at least I knew that I was trying.

I do not remember exactly when, but at some point in time unknown, the class discussion became less and less, and eventually disappeared one day. That was when silence began to occupy our classroom. Only the professor's soft muttering-like restless questions and answers sounded in vain. I really became puzzled. I did not understand why the class became so wordless. The first few weeks, the professor seemed to be patient with that sudden change, but some time later he started to ask for volunteers for the class discussions. He would also try to find out the reason for that silence by posing questions to himself and answering them by himself during the class hours: "... perhaps because many of you are freshmen, so you are still shy ... because this class starts very early in the morning, so many of you are not quite awake ... all my life I was pushed to speak up ...," said the professor with frequent pauses. I suppose that his experience did not allow him to make the students involuntarily talk in the classroom. I felt somehow moved when I saw his gentle conduct, yet my courage was not enough to raise my voice.

Silence still existed in the classroom. It was as if his words never reached to the students' ears. Time passed, but no change was made. Having the wordless students before him, the professor still repeated his soft muttering-like questions and answers during the class hours. Every once in a while, with a serious and painful expression on his face, "Please help ..." asked the professor. Misery and helplessness overwhelmed our classroom. The professor's words would add to my sense of sadness and guilt. When I think about the professor's struggle, my heart ache and I felt that I was committing a crime by not volunteering in the classroom.

One day after the class, I could no longer put up with that silence and guilt. My mind urged me to go to the professor's office. And next I found myself ascending the stairs. I had no idea what I was going to tell the professor, yet I felt obligated to see him anyway. I remember as soon as I reached the floor, I recognized him and I expressed my feelings toward the class and its silence. With a combination of serious and sad looks the professor asked me, "How can I make people talk?" Unfortunately, because it was so sudden, I could not offer any concrete ideas at that time. Yet I promised him and myself that I would make more efforts to speak up in such a dead classroom.

On the following day, sitting with my nervousness and fear, I was listening and waiting for the right time in which I was able to raise my voice. However, I found it so difficult to grab such timing. It was not because of my hesitation; but because of the way the professor talked, which was so smooth just like pouring out torrents of words, I did not want to, or moreover I felt I should not destroy his world of philosophy by using my peculiar language and thoughts. The professor was creating the beautiful waves of self-conversations. How could I mess up his world?

In spite of my feelings, I several times raised my voice with desperate efforts until the end of the semester. But my efforts could not make the following expected waves in the class. The class basically kept that silence, and in my eyes it seemed like everybody got used to the unusual situation. It was, however, easy in a sense. Since the professor did not call on any students, if you did not want to, you did not need to prepare for that course. All you had to do was write good papers based on the readings and our own experiences and opinions.

Now I sometimes look back on those days, and ask myself what I learned in that course. I honestly don't know. I sometimes felt buried under the silence. I sometimes felt like I was drowning at the mercy of the professor's philosophical waves. Since both contrasts were so strong there are no other memories in my mind now. All I remember is silence and words, and words, and words.... It was not because of silence that the professor's words were heard. It was because of the words that such miserable silence was created among the students. I suppose that the professor's words did imprison the students' voice.

THE DISCIPLINE OF THE TEA CEREMONY

When I first started to learn "tea ceremony", (Sa-doo: the way of tea,) I had so many questions about the way tea was served. For me, as a beginner, the many strict and precise movements which have been handed down over four hundred years seemed to be truly futile, especially without knowing and understanding the meaning of each single movement. How many times did I have to swallow my questions about those manners? It is easy to say, "Why don't you ask?" Yet, there is an invisible contract between a master and a student: We students, especially beginners, are not allowed to question what the master says or asks us to do. Questioning is regarded as "disrespectful" behavior toward the master. (This rule is true for other traditional arts as well. At least in places where I learned things.) Once you start to learn it, what you have to do is just copy what the master demonstrates before you, without understanding or exploring of course the meaning of those manners.

Perhaps such a learning style is strange and irrational for Westerners; but for us, Japanese, as my master used to say, tea ceremony is not only practicing the physical movement of tea serving, but also undergoing spiritual training—in other words, searching for an absolute state of "nothingness" in order to achieve the true essence of life. Through rational understanding it is said that one won't be able to acquire that stage. It does not however, mean one will never understand the meaning of each "manner." An alternating succession of tense discipline and memorization, gradually draw you into the world of tea ceremony, and one day it is as if you are hit by lightning when you come to realize and accept each single movement as a whole flow of natural consequence of tea ceremony. No words are necessary. You have just acquired it from the bottom of your soul. When all happened to me, I could finally see the whole picture.

The fall '93 semester, as far as I recall, was the most unforgettable and the toughest semester during my days in UMASS. Not only was I taking five courses, but due to the kind of subjects that I selected, I had hard time to manage my everyday life; especially, the course is called classical sociological theory—really cast shadows in my life.

Since the first day of the course, my struggle with that course began: Basically I had trouble with comprehending the textbook and other materials written by early sociologists. I can still vividly recall myself drawing a big sigh having the textbook before me. The thing was that even though I could read and recognize each single word in the book, I was not able to follow those great sociologist's set of complicated thoughts and ideas. I often recall what Mike Rose said, "I was reading words but not understanding that," like Rose, I was "the human incarnation of language-recognition computer program." If I were merely a machine, I did not need to feel so stupid back then. Yet, in reality I did since I was a senior student with a major in sociology. As a result, I felt wretched, and as usual I started to reproach myself and my English for not being able to keep up with the college level of education.

However, as a realist, I knew that I had no time for lamenting over my incapability. The subject was there, and that was one of the required courses for a sociology major. Not only did I have to pass the course, but I also had to obtain a decent grade. Moreover I did not want to hurt my high GPA. "No matter what, I should not give up this course!" I made up my mind to tackle this course. I started to find the way to wriggle out of the difficulty, and at the same time in order to maintain my interest and motivation for the course, I tried to persuade myself that the lecture would be really interesting and would help me to understand the subject. I believed that the lecture would give me a clue on how to access those great thinkers' complicated thoughts.

The class was basically all lectures. For one hour and half, we students would listen to our professor's interpretation of the materials and would take notes from beginning to end. Contrary to my expectations, the lecture was very difficult to follow. In order not to miss any information, I would devote all my energy to catch the professor's words. I was so intense. Even after I started to record the lectures, I never relaxed. Now I suppose that when all aspects, such as my ideas toward my English ability and the course, the professor's difficult language, abstract subject matter, and the professor's somehow stiff and starchy (formal) appearance and his thunderous tone of voice, combined together, they made my heart harden and eventually closed my mind really tight toward the subject.

to talk in a gentle tone, "I know ... because of the materials. Their concepts are so abstract, it's hard to understand. Even I read the text several times ..." Is it right? So, I really should not have blamed my English so much. I felt the hostility toward my English and toward myself gradually faded in my mind.

On my way home, and even after arriving at home, I constantly repeated what the professor said and that graduate student's words. Their words cheered me up and gave me some hope. I could finally get myself together to prepare for the final examination. But I knew that I should not use the same strategy as before: For a whole semester I attempted to understand the concepts first, and I did not succeed. As a result I had lost confidence in myself and I had lost confidence in strategies that had worked for me up to now.

But what can I do? One idea flashed in my mind. According to an old saying, "Read a book one hundred times, and its content makes itself understood": the idea is basically when you read so many times, you can memorize the whole book. That will make you naturally understand the content. Perhaps the ideas of the Japanese traditional arts such as tea ceremony, calligraphy etc. are the same. I put my faith in our traditional belief, and I started to memorize the textbook.

During the study period for exams, the end of December, I was literally living in my closet for a week. From days to nights, I was sitting on the floor with my small low-height desk before me. I was surrounded by an enormous number of papers, my sociology textbooks, eight different dictionaries, and my clothes. I was studying in that commotion in order to seek enough concentration for my classical sociological theory's final examination. If somebody saw me in such a tiny and dark place, they might think my conduct was eccentric. Yet, I knew exactly what I was doing. I was recreating the atmosphere which is really similar to one in my country—so-called a "rabbit hutch." (Since my country Japan is a small country, typically houses are quite small. Therefore many foreigners call our homes "rabbit hutches.") Though I longed to live in a big house as I do now, though I cherish the luxury of space nowadays, whenever I needed to seriously concentrate or whenever I have to console my soul, I have to have really tiny space surrounded on all sides by walls and a door to take me back to my old comfortable, and familiar atmosphere. From days to nights, I tried to memorize as much as I could. It was really hard though ...

Probably on the fifth day of my concentration study, I was struck by a familiar feeling that I experienced when I was learning the tea ceremony. I discovered those memorized words started to fill blanks among the existing fragmented information, and each of them began to connect to one another. They eventually showed me the whole picture of those great thinkers' concepts. I became really excited because I did not really expect to have such strike like a bolt from the blue. But now everything started make sense. Of course I should not say that I completely understood the concepts, though vague still, the whole picture was in here my brain.

From that point on things worked so fast. I made some questions for the essay exam by myself, and answered them by using the new information. On the day of the final, we were given two hours to write two essays. I used all two hours to answer the questions carefully and precisely. In fact I wanted show my effort to the professor. This time my effort was not in vain. My desperate effort yield the good result—I got an A on both essays.

My final grade of that course was a B+. It was still lower than other grades, but I felt that I really earned it this time. I felt a little proud of myself and my English. Yet I think the most interesting discovery here is that even though I am in the Western world, I can use my traditional learning strategies and discipline on occasion.

THE MYTH OF QUIET CHINESE

> After American school, we picked up our cigar box, in which we had arranged books, brushes, and an inkbox neatly, and went to Chinese school, from 5:00 to 7:30 p.m. There we chanted together, voices rising and falling, loud and soft, some boys shouting, everybody reading together, reciting together and not alone with one voice.... The boys who were so well behaved in the American school played tricks on them and talked back to them. The girls were not mute. They screamed and yelled during recess, when there were no rules.... (Kingston, *The Woman Warrior*, p. 167)

I could hear somebody's chattering and laughter. But, it was not in English. Whenever I approached the corridor which led me to my Chinese literature classroom, the sounds from that particular place gave me the false impression that I was in a Chinese school. Upon entering the classroom, I saw four Chinese students talking quite lively to each other in their own language. Since I had taken Chinese 101, I can sometimes pick out some of the words in their conversation. Yet, most of the time, I did not understand what they were saying. So, in order to join in their conversation, I would listen to their sounds with smile on my face. (I don't know why I smiled ... I suppose that perhaps the sign of Asian faces made me smile.) I looked at the people around me. I saw one white student staring at the ceiling, another one looking into space absentmindedly, and other non-Asian students close their mouths really tightly and try to concentrate on their textbooks. It was as though those vigorous sounds from the Chinese students had silenced them. I traced this picture to other classrooms in my mind. There, I saw many Asian students seated closemouthed, intently concentrating on their textbooks, as the white students were in this class.

It is commonly believed that Chinese people, moreover all Asians, are very quiet. But every time I witnessed those scenes in my Chinese literature classroom, I would murmur, "Who said that, who said that Chinese are quiet?" Not only during break time, but also during the lectures, those Chinese students voices were heard, of course this time—in English.

There were only 15 students in my Chinese literature class. Led by a Chinese professor, the class was made up of 7 whites, and 8 Asians of which 6 were Chinese students. As in other courses, from the very beginning of the course, the students found their place to sit. Most of the Chinese students took seats in the first or second row, and the white students sat on the right side of the class, close to the exit. Since I am not a psychologist, I do not know what this demographic (or seating choice?) implies, but from what I have observed in other courses, it is usually the minority students who have always occupied the marginal seats or the seats close to the exit. I always wondered where these reversals in seating patterns came from. (By the way, I myself often took the seat in the center of the last row of the classroom to observe everyone else.)

"I would like to invite your comments ..." This was a typical phrase that the professor made after she explained the material that was assigned for each lecture. "Do you have any thoughts?" With a warm smile on her face, she would encourage the students. Most of the time this was enough to initiate the class discussions; yet every once in a while, no reply was made. "O.K. Uhmm.... How about ... do you like this story?" Once somebody broke the silence, the professor encouraged both the student and other students to make more waves in the class. Except for the extremely biased opinions, the professor usually welcomed any and all thoughts if the students had persuasive reasons to support their opinions. After giving the student a brief but concise and thorough comment, most of the time, she would rephrase our words, and transform them into a question for the class. Through the professor, anybody's opinion became useful and important. Even though she was a very intellectual person, her words were not complicated by a confusing vocabulary. Instead, by using familiar words, she made a beautiful, meaningful, and profound statement that would always touch my heart. Every time I witnessed this professor's conduct, I felt warm; the feeling was the same as after having a hot chocolate on a very cold day.

Every time I went to the class, whether I participated or not I felt that I belonged. I do not exactly know how the others felt about the course, but from what I observed, at least it seemed that the Asian students truly enjoyed and appreciated the course. Most of the time, it was the Asian, particularly the Chinese students, who led the class discussion. There, those Chinese female students were unbelievably active and aggressive, which one might not see in other courses. Sometimes their debate became quite exciting, and eventually their power overwhelmed and silenced the other students. No Chinese were "mute" in my classroom.

I often wonder why there is a such huge difference in class participation among Asian students. As far as I observed, that Chinese class really tore down the stereotype of Asian students. But, what influenced those students' attitude toward class participation? Was it the subject matter's familiarity? Was it the class size? Was it the professor's ethnicity? Was it the number of the students who had the same background? Was it their level of English ability? Or, was it the professor's teaching method. I am still looking for the answers. Perhaps our professor used an ancient Chinese trick to open the students minds …

COMMENTARY: WHAT MOTIVATED ME THE MOST

Hattori sensei (teacher) was the best and the most memorable teacher of my school days in Japan. Not only was she the first teacher for my compulsory education, but the unforgettable commentary that she made on our school work also made her existence very special in my mind.

I still remember the first long essay that I wrote in my elementary school. I was six years old. Because Hattori sensei assigned her pupils to write an observational essay, my mother and I went to a fish-store together and bought about a pound of Asari (short-necked clam) for both my observation and the following morning breakfast—miso-soup. Right after my mother put the Asari into a bowl of salty water to soak and remove their sand, my observation had started. I was sitting before the bowl and watching their action very patiently. As if my eyes were "glued to the bowl," I settled down for a long wait.

"Spit … Spit … Spit … " How many times my face was squirted by the Asari whenever I put my face too close. It was as though they were attacking me: Did I surprise them? Did they have eyes to recognize my face? Did they know their destiny? By the time I finished my observation, I found myself attached to the Asari—which was an emotion that I never had when I ate Asari before. With detailed descriptions, I put all my reactions and emotions on my paper. When I finished all my work, the Asari were cooked and eaten, despite my attachment. I had a vague sense of sadness.

However, that little bit melancholy was blown off by Hattori sensei's comment on my essay, which was called "The Observation of Asari." She said that she was very impressed by my vivid descriptions, emotions, and patience toward my observation, etc. I was a child; her commentary put me in Seventh Heaven. From that point on, I always put forth all my effort whenever I wrote. I also started to gain confidence in my writing.

Hattori sensei taught not only composition, but also other subjects like music, calligraphy, drawing, calculation, science, social studies and Japanese to about her 40 pupils. Every single subject was treated as important as the next. And what made her so special was, as I said, her commentary on every single subject: sometimes it was her questions, sometimes it was her reactions, compliments, or a little critique. Sometimes it was even her observation of our behavior in the classroom. (She

III

Engaging Students in Learning:
Through the Eyes of Faculty
Across the Curriculum

The chapters in Part III are written by faculty who discuss their own attempts to address the needs of multilingual learners in their classrooms. Representing a variety of academic fields—Anthropology, Philosophy, Nursing, Literature, Sociology, and Asian American Studies—these instructors acknowledge the challenge of working with multilingual learners, describe how they promote the learning of these students, and analyze their efforts to make their pedagogy more inclusive. Together, the chapters show that students' progress and success as language learners, readers, and writers in college classrooms are inextricably linked to course-specific factors and conditions. These chapters further demonstrate that when faculty recognize students' struggles, value students' insights, make knowledge accessible by building on students' understanding, and provide meaningful input in response to students' work, they not only promote learning but also foster further language and literacy acquisition.

Chapter 8

Excelling in the Critical Study of Culture: The Multilingual-Multicultural Student Advantage

Tim Sieber

Tim Sieber shares his appreciation for the increasing numbers of ESOL learners in his cultural anthropology course who bring firsthand knowledge and understanding to the study of cross-cultural issues. He notes how these students' life experiences give them critical insights into the analysis of culture, thus making it possible for them to question unexamined assumptions and beliefs. Tim describes the kinds of informal and formal writing assignments that are central to his teaching and discusses his approach to reading and responding to students' texts.

At the urban public university where I have taught for 27 years, I'm fortunate regularly to encounter in my classes large numbers of students who are gifted learners in the subject that I teach—cultural anthropology. I have always taught at all levels of the university's curriculum—lower-division general education courses, upper-division courses oriented to undergraduate majors, and master's-level courses—and consistently find that, whatever the level, this same group stands out in their advanced understanding of the subject matter. Who are these students? They are the growing numbers of mostly multicultural-multilingual people—immigrants, refugees, and international exchange students—that we often refer to as "ESL students," entering our university today.[1]

When I started my teaching career in the mid-1970s, ours was a different university, with many fewer foreigners, immigrants, and minorities, and a considerably more White student body. It's hard for me to believe now that I saw my role as an anthropologist as helping students from backgrounds similar to mine (Judeo-Christian, U.S.-born, White, and English-speaking) to understand the "other," exotic cultures of the world. Asian, Caribbean, and Latino immigrant students were only beginning to enter the university and were easily classed as anomalies, presumably willing to adapt themselves to an essentially Anglo U.S. education. Speaking to all students as if they and I together constituted a common group, a "we," I even used to make common comparisons between the assumptions of those "other" cultures we studied, and what I would refer to as "our usual Judeo-Christian understandings of the world."

Through my interactions with an ever changing student body during the 1980s, I began to recognize that this paradigm was misguided and inappropriate where the students I was teaching were concerned. As our student body grew more multicultural, I was able to identify in just one of my classrooms Hindus, Buddhists, Muslims, Jews, and Christians (each group also with its own internal diversity), as well as many nationalities, ethnicities, and native languages. All these changes, of course, simply reflect the growth of the "New Immigration" to the United States and the resulting growing cultural diversity in Boston and its metropolitan region. This demographic shift has, of course, been mirrored throughout the nation in the trend toward more diverse enrollments in universities, and indeed the entire education system. Some of the traditionalists on our faculty were alarmed by this influx of students who were perceived to be "underqualified," especially non-native speakers of English who use the written and spoken language in ways sometimes different from native speakers. Fortunately I have colleagues who shared my own positive assessment of these new arrivals, and the opportunity they have given our university to move toward being a more universal community of teachers and learners engaged in even more productive, fresh, democratic dialogue with one another about the important intellectual issues of our time.

GOALS OF CULTURAL ANTHROPOLOGICAL STUDY AND THE ESOL STUDENT

The major goal of cultural anthropological study in a liberal education is to develop an understanding of culture as a defining context for human behavior, thought, and feeling, and for the patterning of human variety across time and space. Through the exercise of cross-cultural comparison—confronting, examining, and explaining the cultural differences found among various human groups, including one's own—the learner can become aware of culture as a matter for critical reflection; thus, one can gain some purchase on one's own unexamined cultural assumptions, that is, one's own ethnocentrism. At its best, then, cross-cultural comparison always yields simultaneous, reciprocal, critical insight into both the cultures of others, as well as one's own. In this sense, cultural anthropology's view into others offers a "mirror" for the observer. It is not surprising that Margaret Mead (1989) and others have long noted, in this respect, that anthropology's critical and relativist frame of mind about culture also comes more easily, and appeals as more sensible, to people and groups who have experienced cultural transitions, or participated in multiple cultures, in their own individual biographies and collective histories.

A few other fundamental maxims of today's cultural anthropology also warrant mentioning in any inventory of the field's key ideas; with these themes, as well, multicultural histories and experiences tend to deepen a learner's understanding. First of all, "cultures" are no longer understood as static, essentialized, homogenous units, but instead as historically contingent, always changing, and constructed through the praxis of everyday life. Second, among the carriers of a culture we now expect to find diversity and behavioral and ideological fluidity, rather than homogeneity and purity, which seem less and less evident in the reality of today's rapidly changing, postmodern, and globalizing world. Third, in anthropology as in all of the human sciences today, as well as in society in general, the question of identity looms as a central matter for inquiry—chiefly because of dramatic collision and mixing of cultural elements everywhere, promoting the new forms of hybridity, multicultural identities, cultural exchange, and creolization so striking in today's cultural scene. Fourth is the central focus in today's anthropology on how cultures interact and coexist with each other, in the past as well as the present, especially in response to the overarching hierarchies of power and economic control that have structured relations among them.

It should be obvious that all of these are challenging concepts not easily problematized or studied in the U.S. academy today. The culture of the academy itself does not offer fertile ground for this study either, because much of higher education prides itself on privileging ("conserving") an older, fairly rigid notion of erudite, academic culture that is ruthlessly monocultural and monolingual. Most U.S.-born students entering higher education are also veterans of a strongly monocultural and monolingual education at the elementary and secondary levels, where unfortunately any elements of multiculturalism or bilingualism that are present are normally seen as "remedial" or as "frills." The markedly conservative political climate in the United States for the past generation, as well, has been quite congenial to renewal of older essentialist definitions of cultural groups, and to ignoring, rather than critically interrogating, the ways that power relations shape culture and human behavior. After 35 years of studying anthropology, I can see how this recent conservative ideological climate has changed students' consciousness of some social and cultural realities. It has limited the horizons of many students' educations, and hampered critical inquiry into many cultural issues that were much more actively investigated and understood by young people only a generation ago.

Although no group generalization can hold for every individual, in my experience ESOL students as a group are more capable of critically analyzing culture and understanding the aforementioned fundamental contemporary themes in cultural anthropology than U.S.-born monolingual students are. Before even entering my class, ESOL students are already bicultural, bilingual minorities making good progress in negotiating a culturally different, if not alien, university and broader social environment. This *life situation* requires a critical, relativistic approach to cultural issues that is readily evident in students' thinking, classroom conversation, and in particular in their writing. Bilingual students' writing reveals a basic depth of understanding of cultural issues that is, at the outset, well beyond what most monolingual students bring to the classroom. Of course, this is because ESOL students' understanding does not derive only from book learning, always a limited teacher, but also from life experience.

In classroom discussion, ESOL students frequently become information resources—teachers, really—for the whole class. A student from Kenya can explain, for example, how indigenous rural villages appear in her own country, drawing parallels with a reading on Amazonian village life. It is often hard for American students without any direct exposure to developing areas or indigenous peoples to envision and, sometimes, I have come to think, *believe* the truth of what they read about indigenous life. I find that ESOL students frequently spontaneously counter the skepticism of White American students by volunteering confirming accounts of what they have personally seen or heard about in their home regions.

The value of ESOL students' life experiences can be appreciated when we take into account what Dell Hymes argued two decades ago about the overlap of critical cultural, or "ethnographic," sensibility with experiential, commonsense reflections. He was closely echoing Gramsci's own assertions[2] (Gramsci, 1988) about the "organic" embeddedness of critical intelligence among all people in their practice of everyday life:

> Ethnography ... is continuous with ordinary life. Much of what we seek to find out in ethnography is knowledge that others already have. Our ability to learn ethnographically is an extension of what every human being must do, that is, learn the meanings, norms, patterns of a way of life.... [G]ood ethnography ... is an extension of a universal form of personal knowledge. (Hymes, 1982, pp. 29–30)

Their complex, rich multicultural biographies are an asset to ESOL students in learning critical analysis of culture, precisely because their status as boundary crossers sensitizes these students to question a dimension that more monocultural people take for granted. This more complex analytic understanding offered by the minority situation has been noted in other fields, as well, such as history. Rosenzweig and Thelen's (1998) study of historical awareness of American citizens, for example, found African Americans more capable than ordinary White Americans of what they call a "critical" understanding of history, especially in their ability to place their own personal experience within broader historical contexts and currents (see also discussion in Blake, 1999).

USING WRITING TO PROMOTE CRITICAL THINKING IN STUDIES OF CULTURE

I am ashamed to admit that earlier in my career I saw it as a *weakness* when ESOL students brought their own experiences into their writing about cultural studies, and did not write in the abstracted, formal way that is more traditional in the academic world—or that is common among conventional students who see this subject matter as something "curious" that can be studied only in disinterested ways. It is easier for students to leave themselves out of the discussion, and for their discourse to seem more "objective," when they do not see their own culture as problematized, or even understand that they have a culture. But I have learned that students can exercise critical facility in analyzing culture through writing frequently about the contrasts and connections between course materials and their own native cultures, about the history of their own experiences as immigrants, refugees, or international students, and about the contrasts and contradictions between their original cultures and the demands of their lives and their educations within U.S. society—*especially when they are allowed or encouraged to do so*. There is ample material for making critical reflections, comparisons, and connections in writing that can be drawn, in other words, from students' own past and current experiences.

It was a slow process for me to discover the value of encouraging students to do regular informal, critical writing—in other words, to make recording their thinking in writing a regular part of their experience of the course. I was helped much by encouragement from colleagues—especially from my university's English Department—who were more knowledgeable about composition and could suggest new ways for me to experiment with writing. I benefited from many workshops with specialists, as part of faculty training for different "writing across the curriculum" initiatives at my university. Another factor was my own dissatisfaction with the level of students' performance in my courses, and especially by the overly stiff, formalistic, and uncritical ways that students tended to write in response to my assignments. Once I required students to write regular critical reading journals as part of their coursework, I was literally shocked at the lively, fresh, critical writing that students started to produce.

In almost all my courses, I assign several different kinds of writing to students. Sometimes I ask students to write spontaneously on some issue during class time—and either turn it in for me to read, or else keep it to themselves, using it simply as a spur to formulate ideas that we later discuss

efforts by outsiders to appropriate their land and other resources for "development" of the Amazon.

Learning about the ugly particulars of slavery, introduced disease, epidemics, violence, displacement and resettlement, and a broad range of genocidal pressures on Indians is always a shock for students, especially those who have not experienced such turmoil. So many of our university's immigrant and refugee students, however, have themselves fled sites of serious political upheaval, civil war, violence, and dislocation, and thus can easily draw parallels between the Indians' situations and their own. Many ESOL students are quick to recognize, understand and realistically articulate the human costs involved in these historical situations.[4] José, for example, wrote a journal discussing the activity of an indigenous Amazonian leader, Davi Kopenawa Yanomami, who criticized the negative effects of a gold rush on Indians' welfare. In his writing José compared the civil war in his own native country, El Salvador, with the aggressive Brazilian displacement of Amazonian Indians:

> After reading the articles about the Yanomamo of Brazil and the rest of South America I was upset. I was born in El Salvador ... during the civil war many innocent people were massacred. Many of the villains that committed the massacres were battalions trained by the U.S.A. Many people spoke out of the injustices that were implemented on behalf of the Salvadoran government with U.S. assistance.... In the eyes of the government protecting investments over civilian lives was more important. In relating Davi's story to what I have conversed the similarities are that the [Brazilian] government refuses to acknowledge the horrific acts of violence that are being committed on the Yanomamo Indians. They refuse to see what is wrong in order to help the economy grow by letting the miners exploit the lands of the Yanomamo.

The failure of development schemes introduced by central governments also came as no surprise to a student whose family members were refugees from Vietnam. Twi wrote a journal on the parallels she saw after watching a class film on dam construction in Brazil that had flooded indigenous people's land and displaced its population, with disastrous environmental and social consequences:

> Watching the movies in class today remind me of my country view and I feel homesick again. In my country the first couple years when the communist take over the country they cut the river and put damp everywhere. They polluted the water in the countryside and digging up all the graves to make more land so they can move people from the north to the south.... As in the movie the Brazilian government say they want the economy to improve and they promise to help the Indians, but they never did. The same thing that the communist government promise to the people; they promise that they will improve the poor people life by taking the rich property and give it to the poor people and they didn't.... Indians are consider as lower class people

and it's the same as the lower class people in my country many people die of starvation and disease because of poverty.

In another point in the semester, we read Christopher Hampton's play, *Savages*, about Indian genocide. One subtle but critical theme of the play is the idea that poverty and enormous class inequalities in Brazilian society lead the poor to invade the forest in their own struggles to gain land for survival, and even occasionally to hire themselves out for small sums and accept assignments to massacre indigenous people. Tran, another Vietnamese student, wrote clearly about this issue:

> Brazil is an undeveloped country. A very small percent of the population owns the country's wealth. The rest of the population is extremely poor. They live in poverty and have very little to eat. The unequal distribution of the wealth has great impact on the poor working class people. These lower class people can't find job to support their family, therefore they have to seek others alternatives that lead them to the Amazon forest. The Amazon forest is a hug place with rich resources. Both the poor and the rich start to intrude the forest for its resources.... Pereira represents the working class of Brazil. One of the jobs that he took was to kill the Indians. Although his killing the Indian could not be justified, this tells us how desperate these people are.

Through the study of ethnography, history, and the writings of contemporary native Amazonians in their own voices, all of us work together to demystify Indian cultures, to see how indigenous peoples are active agents in their own usually difficult histories, and to understand how as a part of history their cultures have never stopped changing. All this not only requires learning about what is really happening in today's rainforest, but also some critical interrogation of common images of rainforest Indians as exotic, romantic, sometimes tragic figures, who are caught in a frozen, timeless past out of step with the contemporary world. We study how such "exoticizing" imagery of Indians—by local, "civilized" South American people as well as by many academic observers—has often had racist undertones and harmful consequences, in a world unwilling to accept and to live with Indians as "normal" humans. Being bi- or multicultural oneself, as virtually all ESOL students are, is an enormous asset in reaching the sophisticated, analytical understanding of culture that such a critique requires. Raul, for example, addressed the parallels between White people's views of native American cultures in the United States, and his own situation as a Latino:

> What is interesting is that some people don't realize the struggle and inhuman suffering the Native American have gone through. Some people go as far as to make an exotic imagine of them.... They think that having a culture that links them to the past is exciting. They are fascinated by their cultural functions, language, appearance, and history. Yet someone of these people

aren't really interested in embracing the culture. They admire from a distance, but don't take a closer. I for example can relate to that. When in high school I dated an Irish girl. We dated for a while and remained friends after we broke up. I later found out through some friends that she was fascinated by the Hispanic culture. So I wondered, did she go out with me because she really liked me or because of my ethnic background. The reality of it was that me being Hispanic played a roll.

We see it in the music industry.... People get fascinated by the "new" rhythms they hear. They buy the music and evening go as far as to taking dancing lessons to dance to the music. In some instances though, the person who is fascinated by all this new phenomenon doesn't have any friends that speaks Spanish. They read about the culture, but don't get involve with it. They create some sort of romanticism ... in the end, the reality is not an acceptance of culture it is only the admiration of it and nothing else.

Immigrant students frequently address issues of culture by referring to their own struggles to survive and prosper, and to remain bicultural, in often resolutely monocultural high school and university environments that demand they erase cultural traditions and discard older identities. In my Amazon class, for example, many students draw parallels between the demands missionaries make of Indians in the Amazon to accept Christianity and to acculturate to Western ways of living, and their own experiences of public, especially school, disparagement and misunderstanding of their own cultures. Esmeralda, from the Dominican Republic, addressed in one her journals the culture shock she experienced in her previous, private liberal arts college:

A culture shock can also be when you are introduced into a place that lacks diversity. This is when I experienced at Freeland College (pseudonym). Only three percent of the students were minority.... Going to FC's cafeteria was always a new experience. I never knew what was the food nor was I accumstomed to the way it was prepared. I am Hispanic and was raised eating platanos, arroz, yuca, carne, and huevos. It was difficult eating something new everyday. Language is also a huge part of culture. I would sometimes unconsciously speak Spanish to my room mates which were Caucasians. They would tells me things I wouldn't understand even though it was in English.... I would also not go out with my room mates because I wasn't into the music that they like nor were they interested in merengue, salsa, or bachata.... It is good to learn new things about different cultures but it is hard when it is something you are obligated to get into and enjoy. This was one of the reasons I transferred from FC. Not fitting in and feeling unconfortable is not a good environment to be in. Being told by a faculty member at FC that I will not make it at FC if I continued to speak Spanish at home was an eye opener that it was not a place I wanted to be in. I will not change my culture for no one or nothing.

In a society so monocultural and monolingual (and probably more so in higher education than in many other sectors), there has always been a traditional tendency in the United States to "essentialize" cultures, to view them as fixed, sharply bounded units that seldom mix with one another or change in response to their interactions with one another. We realize now that these traditional models ignore so many processes that are important to, even diagnostic of, the cultural scene in today's world, especially hybridity, cultural borrowing and recombination, "borderlands," and maintenance of multicultural or multiple identities. ESOL students like Esmeralda, just discussed, and Bhue from Vietnam, already live such processes in their own experience, and have little difficulty addressing them in their writing. As Bhue wrote:

> My family is one of the many families that immigrate to United States to look for a better life. We came here to seek for better opportunities and freedom that weren't allow to have in the mother country. I came to this country when I was about eight years old. I was young enough to be able to adapt easily to the new environment and custom. But I wasn't young enough to forget what I was taught in Vietnam. I often have difficulties when asked to define my culture. I have always thought that each person is only allow to have one culture. But the reality is that one can have more than one culture (I just know this recently). I often feel like I was force to choose between the Vietnamese and the American culture when asked to define it…. I find it is difficult to be living in two cultures, because you're constantly asked to make a decision.

Being more critically conscious of their own cultural differences, immigrant or international students are quite likely to make cross-cultural comparisons between their own home countries and the newer places and peoples that they study in anthropology, places that seem so foreign and distant to most students born and raised in the United States that they usually have a hard time imagining any similarity with their own everyday world. Chikage, a foreign-exchange student from Japan in the country only 6 weeks, for example, noticed and wrote about similarities between politically autonomous, warring villages of Yanomamo Indians in Venezuela, and the relations between warring kingdoms in feudal Japan. Though her historical comparison was not entirely correct,[5] Chikage was right to notice some key processes that these two societies had in common, for example, the absence of a strong, central state, and the fact that women were often the focus of fighting between groups of men:

> Because kinship is the most important issue for Yanomamo people, abduction and periodical fission of a village makes a relationship multiple. I think this is a very simple and basic system to maintain the group of people. I used to watch period dramas of Japan. These were stories about Japan from 14th century to 17th century. We did not have government to rule the land. People fight each other for their territory. The leader of each group was the top man of its kinship…. Abduction and marriage for political reasons was com-

mon. Women were like political tools. I found these two systems were similar: early modern Japan and Yanomamo. This period ended when black
ships from the foreign countries came to Japan.... Yanomamo is changing.
There are more outsiders visiting Yanomamo villages. They may change like
Japan in the future. I do not know it if is good or not, though.

After a class discussion of American slavery, to cite another example,
Xinh from Vietnam identified with the effects slavery had on children by
remembering his experiences as a refugee in Southeast Asia. He recounted
his experience of flight with his family, and their struggle to survive in a
refugee camp, and the early loss of his childhood innocence:

> The city we would reach, is distant about sixty miles. We only moved at
> night because to avoid danger of bombing and gun. On travel, we took shel-
> ter under big tree, church or temple for sleeping and cooking. This fearful
> travel spend five days. We came city and were welcome to refugee camps
> that built temporary for the communist refugees.... I was eight years old in
> this period. After school's hours I went to market to ask for fish or vegetable
> for family's meal or I went to sell newpaper, peanut every night. Really my
> mother did not require me to do these but I wanted to share hardship of fam-
> ily. After a year U.S. military began entering Vietnam. Every afteroon I usu-
> ally came garbage of U.S. base. It was call "U.S. garbage" to look for thing
> that need for family as wood, paper box for fueling, food, as well as other
> needs.... Although my childhood story is completely different with child-
> hood slavery. There is a common point is the war and slavery that rob my
> own childhood as well as childhood slavery.

To greater or lesser degrees, as can be seen from the verbatim extracts of
student writing just cited, ESOL students commonly make small errors of
grammar, word choice, and more rarely spelling (computer spell-checkers
have largely solved the problem of word-level spelling correctness, as can
be seen in the preceding texts). Often these "mistakes" come from students' transposition into academic writing of essentially oral speech patterns that they have adopted in learning English for everyday use outside
the university. Despite the perceptions of many of my faculty colleagues
at the university, some of whom seem more alarmed by such transgres-
sions in academic writing, I very seldom find that these minor grammatical irregularities obscure the meaning of the student writing. I hasten to
remind them that the content, or meaning, of what students write is usually sophisticated, analytic, and to the point. The *very same life conditions*
that require the student to learn conventions of academic writing usually
only *after* they are already in the university, and after regular writing practice there, also offer a solid foundation—as I have noted earlier—for students' superior intellectual work. It seems like a small trade-off.

I did not always have this mind-set. I used to think that my major responsibility as an evaluator of writing, with respect to ESOL students, was

to be a grammar policeman, to screen for errors, and to mark down students' grades accordingly, regardless of the content of their ideas. Too often I let my concern for proper writing form contaminate my assessment of students' intellectual achievements. Excellent ideas could mitigate grammatical imperfections, I thought, but never really overcome them. I am very grateful to faculty colleagues at my university, and to many students themselves, for helping me to understand how this type of response to student writing was not effectively recognizing and promoting students' intellectual development.

With the help of colleagues, I learned to appreciate how dedicated most ESOL students' efforts really are, that they are likely to expend two, three, or even four times the amount of time and work in preparing papers as native speakers of English usually do. They also make extraordinarily rapid progress if given support for sustained writing practice, especially if they are encouraged to write about their own ideas in authentic, honest ways. The surface grammatical imperfections that sometimes occur do require a teacher's strategic attention and correction, to be sure; but it is important to keep in view that they are temporary, and seldom blemish the outstanding intellectual work that ESOL students regularly do. As I have noted, I think there is little to complain about, and much to be grateful for as a teacher: ESOL students in the study of culture show advanced critical thinking in their work, and seriously use their writing as a tool for clarifying their ideas. What more could a teacher ask?

CONCLUDING THOUGHTS

It is important to point out that not all multilingual students are "naturally" enlightened about cultural issues or tolerant of cultural differences they encounter in their own lives or backgrounds. They are not free of ethnocentrism. About many issues, ESOL students have their own forms of ethnocentrism that are challenged by the teachings of cultural anthropology. Even if students have knowledge of foreign cultures outside the United States, their own class, religious, gender, and other identities can bias their perceptions of what they have "seen" before. Some of the most memorable examples of ethnocentric blind spots from recent students include: (a) the middle-class, urban, Catholic Vietnamese student who viewed tribal mountain peoples in his own country as semihuman barbarians; (b) the Brazilian who saw Amazonian Indians as more naturally sexual and artistic than ordinary urban Brazilians; and, (c) the Chinese student who repeatedly argued for the veracity of a story heard from a relative about a Vietnamese boat girl who, left on an island, mated with a monkey and produced hybrid offspring.

Such stories evince biased, even racist assumptions about indigenous or poor peoples in their previous countries. Students probably surface such stories in journals and class discussions precisely because their meanings are quite discrepant with what they are learning in cultural anthropology about understanding human behavior in parallel situations. As almost all teachers learn, I have come to realize that such cognitive resistance to the course material is part of students' developmental process toward new, more encompassing understandings—that may yet appear before the end of the course, or perhaps not until long after it is over. Resistance is often temporary, a prelude to intellectual growth.

Finally, in regard to their own position in U.S. society, as well, ESOL students face severe challenges. Awareness of their struggles at adaptation and survival in the U.S. context does not always produce tolerance and understanding of other minorities they encounter. Immigrant students are especially uncomprehending, sometimes, about why the United States' own long historically oppressed, "involuntary minorities" (such as African Americans) might see them as competitors.[6] Multilingual students may also learn many racist and ethnocentric ideas and attitudes as of result of their participation in U.S. society. Thus although it is not useful to idealize or overexaggerate the wisdom or tolerance of ESOL students, overall I still have found them more open to relativist thinking and understanding of cultural differences than other students.

Whatever experiential or intuitive understandings ESOL students have of cultural issues, of course, it is necessary for them to study the methods and theories of cultural anthropology in order to develop their understandings in more formal ways, and especially to become more self-conscious and in control of their own critical faculties in this area. Studying anthropology, and especially being supported to write extensively about cultural issues, is a way for students to recognize what they know, to examine its relevance to conventional bodies of academic literature on the subject, and finally to deepen their self-knowledge and understandings of the worlds they are a part of. After beginning intensively to read, write, and think about these issues, there is still thus a long and rewarding intellectual path to follow, toward more profound understandings of culture, and themselves.

In all these matters of the purposes and processes of learning, it should be clear, there is no real difference between ESOL students and students in general. Teaching practices that are good for ESOL students are equally good for all students. Though ESOL students have an edge in basic understandings of the material, as with all other students, the requirements of deeper learning, and of self-knowledge, are identical. Reading the eloquent writing produced by so many ESOL students has been important to me, I should add, in raising the expectations and the standards I set for all students. Whenever I can, I encourage them to strive to reach the same levels of criticality and authenticity in their writing as ESOL students commonly do.

ACKNOWLEDGMENTS

I thank first of all the many ESOL students I have been fortunate to teach in my classes at the University of Massachusetts Boston. They have helped me much in learning to be a more effective teacher, and in raising my standards for student writing, for all the students that I teach. I am also deeply grateful to Vivian Zamel, Donaldo Macedo, and other wise, generous university colleagues, who have regularly offered guidance, support, and good examples where all these issues are concerned. Names of all students used in the text are pseudonyms. I also thank Vivian Zamel, Ruth Spack, and Victoria Nuñez for their helpful comments on earlier versions of this chapter.

REFERENCES

Blake, C. N. (1999). The usable past, the comfortable past, and the civic past: Memory in contemporary America. *Cultural Anthropology, 14*(3), 423–435

Gramsci, Antonio (1988). *An Antonio Gramsci reader: Selected writings, 1916–1935* (D. Forgacs, Ed.). New York: Schocken Books.

Hymes, D. (1982). What is ethnography? In P. Gilmore & A. A. Glatthorn (Eds.), *Children in and out of school: Ethnography and education* (pp. 21–32). Washington, DC: Center for Applied Linguistics.

Mead, M. (1989). *Blackberry winter.* Gloucester, MA: Peter Smith Publishers.

Ogbu, J. (1993). Frameworks—Variability in minority school performance: A problem in search of an explanation. In E. Jacob & C. Jordan (Eds.), *Minority education: Anthropological perspectives* (pp. 83–111). Norwood, NJ: Ablex.

Rosenzweig, R., & Thelen, D. (1998). *The presence of the past: Popular uses of history in American life.* New York: Columbia University Press.

Sieber, T. (2001). Learning to listen to students and oneself. In E. Kingston-Mann & T. Sieber (Eds.), *Achieving against the odds: How academics become teachers of diverse students* (pp. 54–76). Philadelphia: Temple University Press.

NOTES

[1]In this chapter, in keeping with the perspective of the editors, I use the acronym ESOL (English for Speakers of Other Languages) as a more accurate description of this diverse group.

[2]Gramsci (1988) explains the relation between intellectual activity and everyday experience, and the universality of human intellectual capacity, in this way:

> This means that, although one can speak of intellectuals, one cannot speak of non-intellectuals, because non-intellectuals do not exist. There is no human activity from which every form of intellectual participation can be excluded: *homo faber* cannot be separated from *homo sapiens*. Each man, finally, outside his professional activity, carries on some form of intellectual activity, that is, he is a "philosopher," an artist, a man of taste, he participates in a particular conception of the world, has a conscious line of moral conduct,

cannot borrow wholesale the pedagogies that work in remedial or first-year language classes. Rather, my challenge is to retain pedagogies that are appropriate for the majority of students while being sympathetic to the special needs of non-native English speakers.

In this essay, I describe the instructional supports that helped an ESOL pupil, Neha Shah. These are pedagogies that did not require that I divert my attention from course subject matter or slight the majority of students in the class. In what follows, in addition to providing my teacher's perspective, I try, with Lucille McCarthy's help, to present Neha Shah's point of view as well.

AN ESOL STUDENT IN "WRITING INTENSIVE" INTRODUCTION TO PHILOSOPHY

At the time she took my class in fall 1998, Neha Shah was a 23-year-old senior math major who had immigrated to America from India just 2 years earlier. Neha was a particularly challenging test case for my pedagogy because she came to my class reluctantly, experiencing a special type of bicultural tension (Cummins, 1986). That is, Neha came to my class convinced that having to take it was totally unfair. She had already earned a degree from a university in India and hoped to be granted an undergraduate American degree without taking further courses. Unfortunately for her, however, the dean of the college of arts and sciences at my university felt she needed to satisfy more general distribution requirements, including one "writing intensive" class. Thus it was with considerable reluctance that Neha enrolled in my Introduction to Philosophy course.

I mention that Neha experienced bicultural tension because, in interviews with Lucille McCarthy, she explained that she had been taught to view professors and other elders as authorities to whom she owes total respect. Yet at my university she was faced with an American official who contradicted authorities in her native country, an American dean who, in effect, questioned Indian administrators who deemed her already educated. Thus Neha was conflicted and unhappy about having to obey an authority in her newly adopted land whose views were at variance with those in her home culture.

Given this background, Neha came to my philosophy class with only one goal: She wanted to get it over with so she could graduate. This objective is not unusual, of course, among the students I teach. However, Neha faced even greater problems achieving this goal than most pupils. This is because my curriculum is not tailored for someone with her cultural background and interests. I select my readings in an effort to encourage American students to consider some of their deeply held values, ones impacting social issues with which Americans are likely to be already engaged. For example, my early-semester assignments are an effort to help students examine the relationships among racism, colonialism, and capitalism, and to this end we read Carmichael (1966/1995), Fanon (1965/1995), and hooks (1981/1995). But as Neha told Lucille, she was totally unaware of race conflicts in America and, as a result, could not understand her classmates' strong reactions to these texts. Because Neha did not see such contemporary moral issues as relevant to her, my curriculum did little to motivate her to overcome her view that my course was unnecessary "busy work" imposed on her by my dean.

Before discussing Neha Shah's experiences in philosophy and the instructional supports that helped her make progress, I describe my goals and expectations for the philosophy students in my classes.

GOALS AND EXPECTATIONS
FOR PHILOSOPHY STUDENTS

Put most generally, I want students to listen to the ideas of others: the positions of their classmates as well as those presented by authors of the texts I assign. As they try to make sense of these different perspectives and compare them with their own, I hope students will penetrate beneath the surface of moral differences to reflect on the philosophic assumptions that lie behind these differences. More specifically, I have six objectives for student thinking and writing in my courses.

First, I want students to show that they can do *argument extraction,* that is, that they can read texts and identify authors' stances and the ways they defend them. Second, I would like students to demonstrate that they can *evaluate a position,* assessing how and to what extent an author's evidence supports his or her conclusions. Third, I want them to *present and defend their own positions* in a coherent way. All three of these goals are familiar to teachers and students in many disciplines (see Larson, 1991).

In addition, I have two objectives that are more peculiar to philosophy. My fourth goal for students is that they *apply philosophy to their own lives,* seeing ways in which the materials and issues I present in class intersect with their personal concerns. This is crucial if my course is going to be meaningful to students, to be, in other words, a tool of self-exploration. My fifth objective is that students learn to *contextualize* their beliefs, to set them in the context of related arguments and positions that they encounter in the course. This fifth goal is the *sine qua non* of philosophy, at least as I understand it. Gramsci (1971), in *Selections from the Prison Notebooks,* helps me explain why this is so. He says that philosophy allows people to clarify their own beliefs and, thus, make them more consistent with their actions. He also says that by knowing something of the history of thought and various intellectual movements, we are in a better position to be critical of our own views and the views of those around us. As a philosopher, then, I want students to reflect on their own beliefs and the beliefs of others by relating and contextualizing them.

My sixth and final goal for student writing and thinking is, once again, a goal familiar to many teachers across the curriculum. Quite simply, I want *coherence and good organization*. I need to be able to understand what the pupils are saying.

AN ESOL WRITER AT SEMESTER'S START

On the first day of my Intro class in fall 1998, I asked students to do a brief freewrite about their home communities and the values they have taken from them. In addition, I asked how those values have been challenged as students left home to enter larger and more varied communities. After about 10 minutes of writing, I looked around the room trying to decide whom to call on first. Neha Shah was sitting immediately to my right in the class circle, and I thought she might be a good place to start. My hope was that Neha, apparently from a different culture, would present a contrast with my own views as well as those of the other students. So I called on her, and she described something of her personal history and then responded to a number of questions from her classmates and me.

Although Neha spoke very quietly in accented English, I could follow her responses to our questions about her freewrite. That is, her contribution during that initial class period raised no warning flags in me. However, what did get my attention were her first homework assignments. They totally defied my expectations for student writing because they were so different from papers I had typically received during my 31 years of teaching. Although I gave Neha passing grades on these early assignments—not wanting to discourage her and hoping she would somehow improve—concern was building for me in three areas.

First, Neha's surface errors and mismanagements were serious and frequent. For example, on her homework response to an essay by Lin Yutang (1937/1995), she wrote, "On the day of his mother funeral, he felt himself by selfish. This defines his not arrogant. And by Confucian colleague experienced, he felt like he cut off his tie with Christianity. Like this, he calling by himself a 'pagan'."

Although in the preceding example, I could figure out what Neha wanted to say, there were times I could not. So my second area of worry was one Shaughnessy (1977) noted long ago. Discipline-based teachers, Shaughnessy observes, are generally more interested in *what* students say than *how* they say it, and thus they ignore errors when they can. I typically do that. However, when Neha's writing mismanagements made it impossible for me to follow her thinking, I started to realize she presented me with an unusual problem. In other words, the level of Neha's papers seemed shockingly below that of the other 24 students, all of whom were native speakers of English. For instance, I was mystified when, in her homework response to hooks' (1981/1995) claim that women are unaware of the extent to which their psyches have been warped by racism and classism, Neha wrote, "I agree with her because I am a girl. I know how is woman's nature. Woman has a jealous characteristic than man." I was equally confused when Neha attempted, two assignments later, to summarize Holmes' (1929/1973) arguments for immortality. She concluded, "Therefore, for believing in immortality or for being ready to believe in immortality, is the primarily interesting fact that there is no reason for not believing in immortality."

My third concern about Neha's writing focused on those occasions when I realized she did not understand the assigned text. That is, I began to suspect Neha not only had a writing problem but a reading one as well. For example, in response to an essay by Carmichael (1966/1995), she wrote:

> On the behalf of nonviolence and integration, Carmichael used political and economic power term. The Carmichael also argued that racism could be overcome only by sharing economy…. In this article, he gave one example and compare to the real life. When he was a boy, he used to see movie of Tarzan. He saw in movies, White Tarzan used to beat up the black natives because they were black in skin. By this he explained that White Tarzan beat black native in movies, same way it happens in real life that White people hate and ignore black people, not because black are ignorant, or not because they are stupid, only because they are black.

Regarding Neha's first two sentences, it seemed to me that she had misunderstood Carmichael's point. Whereas she describes Carmichael as supporting nonviolence and integration, in fact he argues against them. Regarding her response to Carmichael's example, she again seemed to miss his point. He is less concerned with the fact that Tarzan is beating up Black natives than he is with the fact that he, as a young African American, was rooting for Tarzan.

In pointing out my concerns about Neha's writing—my worries about her mechanics, her inability at times to make herself clear, and her misunderstanding of assigned texts—I do not mean that I blamed Neha. Nor did I take these writing problems as a sign she was not highly intelligent, diligent in her work, and serious about her education. McCarthy had told me that, compared to the other students, Neha came to my class with very little English-writing experience. In her interviews with Lucille, Neha had explained that although her university courses in India had been taught in English, she had seldom written anything because her major was math. In any case, Neha added, she had never liked writing very much, not even in her mother tongue, Gujarati.

However, as sympathetic as I was to Neha's situation, I could not just ignore her reading and writing difficulties. To the contrary, very much in my mind was the fact that my class was designated "writing intensive" and it was my job to certify that students who passed it were reading and writing Standard American English at the college level. I simply had no idea how, in a matter of 14 weeks, I could bring Neha's reading and writing in English up to the level of her better prepared classmates. That is, Neha's problems did not appear to be ones that could be attributed simply to her struggle to become acquainted with the conventions and expectations of philosophy. After all, her fellow classmates faced this same challenge without their reading and writing displaying anything like the degree of underpreparedness that Neha's work showed. To me, this meant that her problems were less the result of her unfamiliarity with philosophic language and methods than of her inexperience reading, writing, and speaking in English. In sum, as I reflected on Neha's early papers, I felt handcuffed. If Neha was unprepared for my course, I, as a teacher, was equally unprepared for her.

THE GHOST OF LOUIS HELLER:
WHOSE ERRORS? WHOSE EXPECTATIONS?

In being taken aback by Neha's writing, I believe my reactions may have resembled those of Louis G. Heller, the CCNY (City College of New York) classics professor alarmed by the way CUNY (City University of New York) implemented its open-admissions policy in the fall of 1970 (Heller, 1973; Lu, 1992/1999; Traub, 1994). Although my university situation nearly three decades later was far, far different from Heller's, my knee-jerk response to Neha was the same as his to the new CUNY students: I viewed her as not belonging in my classroom. My first thought was, "Golly, her work wouldn't get a passing grade from my old high school English teacher, Mrs. Wachs." My second thought was, "With everything else the University is asking me to do, teaching this student to read and write is a particularly difficult burden to add."

However, I could not dismiss Neha, as I have said, for her underpreparedness, nor, in contrast to Heller (1973) and many of his CUNY colleagues, could I blame outside militants and misguided politicians for her presence in my classroom (chaps. 3, 14, 19). Thus, I was, I have to admit, a little embarrassed by my reactions to Neha's work. Obviously, it was people at my own university who had decided that she belonged in my Intro course. So I began to doubt myself. Perhaps the important errors were not on Neha's pages but in my responses to her. Perhaps the unreasonable expectations were not hers but mine. This admission put me in a painful moral vise, trying to honestly evaluate Neha's writing while, at the same time, being sensitive to her special situation. On the one hand, her work deserved low grades because it reflected not only poor command of Standard American English but also limited understanding of the assigned philosophic texts. On the other hand, I knew Neha faced unusual hardships, ones that might justify more lenient or atypical evaluation. But this did not seem right either because I suspected the other students also shouldered hardships, ones that were just less apparent. If this were true, how in the world could I construct a fair evaluation system that would take into account all the apparently relevant factors?

Further compounding my dilemma was Neha's unhappiness with my responses to her writing. My saying anything negative about her work seemed to open an old wound, as if I were a customs official turning her away at the Ellis Island gate. Her passing grade in freshman composition at my own university was a passport I was now questioning. When I first spoke with Neha about her papers, she seemed surprised and offended. She told me that her instructor in composition the previous summer had given her an A because, as Neha put it, "she understood I have been in your country only a short time." I do not know exactly what I expected, but I thought, "Even if she cannot be grateful to me for pointing out her writing difficulties—for not lowering my standards—I wish she would at least acknowledge the importance of improved writing for her future."

Counterbalancing these early, negative conversations with myself about Neha, my sense she was out of place in my Intro classroom, were recollections that I could not put aside of my grandfather, Moishe Gluck. Had this unschooled Hungarian peasant come to America to improve his life so his privileged grandson could, two generations later, prevent other immigrants from improving theirs? If I knew nothing else, I was sure he was not dreaming that dream as he headed in steerage toward the lamp beside Lazarus' golden door.

These were my initial thoughts and concerns about Neha, the undercurrents of uncertainty running through me as I gave Neha passing grades on her first three homework assignments. However, when her fourth assignment appeared to be worse than the previous three, I figured that my strategy of passing her and hoping things would get better was not working. So despite the many conflicts within me, I felt I had no choice but to give Neha an F. This grade led to a conversation with her and to her decision to devote more time to my course. I briefly describe Neha's fourth homework paper.

A FAILED HOMEWORK ASSIGNMENT IN EARLY SEPTEMBER

To encourage greater involvement with course texts and class discussion, I ask for written homework on each reading assignment, and, because our semester began the third week of August, by early September every student had completed three short papers. For their fourth homework, I asked students to write a letter to a randomly chosen classmate about Plato's *Apology* and *Crito*. The purpose of the letter was for each pupil to present a question he or she thought was important and went to the heart of an issue raised by the dialogues. Typically, students ask each other questions like, What does Socrates mean by wisdom? (On the one hand, he says he knows nothing. On the other, he seems to know a great deal about virtues of character and the moral life.) Or, What do you think of Socrates' defense? (He is facing the death penalty, yet he seems to insult his accusers, lecture the jurors, and be very unapologetic, despite the title of the dialogue.) Or, Why will Socrates not escape? (Although he says he is against injustice—and he believes he is being treated unjustly—he makes no effort to leave Athens.)

However, when I looked at Neha's letter, it confirmed for me that she and I were facing a reading problem as well as a writing one. In fact, I doubted that she understood Plato at all. What led me to this conclusion was that Neha seemed perfectly comfortable in the letter genre, one I picked purposely in an effort to make writing about philosophy more informal because of its classmate audience. Yet Neha's questions indicated little comprehension of the texts and the issues they presented.

In her letter about the *Apology* and *Crito,* Neha wrote to her classmate, Robert Bullerdick, a 30-year-old Euro-American, saying that the *Apology* presented no problem to her. She understood it all, she told him, and she understood the *Crito* quite well too, but she did wonder about Crito's comment that if Socrates escaped, letting Crito and his friends bribe the guards, he would be endangering them. Her first question to Robert was, What does the word *endangering* mean? I quote part of Neha's letter to Robert just as she wrote it:

Dear Robert,

Hi, how are you? I didn't get your letter for long time and not even talk by phone. I know you are busy with study and work. I have same situation here; school give me lot of work. In this semester I am taking three classes and going to graduate in December. I am so happy, how about you? How many semesters you left for graduate?

Here, I need your help in my philosophy class. I know you are real good and excellent in philosophy.... Last night I read "The last day of Socrates" book written by Plato. In this book I read the Apology and Crito's conversation with Socrates.

In the Apology I understand everything. In the Crito's I understand pretty much, except Crito's arguments and believe that Socrates should escape.

... In the first argument [Crito] said Socrates should escape, because he is endangering the good reputation of his friends and he need not worry about and risks these friends may be running.... Actually, I do not understand what endangering mean. So, could you please explain me what Crito trying to say?

... At the last, Socrates said, he only wish that ordinary people had an unlimited capacity for doing harm and power for doing well. In this sentence I do not understand what kind of unlimited capacity he was talking about. Because he said only ordinary people had unlimited capacity. I am wondering what about other people.

I hope you can understand my question. Please explain me in brief, So I can go straight. I am really waiting for your explanation letter about my question.

I know it will make you busy, but you are my friend so please help me out. Take a time and write me back.

Your friend,

Neha shah [sic]

After putting an F at the top of this paper, I wrote, "It is a struggle for me to follow your writing. I cannot understand what you are trying to say. *Please* get help at the Writing Center." This failing grade was, at least in part, the result of my own frustration. I was not sure how to teach Neha the vocabulary she needed to follow something like a Platonic dialogue nor how to explain the various rhetorical strategies someone uses in presenting a dramatic piece.

When Neha came to talk to me about her grade, I told her that if she did not get some help, I did not see how she could pass the course. And that was my honest feeling. Although not all of the students come up with great questions in these letter assignments, none of them asks about the meanings of familiar English words. Put differently, I felt that Neha at this point was just not prepared to do the reading in the course, and that left me puzzled, unsure what I could do to help her.

Neha, according to Lucille McCarthy, felt equally at a loss. She told Lucille in an interview that she believed it was unfair of me to suggest she might fail the course, given that we were only 3 weeks into the semester. She also said she considered dropping the course but, after talking to her adviser, decided to stay. Because she was desperate to graduate at the end of the semester, Neha elected to give up one of her jobs—she was working 45 hours per week plus taking two other courses—so she could better complete my homework assignments.

In the long run, this turned out to be a good decision, and I could tell from Neha's subsequent homework papers that she was spending more time on them. In addition, she told Lucille, she was getting help from her family, an older cousin and a younger sister, both of whose command of English was better than Neha's. With her reduced work schedule, she could also spend an hour a week in the writing lab. Thus, despite Neha's lack of American "cultural capital," she possessed significant economic, social, and academic capital (Bourdieu, 1982, p. 392; see also Bourdieu, 1991). That is, she had the financial resources to reduce her job hours, had access to educated family members, and had some well-developed study habits of her own.

However, I do not want to paint too rosy a portrait and say that Neha's writing improved dramatically. It did not. But I began to feel that she was profiting from the course, that she was actually wrestling with difficult texts and succeeding in modest ways in writing about them. With her stronger effort, Neha ultimately made reading and writing progress that, given the place she started, was, in my view, remarkable.

VISIBLE PROGRESS BY SEMESTER'S END

The final exam was the place Neha's reading and writing improvement was most obvious. In one of her answers, in particular, she achieved two of the six goals that I listed earlier as my primary aims for the course. She not only extracted and summarized with some clarity Bertrand Russell's (1929/1970) arguments about patriarchy in *Marriage and Morals* (goal one), she also applied philosophy, relating patriarchy to her own life (goal four). Although Neha's level of writing remained far below that of her classmates, and her application of Russell's concepts was somewhat garbled, she did step back and use Russell's ideas to reflect on her own concerns. That pleased me. I quote Neha's final exam here, just as she wrote it. The test question reads:

> a) What are some of the events and beliefs that Bertrand Russell says provided the foundation for our patriarchal society?
>
> b) In your opinion, what are the pluses and minuses of patriarchy?

Neha responded:

> a) 'Marriage and Morals' by Russel is viewed as a great and famous book. In this book he talked about different cultural, traditions, society and marriages. He mainly talked about patriarchal society, which means the male is the head of the family and female always considered below than male. About his talked it seems to me like all civilized modern societies are based upon the patriachal family, and the whole conception based of female virtue which has been built up in order to make the partriarchal family. I believe that in patriarchal society mother and father have different expression and behaviour for their child. The relation of father and son in a patrilineal society is more closer then any relation between male which is exist in other society, and man inherits from his father. I also believe this society is one kind of "primitive" society. Because in this society a father (man) has everything means power, property, affection and the patriarchal family is more closely. The main provided thing for patriarchal system is that man came to desire virginity in their brides. Men has strongly feelings for this virginity. A father has strong power over his children and wife, child could not marry without their father's consent, and it was usual for the father to decide whom they should marry. In sort, a woman has not period in her life for any independent existence because being above situation first to her father and then to her husband. At last, patriarchal society provided as the DOMINION of the father.
>
> b) About my opinion, our society is patrirachal society. Woman always consider below than man that means male is head of the family. About my family my mom and dad are modern (new generation) but we still have to follow

our society. I think there are all points and which is all minuse. Woman and man both have to have equal rights, power and oppertunity. If father is head in the family why should mother not? The main minuse point is about marriage. Why only father decide to whom child should marry. If men desire for virginity then what about woman. All this should be subtract (minuses) in patriarchy. There is only one pluse in it, and it is about respect. Means woman has to give a respect to her mother-in-law, father-in-law and her husband, and stay with her husband with all equal oppertunity. These all are the pluses and minsues points about my opinion.

Although it was clear to me as I read Neha's final exam in December 1998 that her writing still displayed multiple surface mismanagements, it was also clear that, compared to her Plato letter, she had made progress. Her paper reflected a strong effort both to interpret Russell's text and to relate it to her own social and cultural situation.

INSTRUCTIONAL SUPPORTS THAT HELP AN ESOL WRITER

What were the instructional supports that Neha identified as helping her improve her philosophic reading and writing? Her choices surprised me, although to those who have studied ESOL students, it may be a familiar story. To explain, I see my class as featuring writing-to-learn techniques. That is, in the semester I taught Neha, for every reading assignment, as I have already noted, I assigned homework that had to be typed so that when students arrived at class they were prepared for discussion. And in many sessions I found ways to circulate this homework, asking students to share it with classmates in pairs or small groups. I also frequently had students report the results of their small-group conversations to the entire class. My reason for asking students to write about every assigned reading was that I believed it would provide them a focus, and they would thus take their reading more seriously. My rationale for circulating their homework was that I did not want to be the sole audience for their writing. Instead, I was eager that they have multiple readers. As a matter of fact, on some assignments, I asked pupils to read a draft of their homework to a friend or family member so they could get help from non-class-members as well. My hope was that the students would get into the habit of using various audiences to enrich and complicate their work.

COMBINING WRITING-TO-LEARN TECHNIQUES WITH DIALOGIC INTERACTION

When I realized that Neha was struggling not only with her writing but also with her reading, I wondered if my writing-to-learn homework assignments would help her. What I learned from this study was that, by themselves, they did not. However, when my writing-to-learn exercises were supplemented by in-class, interactive activities, ones in which pupils played teacher and learner to one another, Neha came to understand the material better. In a December interview, she told Lucille McCarthy that although she worked hard at home, sometimes as much as 6 hours on an assignment, she would still come to class confused and uncertain about the readings. However, she realized that when she discussed her homework with classmates, she developed a better grasp of the texts and the issues they raised. Neha explained: "We had already done the assignment, right, and after assignment he will talk about what the assignment about. Then, [in pairs or small groups or class discussion], I hear what my ideas are and what other people's ideas are, and I finally understand the material better. My mind clicks on ... and I clear up some of my confusions."

Again, Neha's need for in-class conversation with peers may come as no surprise to scholars who have carefully studied ESOL students. Such researchers often advise teachers to provide meaningful opportunities for their ESOL students to practice the target language—in this case not only English but also philosophic talk (see Cummins, 1986; Dean, 1986/1999; Zamel, 1995). Neha's interactions with her classmates allowed her to do that. She told McCarthy that in these small-group situations she was less embarrassed to speak up than in whole-class discussions where she rarely volunteered.

In sum, writing-to-learn, which is dependent on a certain level of comfort with Standard English, was not, by itself, helpful for Neha. However, when combined with the sorts of peer dialogue that often went on in my classroom, the writing-to-learn homework became worthwhile. Although Neha never became excited about my subject matter, nor did she ever see any intrinsic value in my class, in the end she felt as I did: that she had gotten something out of my course. In fact, she told Lucille in an interview a year and a half after the course concluded that she had recommended it to her younger sister, a freshman about to enroll at my university.

I turn now to three specific assignments—examples of writing-to-learn combined with student-to-student dialogue—that Neha identified as most helpful. The first of these is the letter exchange with classmates that I have already mentioned. Second were student-generated exams and, third, student-generated questions for class discussion.

THE LETTER EXCHANGE: HELPING STUDENTS TEACH ONE ANOTHER

The letter exchange is an activity I used four times across the semester. For the final letter, in early December, Neha was randomly paired with an African American student, 36-year-old Ellen Williams, a criminal justice major whom she knew and liked on the basis of their previous interactions in class. In this letter, which focuses on the first chapter of Dewey's (1920/1962) *Reconstruction in Philosophy,* I again asked students to formulate a question about some aspect of the work that puzzled them. In contrast to her letter to Robert Bullerdick 3 months earlier, in which she asked about the meaning of the word *endangering,* Neha wrote about the Dewey chapter in more sophisticated ways. She asked Ellen about Dewey's view of the relationship between science, practical knowledge, and philosophy. Neha was confused, she told her classmate, about the importance of science for philosophy, and she was not clear what Dewey is saying. Does he say science is important, or does he say it is not important? Although the language that Neha used in her letter was far from polished, and there remained many surface mismanagements, it is obvious that she was getting to issues that are at the heart of Dewey's chapter. (See the Appendix for her letter.)

In fact, I found Neha's letter to Ellen exciting because Neha shows sensitivity to Dewey's own ambivalence in the opening chapter of *Reconstruction in Philosophy*. On the one hand, he says that philosophy is born in the conflict between practical knowledge and tradition, between burgeoning science and long-held customs that are accepted without careful examination. However, on the other hand, Dewey also suggests that science abstracted from human values and concrete situations is not as valuable as it would be if it remained tied to everyday life. Neha's letter captured something of this conflict.

In an interview on the afternoon this letter was completed, Lucille asked Neha about this assignment. Neha's answer indicates the importance of this homework's dialogic component. Her primary concern was not Dewey's chapter or the teacher or her grade: It was her letter partner, Ellen Williams. When Lucille mentioned she had just spoken to Ellen, also a research informant, Neha asked, "Did Ellen understand my question?" (Lucille had not discussed this with Ellen.) Neha's concern indicates her genuine desire to communicate with Ellen, to keep up her part of their teaching–learning bargain. She told Lucille how she had struggled to shape a good question for her classmate:

> I have to read [Dewey's chapter] twice because when I read first time I don't understand. I'm lost. After the second time my mind is clearer. I highlight, and I put in the margin what I'm going to ask Ellen.... My question is I'm not sure if [Dewey] believe in science or he just believe in philosophy.... I mean does he believe philosophy is related to science or not? Because I'm not sure. At first he said philosophy's just imagination, but later he said philosophy is a science experience, and then he says philosophy is also like a social tradition. I was lost, so I just asked her what Dewey believes....

I find Neha's comments significant not only because they indicate that she understood something about Dewey's text but also because she was developing an additional—and more self-generated—motive for doing the work in my course. As I have explained, Neha entered my class simply

semester I was so distracted by Neha's surface mismanagements that I forgot Banks' advice, by the close of the semester I once again saw its wisdom. I realized that more important than instruction in writing mechanics was a pedagogy that provided Neha with opportunities to write and to share her work with others. In this way her fluency, her ability to compose with fewer errors, occurred spontaneously, as part of a context in which she was trying to clarify her ideas. For example, Neha really wanted to communicate successfully with fellow classmates and to bring useful questions to her small groups. These motivators were important in enabling her to continue to practice, to work on both the content and form of her writing.

In sum, I recommend the instructional supports I have described because they worked for Neha Shah. However, in celebrating this sort of indirect teaching, I am aware of cautions by Delpit (1995) and Lazere (1992) that underprepared students also need explicit writing instruction. According to these researchers, novice writers need to know the rules for paragraphing and sentence structures as well as the conventions within particular disciplines. Yet I believe that only where direct lessons in rules and conventions can be delivered briefly should discipline-based teachers offer such lessons. My experience with Neha suggests that focus on course content, writing-to-learn, and student dialogue—rather than sentence structure and mechanics—is the appropriate emphasis for discipline-based teachers of ESOL students.

APPENDIX: FINAL LETTER ASSIGNMENT (DECEMBER 3, 1998)

I reproduce Neha Shah's letter to her classmate about the first chapter of Dewey's *Reconstruction in Philosophy* just as she typed it.

Dear Ellen,

Hi, how are you? How do you feel about this article? Did you like it? I want to say that I found this article interesting after completing whole chapter. At first, I was having a hard time making connection with the reading but it finally started clicking. However, on the other hand I still have some confusion. So, can you explain to me? I would like to know does Dewey believe philosophy is relevant with science and the practical experience? Because on pg. 23 he said "philosophy is the possession of a higher organ of knowledge and than is employed by positive science and ordinary experience" that means he said science is the organ of general social progress. Dewey also saw science as giving human control over nature. He said science is very near the core of philosophy or human beings, and science is the "Ultimately philosophically". But later on he said, philosophy finally emerges is irrelevant to science, to explanation, and it is related with figurative, symbolic of fears and hopes, imaginations, primitive life, the history of religion, social tradition, and literature. At this point, I am totally confused. So, could you please help me to get rid of it?

Sincerely,

Neha shah [sic]

ACKNOWLEDGMENTS

Expanded versions of this research appear in *Written Communication,* 2001, vol. 18, pp. 180–228 and *Whose goals? Whose aspirations? Learning to teach underprepared writers across the curriculum* (Fishman & McCarthy, Utah State University Press, 2002).

REFERENCES

Banks, J. A. (1968). A profile of the Black American: Implications for teaching. *College Composition and Communication, 19,* 288–296.

Bourdieu, P. (1982). The school as a conservative force: Scholastic and cultural inequalities. In E. Bredo & W. Feinberg (Eds.), *Knowledge and values in social and educational research* (pp. 391–407). Philadelphia: Temple University Press.

Bourdieu, P. (1991). *Language and symbolic power* (J. B. Thompson, Ed.; G. Raymond & M. Adamson, Trans.). Cambridge, MA: Harvard University Press.

Carmichael, S. (1995). Excerpt from What we want. In M. Hallman (Ed.), *Expanding philosophical horizons: A nontraditional philosophy reader* (pp. 193–199). Belmont CA: Wadsworth. (Original work published 1966)

Cummins, J. (1986). Empowering minority students: A framework for intervention. *Harvard Educational Review, 56,* 18–36.

Dean, T. (1999). Multicultural classrooms, monocultural teachers. In I. Shor & C. Pari (Eds.), *Critical literacy in action: Writing words, changing worlds* (pp. 87–102). Portsmouth, NH: Boynton/Cook Heinemann. (Original work published 1986)

Delpit, L. (1995). *Other people's children: Cultural conflict in the classroom.* New York: The New Press.

Dewey, J. (1962). *Reconstruction in philosophy.* Boston: Beacon Press. (Original work published 1920)

Dewey, J. (1967). *Democracy and education.* New York: The Free Press. (Original work published 1916)

Dewey, J. (1990). Attention. In J. A. Boydston (Ed.), *The collected works of John Dewey: The later works, 1925–1953* (Vol. 17, pp. 269–283). Carbondale: Southern Illinois University Press. (Original work published 1902)

Fanon, F. (1995). Excerpt from *Wretched of the earth.* In M. Hallman (Ed.), *Expanding philosophical horizons: A nontraditional philosophy reader* (pp. 188–193.) Belmont, CA: Wadsworth. (Original work published 1965)

Freire, P. (1997). *Pedagogy of the oppressed* (M. Bergman Ramos, Trans.). New York: Continuum. (Original work published 1970)

Gramsci, A. (1971). *Selections from the prison notebooks* (Q. Hoare & G. N. Smith, Eds.). New York: International Publishers.

Heller, L. G. (1973). *The death of the American university: With special reference to the collapse of City College of New York*. New Rochelle, NY: Arlington House.

Holmes, J. J. (1973). Ten reasons for believing in immortality. In P. Edwards & A. Pap (Eds.), *A modern introduction to philosophy* (3rd ed., pp. 250–260). New York: The Free Press. (Original work published 1929)

hooks, b. (1995). Excerpt from *Ain't I a woman: Black women and feminism*. In M. Hallman (Ed.), *Expanding philosopical horizons: A nontraditional philosophy reader* (pp. 199–209). Belmont, CA: Wadsworth. (Original work published 1981)

Larson, R. L. (1991). Using portfolios in the assessment of writing in the academic disciplines. In P. Belanoff & M. Dickson (Eds.), *Portfolios: Process and product* (pp. 137–149). Portsmouth, NH: Boynton/Cook-Heinemann.

Lazere, D. (1992). Back to basics: A force for oppression or liberation? *College English, 54*, 7–21.

Lu, M-Z. (1999). Conflict and struggle: The enemies or preconditions of basic writing? In B. Horner & M-Z. Lu, *Representing the "other": Basic writers and the teaching of basic writing* (pp. 30–55). Urbana, IL: National Council of Teachers of English. (Original work published 1992)

Plato. (1993). *The last days of Socrates* (H. Tredennick & H. Tarrant, Trans.). London: Penguin Books.

Russell, B. (1970). *Marriage and morals*. New York: Liveright. (Original work published 1929)

Shaughnessy, M. (1977). *Errors and expectations: A guide for the teacher of basic writing*. New York: Oxford University Press.

Spack, R. (1997). The acquisition of academic literacy in a second language: A longitudinal case study. *Written Communication, 14*, 3–62.

Sternglass, M. (1997). *Time to know them: A longitudinal study of writing and learning at the college level*. Mahwah, NJ: Lawrence Erlbaum Associates.

Traub, J. (1994). *City on a hill: Testing the American dream at City College*. New York: Addison Wesley.

Yutang, L. (1995). Why I am a pagan. In M. Hallman (Ed.), *Expanding philosophical horizons: A nontraditional philosophy reader* (pp. 286–292). Belmont: Wadsworth. (Original work published 1937)

Zamel, V. (1995). Strangers in academia: The experience of faculty and ESL students across the curriculum. *College Composition and Communication, 46*, 506–521.

Chapter 10

Writing in Nursing Education and Nursing Practice

Kristine Beyerman Alster

As Kristine Alster reflects on her teaching and questions her past assumptions about assigning and responding to student writing, she acknowledges the problems inherent in the professional texts nursing students are expected to read and emulate. Kristine recognizes that writing is critical not only for communicating ideas and observations clearly, but also for testing out and discovering knowledge, and she explains why a writing-to-learn approach is especially productive for students from non-English backgrounds.

Prospective nursing students inevitably develop expectations about what they'll experience at "nursing school." Enrolled students tell me about having imagined a world in which they acquire sophisticated technical skills, save lives, and console the inconsolable. Over time, those expectations—not entirely unrealistic—are tempered by experience. Because the students at my urban public university are typically older than traditional college students, they seldom entertain "ER" type fantasies about nursing practice. They predict particular educational experiences fairly accurately, reporting that they expect to hear lectures about therapeutic interventions, to practice those interventions in laboratories as well as in actual clinical settings, and to be examined on their theoretical knowledge and technical proficiency. In short, they have a realistic, but incomplete image of nursing education.

Not one of the students in my classes has ever said that he or she expected that writing would be an important part of the nursing curriculum. They accept term papers and other writing assignments as expected requirements of prenursing courses, viewing them variously as unavoidable, enjoyable, or frustrating. However, many students express surprise and even dismay when informed that writing is an integral part of the nursing curriculum as well. Their responses don't surprise me. As a novice teacher, I'd had a parallel set of expectations related to the place of and responsibility for writing in the university curriculum. If I thought about writing at all when I began my career as a nurse educator, I suppose I anticipated teaching students who would arrive on campus with writing skills comparable to mine as a college freshman, and expected that the responsibility for honing students' writing skills would fall to the English Department. I would teach nursing theory and skills.

I was soon disabused of the first expectation. Not only were the writing skills that my classmates and I brought to our freshman courses at a small, Midwestern liberal arts college stronger on average than those of the students I began to teach in 1983, but the students themselves were less diverse. Diversity at my alma mater was represented by a mix of "downstate" students (from farms and small towns in Illinois), students from Chicago suburbs, and a small number of actual Chicagoans and students from "back east." All of the nursing students were White females, most in their late teens and early twenties. In contrast, the students I encountered as a new professor were diverse in terms of gender, race, country of origin, language, educational preparation, and socioeconomic background. At my alma mater, a New York accent was regarded as exotic. At my current university, I met students who not only spoke accented English, but the languages that they first spoke in Uganda, Vietnam, Portugal, China, Haiti, Ethiopia, the Soviet Union, and other countries. Large differences in reading, writing, and verbal skills existed among the students. Some were sophisticated writers. Others wrote so ineffectively that I was surprised that they had been admitted to the university. Duang, for example, was an intelligent and highly motivated young woman who had emigrated from Vietnam. Given enough time, she could express herself well enough in conversation for me to understand her. But when she tried to communicate the same ideas in written English, they were barely recognizable.

My second expectation about teaching writing—that the English Department would do it—also had to be abandoned. My primary assignment in my early years as an instructor was teaching the first clinical nursing course. Students registered for the course after having completed the requisite two English courses. Most would never cross the threshold of the English Department again. Moreover, many had already completed the Writing Proficiency Examination required of all students in the Colleges of Nursing and Arts & Sciences, leading me to conclude that these nursing students were not less accomplished writers than the general population of students on campus. My choices were to bemoan the low level of students' writing skills or to try to help them become better writers. I did both.

For more years than I like to admit, I tried to help students improve their writing with virtually no effect. I gave students a lot of written and verbal feedback. When that didn't seem to help, I gave more. It took me a long time to realize that even massive amounts of feedback were ineffectual with some students. Like the students, I was simply making the same mistakes repeatedly. Worse, when I began teaching upper-division courses, the junior and senior students' writing skills appeared comparable to those of the sophomores, indicating that the "help" that students got from me and other nursing professors was not, in fact, helping. Yet for the most part, students progressed in the program, successfully passed the RN licensure examination, and went on to practice effectively as nurses. Eventually, my question about why my assignments and feedback didn't result in better writing gave way to the more cynical question: "Why does it matter?"

WHY SHOULD NURSES WRITE WELL?

At a conference on higher education outcomes, I once spoke to a compositionist about my attempts to help students write well. She asked me about the type of writing that RNs do in routine practice. I explained that much writing by RNs takes the form of notes: patient progress notes, discharge notes, referral notes. The preferred style is brief, often involving incomplete sentences and abbreviations. Factual information is communicated as directly and with as few words as possible. Metaphor, elaborate description, and creative forms of expression are not considered appropriate. The compositionist responded by saying that it didn't seem necessary to struggle to improve the writing skills of students who would be writing in such constrained forms after graduating. I was speechless. This was the same utilitarian argument I was accustomed to hearing from students, yet it was being advanced by a colleague.

As an RN, I was offended to hear nurses dismissed so casually, as if somehow they belonged to a subgroup of students who could be permitted to graduate from a university without being able to write competently. As an academic, an inveterate reader, and the daughter of two newspaper editors, I was astonished to hear a professor treat writing as if it were no more than a handy tool designed for certain practical uses, like a stethoscope. In addition to her stated belief that nurses needed only limited writing skills, was there also an implied assumption that nursing students were unteachable as writers? If so, she was wrong on both counts. It is true that many of the students have trouble with writing, and that those students whose first language is not English often find it particularly challenging to develop the writing skills that academic and professional settings require. However, nursing students *can* learn to write well and they need to write well for the same reasons that other students do. In addition, they need to write well for reasons particular to their professional development and practice.

Writing to Communicate

The students I teach often identify communicating information as the sole purpose of writing. Certainly that is the focus of most writing that nurses do in clinical settings, where they document the symptoms they observe, the treatments they perform, and the decisions they make, such as to inform a physician about a patient's changing condition. Communicating specific clinical data clearly in writing is a necessary skill for nurses. Non-native English speakers sometimes have difficulty documenting clearly enough to communicate vital information in clinical settings. In other settings, it may be reasonable to expect the reader to infer the meaning of a written statement by guessing at the missing pronoun or supplying the correct verb form. In clinical settings, however, overworked practitioners do not have time to choose among the possible meanings of another practitioner's note. More important, misunderstood written communications can have harmful consequences for patients. Therefore, learning to communicate accurately in writing becomes a vital skill for all nursing students to acquire, and it's natural that they focus their attention on this form of writing.

Problems arise, however, when nursing students regard academic writing and clinical documentation as having identical purposes. In academic settings, students read articles that report clinical research findings and texts that communicate information about nursing practice. Then they write term papers in which they convey that information in an altered form. Students sometimes do and sometimes do not convey facts obtained from source material adequately. However, writing to communicate information that exceeds factual reporting, as often required in academic settings, requires students to have a fairly sophisticated set of skills. They must learn to identify credible sources of information; accurately acknowledge sources; fairly represent multiple points of view; report information without distorting the source's intent; and distinguish assertion, interpretation, and opinion from fact.

All of the students in my classes find these skills difficult to acquire. Because these skills require an ability to appreciate subtle nuances in language, students who are non-native English speakers are sometimes bewildered when I question their representation of source material. For example, students with limited English may not apprehend the different meanings implied by the phrases "The researchers found" and "The author believes." Students may become frustrated and even angry when simple reporting is judged to be inadequate writing for a course essay or paper, believing that they have accomplished the prescribed task if they have displayed substantial amounts of information from approved sources.

Writing to communicate information that exceeds simple transmission of facts is not only an academic nicety, however. It is also a valuable skill for practicing nurses who, for example, may need to write patient information brochures, prepare reports justifying requests for additional resources, or publish papers reporting the results of research or innovative clinical practices. As a result of their broad scope of responsibility for promoting the health of individuals, families, and communities, nurses develop unique insights into health care issues ranging from the concerns of single patients to matters concerning the entire health care system. If nurses cannot communicate those insights in writing, nursing's professional voice will be stilled, and its expertise will be unavailable to the clinicians, health care administrators, legislators, and others who need to learn what nurses know.

For example, one area of growing nursing expertise is how best to care for diverse immigrant populations, whose members may hold beliefs about health and health care that differ from those of the dominant culture as represented by health care providers and who may have acquired limited or no ability to speak English as yet. Who better than nurses who are themselves immigrants to help the nursing profession to develop more effective ways of caring for immigrant populations? One-on-one verbal communication among providers is an important way to communicate culturally appropriate health care interventions. However, those interventions could be disseminated in writing to a much wider audience. Therefore, nursing students who can write clearly in English as well as in other languages will be well positioned to make an extremely important contribution to the health care of immigrants.

Writing to Learn

Like other university students, nursing students also need to write well because writing is a powerful learning tool. They write to convey knowledge, but also to discover and invent knowledge. When students write, they stumble upon gaps in their own understanding that send them back to the library, the Internet, and clinical practice sites. Writing may also help students recognize inconsistencies in their thinking, make connections between seemingly unrelated bits of information, and determine if they have constructed adequate arguments to support strongly held convictions. This kind of writing-to-learn approach may be especially helpful for individuals who are still acquiring facility in English, as it de-emphasizes the use of language written by others, and encourages students to create personal language to express their own developing thoughts. Nursing students are entering a profession still too much characterized by excessive reverence for the expertise of other disciplines. Writing to learn can promote students' confidence in their own authority to develop and communicate clinical knowledge.

However, some nursing students find the idea that they might have something new and valuable to say intellectually arrogant. They passively accept the authority of any published document while discounting their own ability to reason and persuade. Nursing students who gain skill in writing for purposes beyond the strictly informational learn how to evaluate the soundness and significance of their own ideas as well as those of health care "experts."

In addition to enhancing intellectual learning, the writing process may also help students to engage in affective learning. Marlene, one of the community health nursing students, told me that the journal she kept during her field experience helped her to understand what she'd learned about herself, as distinct from the technical skills she'd learned to perform. This is an excerpt from one of her journal entries, written about a mentally ill woman who lived in a rooming house and who'd been resistant to the caregiving efforts of multiple clinicians:

> Today Sadie is in a much better mood. We talk about her getting a phone, and she seems very pleased and excited. "We can talk all night to each other dear!" (yikes!). Anyway, I hope to have the phone installed in a week or so at very little cost to Sadie. This pleases me greatly—I so want to leave knowing that I have given her something. I will also feel better about her safety just knowing she has access to a telephone in an emergency. I have grown very fond of Sadie. She has taught me much and I am grateful to her for that. She has taught me to be a better listener and not to presume I know everything! How many times did Sadie say to me, "You *don't* know, dear … you have *no* idea what it is like to live here!" I no longer use the expression "I know." She is so right. I do not know what it is like to be mentally ill living in one tiny room with only Winnie-the-Pooh to talk to. She has taught me that each of us is remarkable and precious … we all have a purpose … a reason for being here … we are all teachers and students.

Marlene learned some wonderful lessons from Sadie. But she didn't fully understand what she had learned until she reflected on her experience in writing.

Writing to Enhance Professional Status

Finally, nursing students need to learn to write well because they are preparing to enter a practice discipline that aspires to professional status. As much as nurses may wish to be judged solely on their substantive contributions as health care providers, they are judged as well on the presence or absence of other markers of professional standing, such as the ability to write well. Even in the circumscribed form of clinical documentation, poor writing by nurses may be noted by other professionals. For example, a psychotherapist was taken aback by a nurse's written description of a patient: "'She appeared irritable bodily and facially,' wrote a nurse, who, I sensed, carried a lifelong grudge against the English language" (Baur, 1994, p. 300).

Professions are often characterized as requiring a rigorous education (Schwirian, 1998). Nurses represent the only group of health care providers asserting claims to professional status whose members do not receive their primary professional training at the postbaccalaureate level; nurses are therefore often discounted by other health care providers as undereducated. Without arguing the merits of that assumption, it is clearly the case that people who do not speak or write clearly are often perceived by professionals as poorly educated. Fairly or not, if nurses are to be recognized as peers by other health care professionals, they will have to adopt the writing standards used by other professional groups.

TEACHING NURSES TO WRITE POORLY

If learning to write well is an important outcome of the nursing curriculum, why do so many nursing students, including some who speak only English, approach graduation with only limited ability to communicate in writing? And what is it about their writing that is problematic? The difficulties I find in student writing range from simple spelling and grammatical errors to papers that are nearly unreadable. Most worrisome to me is writing that appears to reflect little thought or poor reading skills. I can sometimes help students learn to avoid certain technical mistakes or to organize their thoughts in a way that a reader can follow more easily. It's much more difficult to help students who can barely articulate their ideas at all.

The reasons for very poor writing vary. Both students who do and those who do not speak English as a first language may have difficulty, although ongoing English acquisition certainly poses particular challenges. Some students received inadequate writing instruction in their secondary schools, reporting that they seldom wrote a report or essay until enrolling at the university. Other students seem not to have developed the cognitive and verbal skills that support good writing. And some students simply report that they find writing boring or irrelevant to their interests and that they are therefore are unwilling to put much effort into composition.

At worst, poor student writing is characterized by limited vocabulary, awkward syntax, spelling and grammatical errors, lack of apparent organization, and superficial content. However, genuinely incompetent writers represent only a segment of the student population. I credit the dedicated compositionists in our English Department for encouraging me to observe the significant distinctions among "poor" writers. When my dear friend Ellie Kutz, whose work appears elsewhere in this book, introduced me to the concept of "discourse communities," I began to read student writing differently, noting how the diversity among our nursing students was reflected in their writing. Among the students, I came to understand, were those who undoubtedly wrote well in their native languages, but struggled to achieve the same clarity of expression in English. Others wrote as they spoke, using colloquialisms and informal constructions per-

Although the written code of practice settings is useful, it can impair other types of professional writing. Students who become accustomed to practice setting shorthand are sometimes impatient with what they perceive as the wordiness of academic writing. When students import their clinical writing style into other writing forms, the result is flat, affectless text; it is perhaps suitable for informing, but not for inspiring, challenging, or persuading.

Interestingly, students who are uncomfortable with the discourse style of academia sometimes pick up adequate clinical documentation skills without great difficulty. For some non-native English speakers, the telegraphic clinical style mimics their existing writing patterns in certain ways. The style involves few pronouns (MD, patient, and RN are easily substituted), infrequent changes in verb tense, and little need for idiomatic expressions. Furthermore, clinical documentation has a built-in structure in many settings, so that chart entries are formulaic. Students who cling to writing strategies that they used successfully in clinical settings may be mystified to find those strategies useless for other types of writing.

Rigid Rules

Another way that nursing faculty promote poor writing is by valuing form over substance. We spend much time drilling students on the rules required by style manuals. Students benefit from learning the style most often used in nursing journals. The discipline of conforming their writing to an externally imposed style can help them organize their work and make their ideas accessible to others. However, excessive attention to style requirements decreases the amount of time available to focus on ideas and analysis. Students infer, correctly in some instances, that almost any content fitted into the preferred form will be approved.

Some students, including those who are still developing their English skills, become so anxious about learning the "rules" that they cannot attend to developing their thoughts. They are responding as one might expect them to if they were in a clinical environment in which many rules are absolute prescriptions for behavior. One cannot safely or ethically improvise idiosyncratic rules of sterile technique, for example, but instead must adhere to those accepted by the health care community. Nursing students often have difficulty believing that they may experiment with certain rules. And who can blame them? Nursing is a profession in which simple human error can have grievous consequences. No delete key is available to undo a medication error. Novices may extrapolate from that fact to the notion that there is a "right" way to do everything. Professors may support that notion. In the most extreme cases, the belief that rules are supremely important and universally applicable may lead students to submit beautifully formatted papers that are devoid of meaningful intellectual content. Students who've had some success in learning English by memorizing rules may be especially prone to believing that using rules to produce error-free text is a sure method of creating good writing.

Scientific Writing

Several things happen when we expose students to poor writing and make inflexible demands regarding form. First, students tend to replicate what they've seen. Second, they may lose confidence in their own natural forms of expression, leading to a loss of fresh voices. And third, some students (both native and non-native speakers of English) will resort knowingly or unknowingly to plagiarism in an attempt to write in the approved fashion. Every semester I have a substantial number of students who use source material without attribution. I've tried to avert the problem by spending class time reviewing the university's academic honesty policy and discussing the ways in which academics demonstrate respect for an author's ownership of his or her work. I also have students practice citing various types of material.

Most students experience difficulty in learning to handle quoted and paraphrased material appropriately. I find that those who are still developing their English skills, however, often become adept at using quotations more quickly than they master the use of paraphrased material. This suggests to me that what presents as plagiarism may actually reflect an as yet inadequate ability to handle the more sophisticated translation task that paraphrasing involves. Students who may be silently translating the source material from English into another, more familiar language so that they can fully comprehend its meaning must then translate the original English into a substitute set of English words, a task requiring a sizable vocabulary. Then they must decide how much language substitution is required to paraphrase the author's text adequately. Even seasoned academics argue about how close the citing author may come to the original language before paraphrase becomes quotation. The task must seem overwhelming when undertaken by a non-native speaker of English.

Interestingly, as a group, the students in my classes use unattributed material less frequently early in the semester, when we are working on ungraded and less formal writing assignments, including several preliminary papers leading to a final term paper. However, the closer students get to the final draft of the term paper, the stiffer their writing becomes, as they seemingly become desperate to approximate the opaque language of scholarly journals. In the end, some students simply use huge hunks of material belonging to other authors. I'm convinced that some do so because they remain unconvinced by my assurances that this is not the type of writing I value. Having no faith in their own words, especially if they are still acquiring words in an additional language, they use words belonging to others.

HELPING NURSING STUDENTS TO DEVELOP AS WRITERS

What Professors Can Do

In my early years as a nurse educator, I relied primarily on the traditional term paper as a writing assignment—teaching as I was taught. Many students found writing a term paper a terribly frustrating task; I found the product frustrating to evaluate. Some papers indicated that the author couldn't write well, so I appended voluminous suggestions, which were duly ignored or deemed unusable and we were off on another cycle of "write and wrong," leading to little or no improvement. I still find it difficult—*very* difficult—to help students with their writing, but I've picked up a few useful strategies over time. Because students have difficulty writing for different reasons, no single approach works for all. But I've been able to employ some of what I've learned as a clinical nurse to my teaching activities.

Although I am in no way implying that students who have difficulty writing are ill and in need of a cure, my nursing experience has nevertheless often placed me in the role of facilitator for those having trouble expressing themselves clearly, for example, stroke patients who have trouble with word formation or retrieval. Some of what I've learned with patients I've used successfully with students as well. Not because they are ill, but because, like some patients, they are working hard to communicate. Regardless of whether the struggling writer is still acquiring facility in English, has an impoverished vocabulary, is unfamiliar with the rules of grammar and spelling, or has trouble ordering ideas logically, the result is strained communication. It seems reasonable then, to focus as much on the global experience of frustrated communication as on the particular mechanical difficulties of the writer. I keep in mind that every student writer has something to say, and try to determine what that is before paying too much attention to form. I've employed the following approaches with some success with both patients and students.

Express Appreciation for the Difficulty of the Task.   Communication is a basic human need. When people are thwarted in their ability to communicate, they often become frustrated, angry, and depressed. Struggling writers need to know that their professors understand how hard they must work to make themselves understood through writing, and how frustrating it is when they fail. I often tell students for whom English is not a first language how much I admire them for undertaking the dual task of engaging in university-level study, and doing so in a language other than the one they first learned.

Express Confidence That the Task Will Become Easier.   Students can simply become overwhelmed by a particular challenge and give up. They need to hear from their professors that others in similar situations have succeeded. They profit from having small achievements described as part of a larger effort to become more effective writers. Students may dislike writing or believe that they are not capable of learning to write well. Writing assignments can feel like torture. One semester, after having had students complete a couple of short writing assignments, but before they began work on the major term paper, I asked students to spend 5 minutes writing about how they felt about themselves as writers and how important they considered writing to be in their professional lives. Of the 43 students in class, approximately one third did not speak English as a first language. Perhaps 4 or 5 of the 43 said they enjoyed writing, or at least didn't find it difficult. Most students found writing to be difficult, and many considered themselves to be poor writers. The following is a sample of their responses:

- I am still struggling to improve my writing skills. Because I spent most of my life in Portugal, I had to work on my English and grammar skills twice as much in order to attend college.
- Since the only other writing I do is chart SOAP notes, I have lost confidence and have to my horror found that I can't write! ... I'm actually thinking that my difficulty is not the writing so much as it is my ability to formulate coherent, logical thoughts about a subject.
- Academic writing intimidates me.
- I not comfortable expressing myself writing. I have difficulty just writing this statement.
- I am not that confident due to the fact that I feel I don't use enough sophisticated language. Maybe sophisticated is no the word I am looking for, but more like the statements I write are usually too simple.
- I was born and raised in Ethiopia where English is spoken only in schools. Writing is hard to me, like a labor pain.
- When I hear the word papers, essay and research paper or anything that is over 1 page I get stressed. I get stressed because of the turmoil I go through when starting a writing assignment.... Writing does not come natural to me.
- I have always thought of myself as a terrible writer.

So much discomfort! Such lack of confidence! These students require a lot of support before they can even believe it is possible that they can become competent writers.

Back Off When the Frustration Level Gets Too High.   Sometimes students and I need to take a break, redefine the task or switch to another, have a laugh. Continued efforts to communicate without success lead to a sense of futility. I find that there is nearly always some type of writing that a student can do well, and we focus on that for a bit.

Use Different Methods of Communication.   Thanks to Ellie Kutz, Vivian Zamel, and other colleagues, I've come to understand that some students who I had previously classified as "poor writers" might be unskilled in one form, but competent or even elegant writers in another form. When I began to offer more types of writing assignments, I discovered the eloquence obscured by forms that certain students find uncongenial. For example, the clinical students keep a journal in which they record their responses to their clinical experiences in community health nursing. Some of the best student writing I read appears in these journals. I don't grade entries or impose formatting rules; I simply respond to the feelings, questions, and opinions offered, entirely ignoring writing errors. I tell students that this is a conversation between the two of us. Freed from the constraints of other forms, they often write passionately, and sometimes beautifully about their clinical work. Here are the words of Martina, a student who emigrated to the United States from Ukraine:

> This week, even air smelled as Thanksgiving turkey. Beatrice anticipated the holiday dinner that her housing management organized for all residents. She told me that she already had Thanksgiving dinner in the church that she attends. Before I even opened my mouth, knowing that I am worried about her walking, she cooled me down with the quick frase: 'My friend kindly offered me ride.' At least I know she remembers that she is supposed to be careful. Not that I am sure she is. She talked a lot about her family. She has been living alone for almost fifty years since her husband died. Tears appeared and moved their fast little wheels across the face so quickly that I hardly managed to recall this standard phrase 'I know it is difficult for you.' I guess these words do not really warm, at least they would not warm me. (Is it wrong to try everything on myself?) However they serve the purpose usually. Beatrice tears dried soon after I warmed her hands with mine.

Martina's journal was filled with vivid descriptions of events and thoughtful analyses of her clinical decisions. I rarely see this kind of writing in term papers, but often encounter eloquent writing in less formal assignments.

Work From the Simple to the Complex; From the Familiar to the Novel. This is venerable advice to teachers. As a new professor, I intuitively understood the value of starting with simple clinical assignments before attempting anything more challenging. Yet I regularly assigned term papers without considering that many students didn't have the skills enfolded in the assignment. These days I start out with brief writing assignments that focus on one or two skills, for example, identifying the main argument in a reading assignment. Given the linguistic diversity of the students, some find this an easy and familiar task whereas others find it onerous. But until students have the discrete skills that contribute to good writing, it's unrealistic to ask them to take on more complex assignments. For non-native English speakers, this approach is especially helpful. It usually gives them a confidence-building experience early in the course. Working from the familiar to the novel can help students to be less anxious about writing— maybe even to enjoy writing. I choose first assignments that are brief, focused on topics chosen by the students and relevant to their experience. And I never grade the first paper!

Tout Success. I read samples of student work each time I collect an assignment, pointing out what I particularly enjoy. It might be a thoughtful analysis of source material, an interesting metaphor, or a persuasive argument. This demonstrates to students that no one way of preparing a writing assignment is best, but that good writing is good in different ways. It also gives me a chance to acknowledge the wonderful writing that less accomplished English speakers often produce. For instance, Jia, who first attended college in China, wrote about the connections between what she was seeing in her clinical work and the reading she was doing for class. I asked the other students in her clinical group to "Listen to how Jia compares her work in community health nursing with the way that Lillian Wald described her work a century ago. This is beautiful and intelligent writing."

Institutional Concerns

The techniques I just described may be among the taken-for-granteds of experienced writing teachers. Nevertheless, it took years for me to learn these few simple approaches. Individual professors can help students to become better writers, but it's a lonely activity, and inefficient. I'm not trained to teach writing. I wish I were. Most of my nursing colleagues are no better prepared for the task than I am. We have several concerns that are probably shared by many other professors who aren't trained compositionists.

First, we may be uncertain of own writing skills, having been educated as described earlier, with plenty of exposure to bad writing and little guidance about the appropriate use of various writing forms. I suspect that many of us who teach nursing also fail to help students because we don't always recognize problems in student writing. We don't intervene because the problems are invisible to us. Even those of us who have some confidence in our own skills may not know how to teach those skills to students. For example, I often read something that seems problematic, but either never knew or have forgotten the pertinent rules. Therefore, I'm at a loss to explain to the student exactly what is

REFERENCES

Barry, D. (2000, September 3). Ask Mr. Language Person. *The Boston Globe Magazine,* pp. 8–9.

Baur, S. (1994). *Confiding: A psychotherapist and her patients search for stories to live by.* New York: HarperPerennial.

Hegvary, S. T. (2000). Standards of scholarly writing. *Image: Journal of Nursing Scholarship,* second quarter, 112.

Schwirian, P. M. (1998). *Professionalization of nursing.* New York: Lippincott.

Chapter 11

The Soil Under the Gravel: ESOL Learners and Writing About Literature

Rajini Srikanth

Rajini Srikanth speaks to the ways the study of literature—with its possibility for multiple interpretations, unpredictable connections, and intriguing insights—provides an ideal context for the teaching and learning of ESOL students. Rajini describes the classroom conditions that help create a "comfort zone" for these students (and for her), the written work that encourages risk taking and engages her in a written conversation with them, and the pedagogical approaches that help her understand what has meaning and resonance for students.

Born in India, I grew up with English as my primary language, having from my kindergarten through middle school years attended convent schools run by missionaries, and then in high school, an international school modeled on the U.S. system. I never felt the pain of learning English as a second language and of battling with its contradictory rules. Therefore, the insights I have arrived at with regard to ESOL learners, I have reached haltingly over the last few years—fighting against my own very traditional, prescriptive, and Anglophone educational background and my immersion in teaching environments where grammatical accuracy was prized, and where a full command of the Queen's English (with the right inflections and accent) brought one respect.

When I first arrived at the urban university where I currently teach (and where I have been since 1998) with its diverse student body, including international and first-generation immigrants, I became frustrated. I didn't know how to engage meaningfully with the ESOL students in my

Western-educated readers take for granted explained. I remember that once he asked "Who is Jesus?" On the day that we discussed and attempted to make sense of "Zen Americana," Hideo came up to me at the end of the period and said, "I can write about this poem. I understand the poet. She is talking like Buddhist. I am Buddhist, so I know what she says." This was the first time that Hideo had confidently asserted that he held the key to something that remained shut to others. Whether or not Allen's poem has anything to do with Buddhism is beside the point, I believe. The word *Zen* in the title triggered for Hideo a possible connection to a familiar context and made available to him the knowledge of his Japanese cultural world. That accessibility dissipated Hideo's diffidence and made him approach this text with a confidence that he had not displayed with other texts. In writing about the poem he observed that the poet talks about a state of "nirvana," of detachment from all things worldly. The repeated appearance of the word *un* is, according to Hideo, the speaker's desire to disentangle herself from the cares of the world.

I confess, however, that giving play to multiple reader responses sometimes tests my patience. Yet, I hold my tongue and resist dismissing certain (what I sometimes consider to be untenable) student responses in the interests of encouraging close engagement with the text. Let me explain. A poem by Theodore Roethke called "My Papa's Waltz" not infrequently evokes contradictory interpretations. In this poem, an adult narrator remembers how, when he was a child, his father would come home every evening, somewhat drunk, pick him up and dance with him. Most students see the poem as a happy memory, a fond recollection of a moment of intimacy. However, there is always a small group of students that finds a more disturbing meaning in the poem. Zeroing in on the phrases "hung on like death," "battered on one knuckle," and "right ear scraped a buckle," this group insists that the memory is not happy but that it records abuse.[5] One student once argued that despite the upbeat rhythm of the poem (which imitates the three-beat time of the waltz), this is not a poem of a pleasant memory. In fact, said this student, that the poem adopts the light-hearted meter of the waltz is evidence that the narrator seeks to soften a painful experience. The first time I heard such a response to the poem, I was tempted to demonstrate its unviability. But I desisted. Instead, I spoke about how the concerns of our time—our greater awareness and acknowledgment of child abuse—might lead us to view the poem from such a perspective. These days, I even tell them what I learned from a graduate student who heard a recording of Roethke reading the poem in a light-hearted and uplifting, rather than somber and disconcerting, tone. But I follow up this tidbit by pointing out that once a work of art leaves its creator, it becomes everybody's possession and subject to the perceptions of those who receive it—as in, for example, the controversy surrounding the teaching of *The Adventures of Huckleberry Finn,* with some readers declaring it a satire on racism and others emphasizing the demoralizing effect on African American readers of the repeated appearance of the word *nigger* in the text, or the controversy surrounding author Salman Rushdie for his writing of the novel *The Satanic Verses*, which some devout Muslims see as blasphemous for its ridiculing of the Prophet Mohammed and other Muslim and non-Muslim readers see as humanizing the prophet and thereby enriching his influence.[6] Discussions such as these signal to multilingual and multicultural readers that their contributions matter.

I would argue that in a teaching situation confidence comes not from having all the answers but from anticipating all the variables and likely challenges. There are times when it is actually to one's advantage *not* to know the answers; in fact, every semester, I make it a point to include at least one text that leaves me totally baffled so that I can say to students with perfect honesty, "Help me make something of this." The reward for this display of vulnerability came when one student said at the end of a semester, "I never liked poetry before, but now I like it a lot because it's not easy to understand. Everybody has to work to find meaning, and I like that there are many meanings."

Comfort Zones and the ESOL Learner

Ideally, three conditions need to be present in the classroom to enable ESOL learners to be comfortable with expressing themselves about literature. The first is an atmosphere in which they are recognized to have lives and interests and strengths in areas outside their acquisition of the English language—that is, an acknowledgment on the part of the instructor that these students are individuals with rich and complex backgrounds based on languages and cultures other than English. The second is an attitude to the text, on the part of the instructor, that avoids deifying it, that conveys to the students that literature is more than just a well-crafted work that must be appreciated and revered—that is, an attitude that privileges the reader equally with the text (as I explained earlier). And, finally, a desire, again on the part of the instructor, to liberate the many voices of the ESOL student—to appreciate that the voice of the ESOL student we hear in the classroom or in his or her paper is just one way of responding to the text and may not be the student's most effective or powerful expression; thus, one must stimulate other modes of thought and expression.[7]

The primary objective of the instructor ought to be to facilitate a connection between text and reader. Extolling the virtues of the text—either its form or its content—may be acceptable when dealing with students who are confident enough in their language ability to feel that they can challenge the instructor's perspective and establish an independent relationship with the text unmediated by the instructor. When a student lacks that confidence, then to present the text as inviolable signals to that student that there is nothing that she or he can add that can enrich the text or make the experience of reading the text meaningful.

So I work to create entry points—doors—through which students can enter and explore the text. These doors ideally should be varied in nature, to accommodate the students' different modes of textual interaction and their specific difficulties. Because I work with literature—the realm of the ambiguous, the domain of multiple readings—I am partial to texts with discrepancies, contradictions, unresolved tensions, and inexplicable outcomes. I don't insist that students begin at the beginning; they may seize on an utterance somewhere in the middle of the short story or poem, and that may provide the chute into comprehension.

Unbinding the Restraints

Prompts from the text are one type of entryway I provide. I choose, usually from a short story that we have just begun to discuss, one or two passages that I consider to be rich enough to allow for various types of commentary—an identification with a character, an opportunity to appreciate an image, something that's ambiguous or that might cause confusion to most readers of the text, a significant escalation of tension, a turning point in a relationship, an epiphany, an action inviting judgment. Students are invited to respond to one of the passages. "Does the situation in the passage remind you of something? Do the characters remind you of people you know? Why are they speaking in that fashion? What do you think is happening here?" I don't grade the responses to these prompts, but I do require that students do them. It seems obvious that when any writer is released from the pressure of being graded, ideas and thoughts flow with greater ease. There is also research to support the hypothesis that unmonitored writing is richer, more substantive, and less mechanical than monitored or censored writing.[8]

The responses are a vehicle for beginning a written conversation with students. The objective of this exercise is to create comfort in the students so that they can express themselves about literature, no matter how strained their articulation, how idiosyncratic the wording. The responses allow me to determine what the student sees in the text, what elements she or he finds illuminating, and therefore provide me with a link to the student. They serve a double purpose, then: to release the student from a tongue-tied state *and* to initiate a path of conversation. ESOL students may know what they want to say but feel inhibited from doing so because they are so conscious of appearing incompetent. With a tentative vocabulary and a still emerging mastery of grammatical structures and effective sentence syntax, some ESOL students may find themselves engaged by complex thoughts that hover in their first-language consciousness and yet elude their English-language grasp. In reading their in-class responses to prompts, I ask myself, "Is there heart in what I'm reading—can I detect the passion of the person buried in those words?" I enjoin myself to look deep into the writing for the intelligent and interesting human being whose words they are. So I search for a sentence, a phrase, a word even, that might inspire me to respond. And that's where I begin the conversation. The purpose of these exchanges is to help me discover students' thoughts and for them to know that I'm excited about what they have to say because the text's yield is endless and protean, changing with every mind that has an encounter with it.

Nincis Ascensio, a student from the Dominican Republic, appears to have found her voice through these responses. Relatively early in the semester, I offered a writing prompt from James Baldwin's short story "Sonny's Blues":

> The silence, the darkness coming, and the darkness in the faces frightens the child obscurely. He hopes the hand which strokes his forehead will never stop—will never die.... In a moment someone will get up and turn on the light. Then the old folks will remember the children and they won't talk any more that day. And when light fills the room, the child is filled with darkness. He knows that every time this happens, he's moved just a little closer to that darkness outside.[9]

I was curious whether anyone would explain the paradox in the sentence "And when light fills the room, the child is filled with darkness." The interplay between light and darkness in this passage is indicative of a pattern that runs through the story, and I wondered whether students would pick up on that.

Nincis' response doesn't address the light–darkness relationship. She concentrates instead on what she sees as the "darkness" of the neighborhood in which the story unfolds, and she observes:

> I think the author is trying to imply that these children do *not* want to become like those bad individuals in the their community. They (the children) want to have their parents there always to remind them *what's wrong!* These children will need a strong friendly hand. No matter what the parents of these children do these will become knowledgeable of the darkness surrounding their lives, their neighborhood.

Her underlining of specific words clues me in to the intensity of her feelings, and it is this intensity that I comment upon. Yes, the neighborhood does seem threatening, I acknowledge. And, yes, the narrator is one of those who grew up determined "not ... to become like those bad individuals" in his community. Later, in a formal paper, Nincis develops the theme of the dangerous neighborhood from which one seeks escape. The in-class response gave her, I believe, a safe (because ungraded) opportunity to test out and voice her idea. Nincis goes on to become a discerning reader and a fine thinker.

Form and Content: The ESOL Learner, the How and the What

Susan Sontag, railing against the tendency to find meaning in art, enjoins us to cease interpretation. Don't emphasize the content of work, she pleads, focus on its form. Don't concern yourself with *what* a work says; consider only *how* it says what it says.[10] To a student struggling with comprehension, however, the *what* is the first order of business. Yet, I have learned from Nincis that one should never underestimate such a student's ability to engage with the form of a text in English.

"A poem should not mean, but be," writes Archibald MacLeish, in his lush "Ars Poetica," a poem filled with exquisitely crafted images that elude interpretation—lines such as, "A poem should be motionless in time/ As the moon climbs."[11] That "Ars Poetica" eludes meaning, that it presents itself as a linguistic rather than interpretative experience, suggests that it may be outside the reach of students who continue to struggle with the English language. And yet, I have taught it in my classes because several students are aspiring writers and aficionados of literary craft and also because the poem questions the very practice of interpretation in which the class engages. Nincis, a deep and thoughtful reader, seems to understand perfectly what MacLeish says. In response to an assignment in which I had asked the class, at the end of our unit on poetry, to explain what made something a poem, Nincis wrote this: "I do not agree with analyzing poetry because I believe it loses the essence of being poetry. I see poetry as an art expressed with writing and all its rules (grammar). Poetry is like love. Love cannot be broken down because then it will lose its meaning, the magic would be lost in the process and only appreciation would be left; appreciation of materials no feelings."

Nincis showed me also that craft need not take a complete back seat to content for the ESOL student. She wrote:

> From the many poems discussed in class the one that really inspired me to look through its verses and undress its body until getting to its skeleton was the poem "Independence Day, 1956: A Fairy Tale by James Galvin."[12]
>
> This poem inspired me much curiosity. The first thing that caught my attention was the spacing of the poem. I never thought that a poem could have such way of spacing its lines. The spacing showed in the hardcopy of the poem did not seem to be attractive at all, that was what I thought. But once I heard the poem being read out loud the pauses (represented by the breaks) made a lot of sense. These pauses helped me understand that it was a sad poem.

Nincis is keenly responsive to the aural quality of poetry. Of course, poetry should be read out loud, it goes without saying, but there is a certain aural quality to all literature—the feel of the word in your mouth, the sound of it in the air, and the way it lands on the ear. I first became aware of the impact of literature's aural quality when I was teaching high school. I was at a private institution of high-achieving students, most of whose parents expected them to go on to prestigious colleges and universities. The work assigned to students was rigorous. One semester I taught a class in creative writing to juniors and seniors. As a treat, I thought I would read aloud a short story. My initial objective was just to get them to relax, to get them to experience collectively the power of narrative, the seductive hold a good story has on an audience, and to distract them briefly from the many academic pressures they faced. The effect was amazing. The rapt expression in their eyes, the postures into which their bodies fell, all indicated that they were responding to the reading in ways that were deeper and more complex than I had anticipated. That experiment confirmed for me the value of reading aloud. I have since read aloud myself or had students volunteer to read aloud at least once a week. That the practice is helpful to ESOL learners as well is only now becoming evident to me. Nincis' articulation of the mood or tone of the poem "Independence Day" in response to a reading aloud that was attentive to the way the words were laid out on the page underscores the importance of infusing language with life, of giving to English a dimension beyond its rendition on the page. I include this story of how I have come to value reading aloud in class as an example of the unplanned ways in which we sometimes come by our most successful pedagogical techniques. But again, reading aloud is useful for all learners; I am aware of a palpable change in the attentiveness of the classroom whenever I read a passage aloud. There is a heightened connection with the text, a greater willingness to attend to its many details—diction, tone, and rhythm.

INTERPRETIVE ACTS IN MINIATURE

For many learners, some texts can seem formidable because of their length. Negotiating through the dense profusion of words can create a sense of helplessness, a feeling that they are ill equipped for the task, incapable of undertaking the long journey, or that it will drain them of useful resources. Though I consider poems to be a wonderful antidote to lengthy texts, poems can sometimes, because of the concentrated significance of the words and the genre, the packed meanings, the multilayered import, seem so cryptic as to be even more frustrating than a longer work of fiction. Thus, I have found the exercise of having students read closely and exhaustively the opening paragraphs of short stories to be an extremely productive way of building the skills necessary to tackle longer texts and to understand the important aspects of that particular text—its world, its characters, the tensions embedded in it, the effect of the diction. For students, this interpretive exercise in miniature can bolster confidence, can make manageable the complex task of explication. What do they see unfolding in the opening paragraph? What do they expect will happen—given the title and the first few lines? I emphasize that the effect of this exercise is to render manageable a task that can seem beyond one's control. Furthermore, once students go through the process of examining the significance of seemingly commonplace elements of the opening paragraph,

would make people understand Morton and his family's situation. That would also help people to understand this story.

I also want to ask people what they think about Kaufman's way that [s]he wrote this story because in this story Kaufman gave students a lot of sentences which were visually. For example, Kaufman wrote "He was a big man, and he seemed to be taking up the whole bench as he held the Sunday comics close to his face." Those sentences gave me many visual images about this man. So I would want to ask people what effects of h[er] way of writing were in this story.

Hideo's questions touch on three critical aspects of the narrative: (a) technique—why the female protagonist, the consciousness through whom the story is told, is given no name. In fact, both the woman and the man with whom she has a confrontation remain nameless, whereas the characters who "surround" them are named. This "reversal" of what one might typically expect is a potentially rich vein for discussion; (b) characterization—by having readers imagine how they might act in a similar situation, Hideo is encouraging them to probe Morton's character; and (c) style—Hideo seems to be suggesting that the author's visual images take the reader right into the thick of the situation.

Stage Secrets

A similar objective of giving students a sense of textual control undergirds this next assignment on playwriting. Drama is the genre closest to orality, observes First Nations playwright Tomson Highway, because the dialogue inside one's head finds expression in the external space of the theater.[15] This remark confirmed the value of an assignment I created, in which students are encouraged to write their own one-act plays. In the 3-week period in which they study drama, students learn about the genre not just as a textual product but as a collaborative form that comes alive only when several elements—acting, space, movement, lighting, props, music, costume, directorship, stage management—work together. They learn about the effects of minimal and extensive stage directions and the freedom and interpretive license that each offers a director. We read two rather dissimilar plays: one, a pastiche of monologues with almost no stage directions, the other a more traditional multicast and interactive play with explanatory stage directions.

At the end of this study, students work on an assignment that requires them to imagine themselves in the role of playwright and director. They think of a situation from their everyday life that has the potential for interesting conflict or tension—for instance, how several family members who have to use the same computer decide on the rules for sharing; the same situation with the use of a single car; Thanksgiving dinner and the conversation around the table; an argument among friends studying for an exam. Or they can pick a scene from one of the short stories we've studied. Once they've selected the situation, they write a script for it of between 7 and 10 pages. The script can be a series of monologues, interactions among several characters on stage, or some combination of monologues and dialogues. Students are asked to think carefully about stage directions and to provide a director with the details that they think are necessary to bring the script to life.

The format of the play with its quick back-and-forth dialogue between characters provides students the opportunity to ground speech in the context of human interaction, rather than to see it as text on a page. Moreover, the lines each character speaks are units that can be relatively easily manipulated. This excerpt from Nincis' play demonstrates how well she has learned to deploy the structure of the genre (here, two characters, David and Eve, argue about the wisdom of putting Eve's dog, Elsie, to sleep):

Eve: I do not know what to do with Elsie. I think I will have to put her to sleep.

David: Oh no! Why would you do something like that?

Eve: Well, I will be living in the country soon and I do not know who will be taking care of her.

David: I could take care of her or Nina or Mary ...

Eve: I do not think they will have time to take care of Elsie. They are never home.
(David answers with anger, almost without air and an ugly look, stares at her and then turns his back towards Eve).

David: They have Miko, which means they have to take her out to the park, so they would take Elsie too.

Eve: I just got a new apartment and you know it is too small and I cannot have her because I do not have space.
(David answers with anger)

David: I do not believe that is a good excuse to put the poor animal to sleep. Look at her face and tell her what you are thinking of doing.

Eve: There is nothing I can do now. I will think about it, but I do not believe I have another choice.

Nincis has understood perfectly that drama is a genre foregrounding human interaction. The dialogue between Eve and David signals an escalating tension in their relationship. The point at which Nincis ends the scene indicates, as well, that she has a fine sense of suspense.

It was Hideo who first led me to consider the benefits to ESOL students of writing drama. In a paper on Amy Tan's story "The Rules of the Game," Hideo gives the immigrant Chinese father of the young first-person narrator a greater role than he has in the story because, Hideo explains, "I thought father would be very powerful even though he doesn't communicate with his children usually because in Asian family, father has all rights to decide everything about family." He imagines a conversation among father, mother, and daughter (the narrator), in which the father is trying to ease the tension in the household between mother and daughter:

> Father came into my room, and then he said, "I have to talk with you. Come to the dining room." So I got up then I went to the dining room. Father and mother were drinking tea and waiting for me. He said "Tell me what happened to you today. What was wrong with you?" I said "I couldn't stand that mother talked to people around us about me." Mother didn't say anything. She just glared at me. Father said "Why? Mother was just proud of you so much." I said "I'm happy about that but I don't want her to introduce me to people around us when we go shopping because I'm ashamed of that. That is stupid." Mother said loudly "You don't understand how much we help you to concentrate chess. You don't improve your skill of chess by only yourself. Your honor is not only for you but also us." Father said "Okay, Okay. Calm down." Then he said "Okay, mother will never do that. So apologize her about you rudeness today." He also said to mother "You see why she said that. You must understand her feeling. And never do that again. This becomes our rule today. Okay?" Mother said "I see." Then I apologized to her. She also apologized to me. After that I started to eat late dinner with father and mother. That dinner was very impressive for me.

Hideo boldly rewrites Amy Tan's text by infusing the father with an importance he doesn't possess in the original story. Not hindered by thoughts on the sanctity of the text, Hideo seems to be transposing the aural quality of what he hears in his imagination to the page. It is easy to see how one could transform the dialogue, with its brief and rapidly exchanged sentences, into a play.

SOIL UNDER THE GRAVEL

At what point I began to pay attention to the unique *individuals* behind ESOL students' written essays, to envision lives outside the dimensions of their responses to my assignments, I cannot say with certainty. At what point I said to myself, "Look for the heart in the utterance, the strength of the emotion in the words," remains a mystery. Perhaps it was one student, whose passionate declaration of feeling deflected my attention from the grammatical errors and made me realize what I might be missing by ferreting out mechanical faults. This one student may have made me keenly aware of the soil under what I perceived to be the gravel, of the wealth and depth of thought under the roughly hewn words. To ESOL students goes the credit for making me a more thoughtful teacher.

ENDNOTES

[1]Terry Eagleton, *Literary Theory* (Minneapolis: University of Minnesota Press, 1996), see especially the introduction "What Is Literature?"

[2]"How Can Art Help Us Now?" *The Boston Globe,* Saturday, Sept. 15, 2001: E1, E5.

[3]Lewis Carroll, *Alice in Wonderland and Through the Looking-Glass* (New York: Grosset & Dunlap, 1979), 159.

[4]Paula Gunn Allen, "Zen Americana," *Poems, Poets, Poetry: An Introduction and Anthology,* Ed. Helen Vendler (Boston: Bedford/St. Martins, 1997), 312.

[5]Theodore Roethke, "My Papa's Waltz," *Poems, Poets, Poetry: An Introduction and Anthology* (Boston: Bedford/St. Martins, 1997), 95.

[6]See Lisa Appignanesi and Sara Maitland, eds., *The Rushdie File* (Syracuse, NY: Syracuse University Press, 1990) for a full account of the fallout from Rushdie's *The Satanic Verses,* and the reactions to the Ayatollah Khomeini's call for Rushdie's assassination.

[7]I find it useful to think of the many voices of the ESOL student as akin to the heteroglossia that Mikhail Bakhtin describes as an essential feature of the novel: see "Discourse in the Novel," *The Dialogic Imagination,* Ed. Michael Holquist (Austin: University of Texas Press, 1981), 262–263.

[8]See Marie Wilson Nelson, *At the Point of Need: Teaching Basic and ESL Writers* (Portsmouth, NH: Boynton/Cook, 1991), especially 32–41.

[9]James Baldwin, "Sonny's Blues," *The Story and Its Writer: Introduction to Short Fiction,* Ed. Ann Charters (Boston: Bedford/St. Martin's, 1999), 90.

[10]Susan Sontag, "Against Interpretation," *The Critical Tradition: Classic Texts and Contemporary Trends,* Ed. David Richter (Boston: Bedford/St. Martin's, 1998), 691–696.

[11]Archibald MacLeish, "Ars Poetica," *Poems, Poets, Poetry,* 466.

[12]James Galvin, "Independence Day: A Fairy Tale," *Poems, Poets, Poetry,* 421.

[13]Toni Cade Bambara, "Gorilla, My Love," *The Norton Anthology of Short Fiction,* Eds. R. V. Cassill and Richard Bausch (New York: Norton, 2000), 45–49.

[14]Bel Kaufman, "Sunday in the Park," *Sudden Fiction: American Short Short Stories,* Eds. Robert Shapard and James Thomas (Salt Lake City, UT: Peregrine Smith Books, 1986), 20–23.

[15]This remark was part of "Reclamation as Resistance: Issues in Native Canadian Drama," a paper delivered by Pankaj K. Singh at the July 2001 conference of the Association of Commonwealth Literature and Language Studies.

goal, I have needed to question my own assumptions in order to make sense of the way each individual's complex educational and social experience impacts the communication process. Two cases in point are the stories of Toko and Mia.[1]

Toko, a student in my internship class, was anxious about the process of finding a community placement. Because of what I perceived to be his limited oral communication skills, I had suggested that he consider an internship in an agency that assisted Asian immigrants, thinking that he might be able to use Japanese, his first language, some of the time. Yet he couldn't locate an agency that provided services to Japanese immigrants, and, furthermore, was reluctant to pursue an internship in a program that provided services for Chinese immigrants. After I advised him to apply, he mustered the courage to visit the agency and he was accepted as an intern. Much later, I learned that Toko's anxiety about his placement was related to cross-cultural concerns. He was hesitant to volunteer in an agency that served Chinese immigrants because of the historically based conflicts between China and Japan. And because he felt "totally ignorant" about Chinese culture, he had assumed that he would not be welcome. My assumption that his oral proficiency was the source of the problem meant that I did not help him address his anxiety. He was, in effect, on his own, because of *my* cultural illiteracy. Fortunately, his self-described "shamefully limited" beliefs about Chinese immigrants gave way to empathy and warmth, and he developed effective relationships with the clients. Reinforced by his supervisors' appreciation, he gained self-confidence. The anxiety that had made his oral skills appear weaker than they actually were disappeared. His communication with me improved, and, as the semester progressed, he even spoke occasionally in class.

Mia spent most of the semester rarely speaking in class. She participated in her required group presentation and spoke to some extent in small groups, but she was otherwise silent. I assumed that she was afraid to speak because of her insecurity with oral English. My perception changed, however, when we read a book that spoke to Mia's cultural experience. *The Spirit Catches You and You Fall Down* provides a compelling examination of a Hmong family as it interfaces with the U.S. medical system. Mia had grown up in Cambodia in a family whose cultural patterns were similar to those of the Hmong family described by author Ann Fadiman. As we began to discuss the book, Mia became involved in the discussion, speaking freely and confidently. She shared stories about her own family, lending credibility to the text. My assumptions had been wrong. Mia's silence was not related to her inability to speak in a group; it was related to her not connecting meaningfully to the other subject matter in the course.

One of my goals as a teacher is to establish a democratic classroom—one in which each student is seen and respected and in which all students have equal time to share their reactions to course materials—to cast their ideological votes, so to speak—if they choose to do so. In classrooms that are not democratic in this way and instead are teacher centered, with limited input from a few confident students, there is little space for ESOL students, women in general, or shy men. Typically the assertive student voices belong to men from the dominant group (whatever that is in various settings) and much has been written about that dynamic (Bernstein, 1995; Disch, 1999, 2001; Lewis, 1990; Orenstein, 1994; Sadker & Sadker, 1994; Sandler, 1987). My classroom approaches a feminist/participatory model described by many faculty in women's studies (see, e.g., Belenky, Clinchy, Goldberger, & Tarule,1986; Davis, Crawford, & Sebrechts, 1999; Maher & Tetreault, 1994; Shapiro, 1991). In the tradition of feminist pedagogues, I aim to increase women's participation, to examine closely the classroom power structure, and to move into the center of discourse voices that have traditionally remained outside (Doan, 1991; Stimpson, 1988; Thompson & Tyagi, 1993). I try to create a safe, comfortable, and productive learning environment in the classroom. Respectful, empathic, attentive discourse is paramount. Without that, too many people are afraid to join the conversation. Without it, the classroom tends to be dominated by people accustomed to speaking publicly in English, especially those confident enough of their ideas to risk stating them in front of strangers. This practice leaves out the vast majority of ESOL students. I assume that within a relatively friendly and respectful atmosphere, students can openly engage with each other about what they are learning, identify allies, and address differences directly. My goal is not simply to provide equal time to speak. Rather, the purpose is to challenge the White U.S.-focused view of life that pervades so much of mainstream U.S. society. When ESOL students and students of color enter the conversation, the dominant view can shift to include a wider range of perspectives and experiences. The power implications that accompany various people's positions can be made explicit once they all share their experiences.

The strategies I use to encourage students' oral participation and engagement allow for a range of participation options and, important to note, are effective not just for ESOL students but for all students. Although there are many cultural factors that might limit students' participation (Vandrick, 1997), I believe that teachers can do much to engage a greater proportion of students in the classroom discussion. Though I hope to welcome a wide range of voices into the classroom discourse, whatever their message, I do not assume that everyone will feel comfortable with everyone else in the room. Rather, I aim to help people find a small cluster of others with whom they can talk relatively freely, and I try to establish an atmosphere in which differences—of self and opinion—are respected. I refer here to differences of all sorts—including those related to race, ethnicity, native language, class, religion, sexuality, gender, age, ability, and ideology. As I attempt to build a sense of community in the classroom, I am continually attentive to diversity and inclusion, both in the reading assignments and in the manner in which I structure the discussion.

THE INTERNSHIP COURSE

Though I use similar strategies in all of my courses, I focus here on the senior-level six-credit internship course I teach, which is a capstone experience for majors in sociology. With its emphasis on critical thinking and research, the course is designed to prepare students for graduate school. In addition to fulfilling substantial reading and writing assignments, students work at least 10 hours per week in a social service agency. The course content is multicultural, and the course attracts students from a wide range of cultures in the United States and abroad.

Getting Started

I begin the internship course with a set of ground rules, an icebreaker related to diversity, and the distribution of a class list. The ground rules for the course, embedded in a handout entitled "Student/Teacher Rights and Obligations," describe student rights and obligations, teacher rights and obligations, and human rights and obligations. The ground rules are also concerned with issues of confidentiality and respectful behavior. I encourage people to remain silent when what is most pressing on their minds is something they don't feel comfortable sharing. This is particularly relevant to trauma survivors, including people who have left their countries of origin under terrorizing conditions. Finally, the handout mentions that there are potentially many hidden diversities in the room of which we should be mindful, including the high probability that many people grew up in abusive families; have been victims of violence; are gay, lesbian, bisexual, or transgendered; have invisible illnesses or disabilities; or have religious or political views outside the mainstream values in U.S. society.

The icebreaker focuses on diversity and by the end of the exercise each person has talked individually with about six other people. In the final pairing students introduce themselves in preparation for introducing each other to the class. By the end of this process, each person has talked and has been introduced. Students who are shy about speaking in front of the group have their notes to depend on and do not have to talk about themselves.

Given that it is close to impossible to develop any effective sense of community without knowing people's names, I take this issue seriously. I have students place their names over the edge of their desks for the first few sessions and we learn the names and their pronunciations. With students' permission, I create a list of names and street addresses, phone numbers, and e-mail addresses to circulate to the class. This list encourages communication outside of class. I find that many ESOL students who are quiet in class are comfortable communicating with me and others via e-mail. The list encourages contact among us.

Writing—Formal and Informal, Graded and Ungraded

The formal writing assignments in the course include both graded and pass–fail papers. I assess weekly responses to the reading, a "differences" journal, and an agency journal on a pass–fail basis. The reading responses are designed to help students prepare for the graded papers and also give me insight into how students are responding to the course texts. In addition to assigning formal writing, I also incorporate unevaluated informal in-class writing.

The frequent writing required in this course opens a channel of communication between each student and me. Students who are too shy or insecure to speak up in class can let me know what they are thinking through their writing, and I can respond. If I see that someone is having a difficult time understanding the reading, I can invite the student to come talk with me about the difficulty before too much time has passed. The weekly writing also serves to prepare students for class discussion. Once they have done the reading, reflected upon it, and written their reflections, they share those reflections in a small group in class; many are then prepared to share their ideas with the larger group. The writing thus serves as a "rehearsal" of sorts. Without this "rehearsing" a class can often be quiet.

Another technique I use in order to foster communication is a variation on the "one minute paper" developed by Angelo and Cross (1993). This exercise asks students to write briefly about what they understood or what they found confusing regarding some aspect of what has occurred in class. I have adapted this exercise to ask students to name what additional information they would like to know, what points they wish had been made in the discussion, or how they are feeling about what transpired in the class. These anonymous responses provide an opportunity for students who are afraid to admit confusion, ignorance, or disagreement publicly to have a voice, for I review in the next class what students report.

Other Ways of Engaging Students and Gauging Their Understanding

When I want to discuss specific aspects of the reading with the class in an interactive way, I frequently create a short ungraded quiz for students to respond to individually and then ask them to compare their answers with those of one or two other students and to try to come to agreement about the answers.[2] I design the quiz to address the issues that I think are most important in the reading and set up the questions in the order in which I want to address them. After working alone and then in twos or threes, a greater proportion of students is ready to join the conversation when discussion is opened to the whole class. At a minimum, they are willing to "vote" for the answers they have chosen. Students seem to enjoy being "tested" when there are no negative consequences and to appreciate the opportunity to discuss the answers together. They can clarify misunderstandings among themselves while looking in their texts for evidence. For students who have difficulty taking notes and listening at the same time, the quiz process effectively provides a set of lecture notes so that students can put more of their energy into listening, thinking, and talking.

The midsemester evaluation of the course, an anonymous questionnaire, provides yet another opportunity for students to contribute their perspectives on the course and to reflect on its assignments, classroom interactions, and their particular needs and struggles. In classes of fewer than 35, I typically hand one back to each person and we read them aloud together. This gives voice to everyone's experience. Within the questionnaire I provide a 10-point scale asking how comfortable people feel talking in both small groups and large groups and also asking students to check the reasons that explain why they are quiet when they are. Two of the reasons on the checklist relate to insecurity about speaking English, but there is space for "other" explanations as to why a person may be silent at times. A close analysis of this scale helps us to understand the source of students' insecurities. This gives us an opportunity to acknowledge that the classroom is not equally safe and comfortable for everyone.

Collaborative Learning—
The Multicultural Literacy Assignment

Classroom research as well as my own experiences suggest that collaborative learning is one of the most effective learning methods for college students (Light, 1990; Matthews, Smith, & Gabelnick, 1996). The goal of the collaborative Multicultural Literacy Assignment (Disch, 1998) is to help students work together in order to learn about and become more sensitive to the needs of a particular cultural group. I present case scenarios of people representing five or six different cultural groups (e.g., African American, Cambodian, Irish, Jewish, Navajo, and Puerto Rican). By the second class, each student becomes part of a study group focused on learning about a culture other than their own and about which they know very little. Ultimately, they make a group presentation to the class outlining a set of intervention strategies that they think will serve the people in the hypothetical case. They need to do library research, use course readings, interview several members of the group they are studying, divide the tasks involved in the presentation, share resources, and each write an individual paper that is due at midsemester.

This assignment serves many purposes. Although frequently from diverse backgrounds, group members are united by their need to learn quickly about the group they are studying. They spend part of several class sessions working together and often visit an agency whose work is relevant to their study of a group (such as the Irish Immigration Center or the Hebrew Rehabilitation Center). If there are students in the class who belong to a cultural group that is being studied, there is an opportunity for the other students to learn from them and added social pressure to be accurate. The written and oral assignments are complex, demanding that the students in each group work carefully with the course readings and help each other think through the assignment. ESOL students are an excellent resource for others as they work on this assignment because they have lived a bicultural/bilingual experience and have a sharpened understanding of what it means to learn about cultures other than their own. Many native English speakers have been so culturally isolated that they have more to learn than do the ESOL students in order to produce an adequate paper. In a sense, the roles are reversed, as ESOL students can provide some expertise that the native speakers often lack.

CONCLUSION

As I listen to the experiences of ESOL students in my classes, I find myself in awe of what many of them have been through. I feel especially moved by refugees and others who were forced by political and economic realities to live in the United States. When I put myself in their shoes, imagining, for example, what it would be like if I had to move to another country, I can barely begin to imagine such circumstances. As I consider here what I do to encourage the participation and intellectual/emotional engagement of ESOL students in my classes, I am reminded of my own experience as a non-native speaker of Spanish. I can speak freely in Spanish with friends and family. In a public setting, however, I silence myself in fear that my grammar will fail, my accent will offend, or my point will be contested and that I will not have the skill to engage in a coherent (I really want to say "intelligent") conversation. The exception to this is when I give a talk in Spanish. In that situation I prepare intensively, get help with grammar and pronunciation, and practice until I have the talk almost memorized. Although I am still nervous, at least I have my notes and oral practice to lean on. Thus, for me at least, spontaneous discourse in a public setting is the most frightening situation I encounter when speaking Spanish. In an effort to structure a range of participation opportunities for ESOL students, I have tried to include both lower risk and higher risk possibilities, in the hope that everyone will find ways of participating at least some of the time.

The informal writing students do in preparation for my classes can serve as their "speaking notes," giving a sense of confidence to otherwise insecure speakers. And their written work can give them a voice— both directly to me and through me as I bring their ideas (anonymously or identified, depending on whether I have their permission) back to the class. Even when students do not participate in class discussions as much as I would hope, their experiences in the larger community offer new possibilities to strengthen their oral communication. The woman from Japan quoted at the opening of this essay had a difficult time talking in class, indicating that, even after 4 years of college, she "still cannot solve it." Yet she brought high motivation to the field of human services, choosing an agency that was outside the realm of her experience. Having previously worked only in Japanese-owned businesses, her choice to volunteer in an English-language agency that served people with AIDS was courageous. Although she continued to feel self-conscious because of her weakness in English, and even though she was challenged to communicate in a second language with "stressed-out" clients, she worked well in that setting.

The face of higher education is changing with the changing demographics of the U.S. population. Students of color, including many who are ESOL students, will become an increasingly larger presence, bringing a wealth of experiences and perspectives to communities that can welcome and embrace them. I hope that my classroom is that kind of place.

ACKNOWLEDGMENTS

Parts of this essay appear in Disch, E. (1999). Encouraging participation in the classroom. In S. N. Davis, M. Crawford, & J. Sebrechts (Eds.), *Coming into her own: Educational success in girls and women* (pp. 139–154). San Francisco: Jossey-Bass.

REFERENCES

Angelo, T., & Cross, T. P. (1993). *Classroom assessment techniques: A handbook for college teachers* (2nd ed.). San Francisco: Jossey-Bass.

Belenky, M., Clinchy, B., Goldberger, N., & Tarule, J. M. (1986). *Women's ways of knowing: The development of self, voice, and mind.* New York: Basic Books.

Bernstein, S. (1995). Feminist intentions: Race, gender and power in a high school classroom. *NWSA Journal, 7*(2), 18–34.

Davis, S. N., Crawford, M., & Sebrechts, J. (1999). *Coming into her own: Educational success in girls and women.* San Francisco: Jossey-Bass.

Disch, E. (1998). Multicultural literacy assignment. In T. M. Singelis (Ed.), *Teaching about culture, ethnicity, and diversity* (pp. 47–55). Thousand Oaks, CA: Sage.

Disch, E. (1999). Encouraging participation in the classroom. In S. N. Davis, M. Crawford, & J. Sebrechts (Eds.), *Coming into her own: Educational success in girls and women* (pp. 139–154). San Francisco: Jossey-Bass.

Disch, E. (2001). Gender trouble in the gender course: Managing and mismanaging conflict in the classroom. In E. Kingston-Mann & T. Sieber (Eds.), *Achieving against the odds: How academics become teachers of diverse students* (pp. 180–203). Philadelphia: Temple University Press.

Doan, L. L. (1991). Difference 101: The pedagogical other in the feminist classroom. *Work and Days, 9*(1), 29–36.

Lewis, M. (1990). Interrupting patriarchy: Politics, resistance, and transformation in the feminist classroom. *Harvard Educational Review, 60*(4), 467–488.

Light, R. J. (1990). *The Harvard assessment seminars: Explorations with students and faculty about teaching, learning and student life.* Cambridge, MA: Harvard University Graduate School of Education.

Maher, F. A., & Tetreault, M. K. T. (1994). *The feminist classroom: An inside look at how professors and students are transforming higher education for a diverse society.* New York: Basic Books.

Matthews, R., Smith, B. L., & Gabelnick, F. (1996). Learning communities: A structure for educational coherence. *Liberal Education, 82*(3), 4–7.

Orenstein, P. (1994). *School girls: Young women, self-esteem, and the confidence gap.* New York: Anchor Books.

Sadker, M., & Sadker, D. (1994). *Failing at fairness: How our schools cheat girls.* New York: Simon & Schuster.

Sandler, B. R. (1987). The classroom climate: Still a chilly one for women. In C. Lasser (Ed.), *Educating men and women together: Coeducation in a changing world* (pp. 113–123). Urbana: University of Illinois Press in conjunction with Oberlin College.

Shapiro, A. H. (1991). Creating a conversation: Teaching all women in the feminist classroom. *NWSA Journal, 3*(1), 70–80.

Stimpson, C. (1988). *Where the meanings are: Feminism and cultural spaces.* New York: Methuen.

Thompson, B. W., & Tyagi, S. (1993). A wider landscape ... without the mandate for conquest. In B. W. Thompson & S. Tyagi (Eds.), *Beyond a dream deferred: Multicultural education and the politics of excellence* (pp. xiii–xxxiii). Minneapolis: University of Minnesota Press.

Vandrick, S. (1997). Feminist teaching in the mixed classroom. *Peace Review, 9*(1), 133–138.

NOTES

[1]The students' names are pseudonyms.

[2]Professor Eric Mazur uses this technique in a large lecture course in physics at Harvard University. In the middle of his lecture he puts a single multiple-choice question on an overhead slide and asks students to answer it. Each student then has 1 minute to convince another student sitting nearby that she or he has chosen the correct answer. Mazur reports that after this short conversation, students who change their answers do so in the correct direction a large majority of the time. A secondary effect of this interactive strategy includes higher attendance. Videotape "Thinking Together: Collaborative Learning in Science," Derek Bok Center, Harvard University, Cambridge, MA.

Chapter 13

Voicing Names and Naming Voices: Pedagogy and Persistence in an Asian American Studies Classroom

Peter Nien-chu Kiang

Noting that many Asian immigrant and refugee students may not be socially or academically integrated in college, Peter Nien-chu Kiang underlines the critical role that culturally responsive approaches can play in supporting students' persistence in their college careers. Describing one such approach, an assignment that engages students in an exploration of their names, Peter demonstrates that when content and pedagogy affirm connections to reference points that matter in students' lives, classrooms provide a space in which students can experience academic as well as social integration.

Student persistence is increasingly a focus of critical importance in higher education, not only because of the specific costs to both individuals and institutions when students do not complete their degrees but also because student retention rates are among the criteria targeted by policymakers who are demanding greater accountability from colleges and universities. The literature on student persistence suggests that student integration into the academic and social domains of college is essential. In his highly regarded synthesis of research, *Leaving College*, sociologist Vince Tinto (1993) concludes that persistence is possible with integration in one or the other but is substantially enhanced if integration occurs across both domains. In previous ethnographic work at

207

my urban commuter university, however, I have shown that many Asian immigrant and refugee students are integrated in neither domain, yet still survive in school and eventually graduate (Kiang, 1996, 2002b). These students' stories and strategies—defined in relation to classroom dynamics as well as issues such as course selection, academic advising, career preparation, and major choices—express not only how students view their reality within the university but also how they attempt to survive academically within it.

For example, students typically report that they neither ask for nor receive direct assistance from family members, friends, or school personnel. Like most informants in my studies of students' survival strategies, Khamkeaw, a Chinese Cambodian refugee, admitted, "since I came to this school I never tried to look for any help. Everything I do is on my own." Students' feelings of social isolation, in both school and the larger society, are equally striking. Danielle, a Chinese Vietnamese woman, noted about school: "In the classes, like most of the American students, they don't like to be your friend … even when you walk in the hall, you see them, they don't even say hi, or probably they don't recognize me."

To survive in school, then, these students turn to reference points outside of the university for motivation and direction. Their reference points, described in stories of refugee flight, family life, and race/gender discrimination, have enabled them to persist in college, despite their marginal relationships to the academic and social domains of the university (Kiang, 1996). It is exactly these same reference points that are explicitly recognized and affirmed in Asian American Studies courses—making the curriculum and pedagogy of these courses, or others with comparable commitments, a powerful institutional intervention that supports student persistence. Asian American Studies classrooms represent a significant space in which students do experience academic as well as social integration because the course content and pedagogy affirm connections to those family-centered and community-centered reference points that matter in students' life histories.

In previous work, I have described other aspects of Asian American Studies content and pedagogy that facilitate learning/teaching in our classrooms with working-class, immigrant students (Kiang, 1997, 2002c, 2003). In this chapter, I share examples of students' responses to one specific writing assignment focusing on their "name stories" in order to illustrate how a simple prompt in an introductory Asian American Studies course can serve not only to affirm students' identities, but also to motivate their persistence in the university by connecting directly with those same critical reference points of refugee flight, family, and discrimination. Because of its pedagogical power, I have used the following *Meaning of Names* assignment each semester whenever I have taught the course, *AsAmSt L-223 Asian Minorities in America,* during the past 10 years:

Memo #2: The Meaning of Names

Parents give children specific names for many reasons. Sometimes the meaning of a name embodies qualities that parents hope their child will become. Sometimes a name is given in honor of another individual who has been important to the family or society. Sometimes a name is chosen simply because it sounds good. In any case, everyone has stories that accompany their names.

Furthermore, when immigrants and international students come to an English-dominant society like the U.S., they often face the dilemma of either having their names mispronounced (by teachers, neighbors, co-workers, friends, etc) or having to change to new names in English. These experiences can be very powerful because one's name has such a close relationship to one's identity.

With these ideas in mind, please address the following questions in a 2–4 page memo:
1. *What is the meaning and origin of your full name? Why was it given to you?*
2. *Were you ever embarrassed by your name? If so, describe some specific examples and how you dealt with them. Also, please include any examples that have occurred here at the university.*
3. *Did you ever change your name or adopt a new name? If so, describe when and why. What did you change it to and how did/do you feel about doing it?*

THE PEDAGOGICAL POWER OF NAMES

Students have consistently responded to this assignment with deep engagement and breathtaking richness—sharing intimate, individual voices with compelling cultural insights and profound lessons about the social/historical context of teaching and learning. One student noted:

> I am usually interested in the meaning of a name but I did not think about meaning in a context. Writing this memo is a chance for me to consider and find an interesting relationship between a name with language and culture of the country. A name is not a dead word. It has an ability to tell me the origin of a language and culture as well.

By sharing stories in class about both the meaning and pronunciation of their names, students learn to recognize and refer to each other in ways that only their closest friends and family members may have practiced in the past. This process directly breaks down the social distance between students in the classroom, while also enabling them to connect an academic requirement of the course to important reference points in their own lives.

Name stories have special pedagogical importance for Asian and Asian American students, and provide significant insights for all students about issues of language, culture, identity, and power. Many Asian immigrant/refugee and international students, for example, indicate that they do not challenge the authority of their teachers or even their classmates when their names and identities are mispronounced or misunderstood. According to a Vietnamese refugee student:

> Yes, I was embarrassed by my name. My name is a hard name to pronounce because it looks deceiving. In Vietnamese the letter D can make a "D" sound or a "Y" sound. My name is pronounced with a "Y" sound. Americans only know the "D" sound. Even after they find out, they still can't say it correctly. Since the start of my education in America, I had to deal with the mispronunciation of my name. I used to hate the first day of school because the teacher would read off the name list and I would dread to hear the different pronunciation from each teacher. I would have to say my name three to four times. The whole class looked at me. I had all the attention. None of my teachers ever got my name correct. Some came close to the correct pronunciation and others didn't bother to ask me if it was correct. My ears had to bear the mistake. I hated it. I never spoke up to the teachers because they were older than me. I had to be respectful. I didn't have the courage then. America was new to me. I didn't know the language, the culture, and the food. Speaking up would create more attention. As an Asian immigrant, I didn't want any more attention in the classroom. I already look weird to my classmates. I remember one hurtful incident. Some Caucasian children made fun of my name. They left the "o" out of my name. They were all laughing and I didn't know what they were laughing about. What did "dung" mean in English? I finally found out. I was injured severely. They related me to that disgusting term. The experience was so degrading. I believe my father had given me a beautiful and meaningful name. But everybody in America makes my name sound so ugly by their mispronunciation.

Frequently, students adopt new names in order to make pronunciation and recognition easier for others. Yet, this is not an easy change to make, according to an Indian American student:

> I feel that I have had to change my name to a simpler Americanized form. Not only have I changed the pronunciation, but the meaning is lost. People do not realize the legacy and spirituality my name carries, rather it is pigeonholed as another "weird" South Asian name. I have realized that the experience of my name signifies much of my changing identity as an Indian American. As many groups who are label "not American," I tried my hardest to fit in and be as "American" as possible. This included hiding my middle name, changing the pronunciation of Ravi, and changing the pronunciation of Dixit. But after I became more comfortable about being different and realizing I would not be able to ever completely "fit in," I attempted to reclaim and celebrate my Hindu roots. And in doing that, I have rediscovered the meaning of my name.

On the other hand, when teachers do make the effort to learn and pronounce students' given names correctly, the positive emotional and educational impact on students is clear. Nguyet, a Vietnamese immigrant student, for example, wrote:

I have been in America for about five years, three years in High School and two years in University. But, not any teachers and professors can say my name exactly like the way you say. I felt surprised and happy when the first time you (the professor) called my name so clearly. I wish the rest of my professors and my American friends could say my name clearly like my "professor" so I do not have to change to American name.

These various *Meaning of Names* examples highlight an important domain of connections between students from diverse immigrant/refugee backgrounds and students with international visa status, despite their having significant linguistic, cultural, and class differences. By appreciating the power of names, we can build on the excitement and motivation expressed by Nguyet, and redirect the frustration and alienation experienced by other students—not only Asian and Asian American students but students from all cultural groups in our classrooms. In the process, we can learn much about similarities and differences in language, culture, family, and society in profound and personal ways, while modeling a fundamental commitment that respects students' identities, regardless of background.

NAME STORIES AND FAMILY EXPECTATIONS AS REFERENCE POINTS FOR STUDENT PERSISTENCE

The context of family has significant meaning for Asian immigrant/refugee and international students in relation to their responsibilities, expectations, and roles as the first generation in their families to go to college in the United States. In students' name stories, the links between culture, family expectations, and educational achievement often become clear. For example, a Chinese Vietnamese immigrant woman wrote:

> My original name was Thi Liem Dang. The name was given to me by my father. In my language it means memorizing a poem or story. My father gave me the name because he wanted me to like learning. He always tells me that it is important to work hard in school because it is the only way I can become someone important some day. Therefore I was given that name. Thi Liem Dang is a very beautiful name in my language. However, it is not so beautiful in English, because people like to mispronounce my name, and I don't like it at all.

For international students, most of whom are separated physically from their families, the name story assignments similarly remind them of connections between their given names and their families' wishes, which often relate to themes of peace and learning/teaching. Rina, a student from Japan whose parents were working in Africa for several years until just before she was born, explained:

I was born in Kanagawa, Japan where my father was raised. They [parents] gave me "Rina" from where I originated; Africa and Kanagawa. They wanted me to have a grand warm heart like the field of Africa. Whenever I asked about Africa, their eyes sparkle and say, "I never saw such a beautiful place" ... they wanted me to have such beauty inside of me. When I was in elementary school, I was too young to understand my parents' thought. Now that I am a person who is able to understand the meaning, I like my name and feel proud of knowing the profound concerns of my parents which I deeply appreciate.

Students from working-class, immigrant/refugee backgrounds also typically do not have intact families in this country. Nevertheless, family expectations motivate student achievement by exerting powerful influences through guilt and grief as well as love and pride. Reflecting on his family's survival story from Cambodia and his deceased father's continuing influence, Sokal noted:

I look through my past, you know. I say, well, I've been through this and I've seen many things. I've been through a lot of stuff that, you know, I thought I never come out of it alive. And then, you know, here's my father who brought me here ... he want you to get through education and he struggle to get here, and, you know, you don't want to disappoint your parents. It really motivates you, you know. Psychologically, that's what I live by.

For students with refugee backgrounds, in particular, their name stories also connect with family expectations that resonate deeply as motivating forces for persistence within the university.

NAME STORIES AND REFUGEE FAMILY LEGACIES

Students from Vietnam and Cambodia often carry powerful name stories that connect their identities, survival, and achievement to the wishes and legacies of parents—especially fathers—and their experiences of war, loss, and refugee migration. A Vietnamese student, for example, wrote:

My given name, Gia Thuy, came from a South Vietnamese town where my father was on duty there. "Vinh Gia" was the name of the town. "Thuy" was the name of the little boy my father happened to hear his mother calling when he was badly injured by a stray bullet. I was later told that a decision came to my father's mind that the next child, (my mother was pregnant at the time) would have that name or a combination of those names regardless of sex. This decision was like a reminder to my father that no one wanted fighting. Everyone wanted peace—lots of it. It also told my father how dire that war was, and that people, not only in Vinh GIA, but all around Vietnam, were always with THUY.

Many non-Asian immigrant and refugee students taking the Asian American Studies introductory course reveal similar connections in their own *Meaning of Names* memos each year. Indeed, their stories deserve far more attention than what is presented in this chapter. For example, the name story of one student from the Democratic Republic of Congo exposes the intersections of revolution, state policy, family legacy, and personal identity that frequently appear in name stories of Cambodian and Vietnamese students and classmates from El Salvador, Guatemala, Bosnia, Somalia, or elsewhere:

> Things change in 1974. That time I was already 14 years old. Our government decided to change all the names brought to us through colonization. None of the official documents in the country will carry those names anymore. I mean documents like birth certificate or passport or other school document and so on. So our parents have to rename us again with our ancestral names. They have to get rid of the Christian's names like in my case LEON has to disappear in all my official documents. I became KALOMBA PAKAFUA KAZADI. Here, basically I maintain my grandfather's last name as my first name and took my father's last name as our last name for the whole family. My middle name PAKAFUA means if people die in the family, still there will be someone left to carry on the continuity. That means family never die at once. This has a lot to do with my father's family; he was the only child left after losing all his siblings.

NAME STORIES' CONNECTIONS TO REFERENCE POINTS OF DISCRIMINATION

As with their refugee stories, many students in my ethnographic research have shared discrimination stories that illustrate their own and their families' experiences as urban, racial minorities and low-wage, immigrant/refugee workers. Racism in school and the workplace has acted as a powerful motivating force for students to complete their higher education. Lien, for example, recounted the sentiments of her parents' generation that served as reference points for her own educational persistence:

> They all complain that they were treated like a stupid person. And they said if they were in Vietnam, probably not the same here. Because some of them, they were teachers or dentists or somebody in Vietnam. But they went here. They was nothing. Just do something, wash dishes, something like that. Because they didn't pass the test for the dentist or something like that. And they feel terrible.

Interestingly, students' name stories frequently articulate with these reference points of discrimination as well. A Chinese Vietnamese student explained:

> I always feel that the minorities have to change much of their culture in order to survive in the American world. One of the well known example is the

name changing. I am just one of the many people who change their names. Some even change their last name, so they can find work easier. I know a person who changed his last name from Chin to Smith. Can we blame him for changing his last name and betraying his ancestors? I think he is not the person to be blamed; we can only blame on the society. You will not get equal chance to be interviewed for a job if your name is different. This is how the society is structured and the minority have to deal with it in our own ways every day.

Within a social context of both material inequality and mono-cultural hegemony, students' name stories reflect multiple strategies, priorities, and beliefs about what is best for their life in the United States.[1] Accommodation for some may represent resistance to others. Retaining one's given name might reflect family loyalty for some, whereas others view the choice as one of resisting assimilation and de-manding reciprocity in the acculturation process. A Korean interna-tional student stated:

Why didn't I Anglicize or replace my Korean name though I was the one who was eager to change my ugly Korean name to a pretty American name? At first, I wickedly enjoyed that people mispronounced my name. I wanted to let them know that speaking and pronouncing another language was not easy. I wanted to give them a hard time because I had the same.

Alternatively viewing her own name change as creation rather than sur-render, especially in the context of claiming U.S. citizenship, a Cambo-dian woman student, "Rath" explained:

I did add a new name when I became a naturalized citizen. I added "Annieratha" as my first name and I left Saroath as my middle name. I de-cided to pick a new name because I have to make my name unique and easy to pronounce. I kept the originality of my name which is "Ratha" in my new name and added "Annie". "Rath" is a very common name in Cambodia as well as with the Cambodian people in the United States. I am known as "Rath" in the Cambodian community as well as to my family here and in Cambodia. But because of all the "Rath" in Cambodia and in my family, I decided to make my name different. The reason I chose "Annie" is because it is a reminder for me of the day that I became a United States citizen, and also a new highlight of my life. It took me a very long time to actually think

---

[1]Indeed, a remarkable, recent experimental study conducted by Bertrand and Mullainathan using randomized sets of resumes with names commonly associated with either Blacks or Whites that were submitted for nearly 5,000 job openings in Boston and Chicago found that applicants with White-sounding names were one and a half times more likely than those with Black-sounding names to be invited for interviews, even though levels of experi-ence, education, and skills on the resumes were controlled to be equivalent. For further discus-sion, see: Krueger, A. (2002, December 12). "What's in a Name? Perhaps Plenty If You're a Job Seeker." *New York Times,* www.nytimes.com/2002/12/12/business/12SCEN.html

of a new name and yet keep the originality of the name. I'm very satisfied with this name and glad that I made the change and not lose the meaning nor the word of my name.

VOICING NAMES AND NAMING VOICES OVER TIME

In recent years I have coordinated one strand of our Asian American Studies Program's research agenda to assess the long-term effects of our courses in the lives of our graduates. The richness of data collected from our Alumni Research Project points to the value of sustaining connections with former students (Kiang, 2000). As one example, the following "updated" name story shared by a Cambodian American alumnus offers important longitudinal insights about constructions of identity and citizenship:

When I escaped from Cambodia with my older brother to Thailand camp, I got there and didn't know anybody at all. I had no other family members, but, fortunately, I meet one of my neighbors who lived in the same village who knew my parents, who knew my mother and father. And he said, "Since you don't have any family here, why don't you just join us? … in order to do so, you have to change your name, so you have to use my last name." I have no problem with it because being in the camp was just so hard. I mean, I would do anything just to get out …

That's my official name from that point on, but, I wasn't really conscious, I didn't have any feeling about changing my name. The reason is because nobody call me Saveth. Nobody. Even though the papers [say] Saveth Noun, but that's not me. I mean, my family, they kept calling me … they still call me Chheub. And I wasn't really conscious at all, not until I come to this country … It take me a long time to be aware that this is my name. Even though I knew that Saveth Noun is my name, but I still don't get used to it, even now. Not at all …

[At one of my first jobs in the United States] I was the only Asian who actually worked there. The first time I went there to meet the captain, and I introduced my name, he said "what's your name?" and I said "Saveth. Saveth Noun". And so, they had a hard time trying to pronounce it, and suddenly one of the guys who really liked me said, "oh, why don't I just give you a new name". He is Italian. I say "why?" and he said "it's easy to call, why not 'Frankie'? You look like Frankie". I said, "Okay, if that's what you like. Okay, you can call me Frankie". Since then they've been calling me Frankie, and I keep on introducing myself as Frankie. I never say Saveth Noun …

But not until recently, I have come to understand the meaning of homeland … homeland and [my] real name. Not until I went back to Cambodia and come back, that's when I feel like I really have to change my real name. I really have to get my real name back … The only thing that keeps me attached to my homeland is my real name, you know. When I sent my application for citizenship, I know for sure that I will lose something and get something, so when I was interviewed by INS official. We just looked at the name change and she looked at me and asked, "are you sure you want to change the whole name?" And I said, "yeah". And then before she did that, she asked me to sign the form to denounce my [Cambodian] citizenship, and then I was like, I look at it, and then suddenly I was thinking of my mother. And then she asked me, "what's going on?" I have to give up my nationality in order to become an American citizen and then I get my real name back. So it has been hard. It's really emotional at this moment, but right now I'm really excited when I go to take the oath. It will be the first day I get my real name back. I will be really proud … I have my real name, this [Heng Bun Chheub] is my real name. I want my family or people in my village to be proud. So I think that it is important to be Heng Bun Chheub, you know. It is really important.

I had three main reasons [to become a U.S. citizen]. One was definitely to get my real name back. And the second thing is it is easy to travel. I like traveling a lot. If Cambodia became peaceful and then everything is stabilized, I could always go back to reclaim my nationality. And then the third thing is that I can vote and there are a lot of things I can do with citizenship, like I can sponsor my family. Being a citizen, I have some kind of priority. Now, I'm just waiting to be officially, to become Heng Bun Chheub, you know. This is my real name now. I don't want to assume that Frankie name anymore. This is it: no Saveth, no Frankie. It's just gonna be just one. Just me, Heng Bun Chheub. For now, it's not official. I'm not official yet. I'm just waiting for that moment to come, so I can say okay, this is it.

As Saveth Noun, Chheub had taken my Asian Minorities in America course in 1991. By the time of his graduation in 1995, Saveth/Frankie was a campus student leader and an Asian American Studies teaching assistant. His alumni narrative, recorded through an interview three years later, illustrates how issues and feelings associated with his name story continue to carry profound meaning long after his graduation from college.

Clearly, a name story collected through a course assignment captures an individual's perspective at only one moment in her/his life. But the issues and meanings associated with one's name emerge and recede throughout the lifespan, particularly in response to changing contexts such as gaining citizenship, having children, or beginning jobs in new settings. By academically affirming the process of articulating and analyzing students' name stories in Asian American Studies courses, individuals gain individual precedents and collective models to reflect on and extend as they continue to construct their own lives and futures (Kiang, 2002b). There is no doubt about the clarity and conviction of Saveth/Frankie/Chheub when he asserts at age 30, "it is important to be Heng Bun Chheub, you know. It is really important."

The developmental perspectives over time reflected in Chheub's narrative also reveal how the act of seeking state-sponsored citizenship intersects with the daily activities of claiming what Chicano/Latino Studies scholars Renato Rosaldo, Bill Flores, Rina Benmayor, and colleagues have called cultural citizenship:

> Cultural citizenship can be thought of as a broad range of activities of everyday life through which Latinos and other groups claim space in society, define their communities, and claim rights. It involves the right to retain difference, while also attaining membership in society ... It includes how excluded groups interpret their histories, define themselves, forge their own symbols and political rhetoric, and claim rights. It includes how groups retain past cultural forms while creating completely new ones. (Flores and Benmayor, 1997, 262–263)

Chheub's narrative suggests that the power of names extends far beyond the context of teaching/learning, and involves a very personal but highly meaningful domain in which cultural identity and civic engagement co-mingle. And, unlike students who use the moment of gaining official U.S. citizenship to change or adapt their original given names, Chheub seizes the opportunity to reclaim his.

Furthermore, at the time of his alumni interview in 1998, Chheub was a classroom ESL teacher in an urban middle school with refugee and immigrant students from Bosnia, El Salvador, Mexico, Korea, Vietnam, Colombia, and a dozen other countries. Drawing on both his own survival skills as a refugee student and the content/pedagogy he had internalized from his undergraduate concentration in Asian American Studies, Chheub successfully developed a range of ways to motivate his own classes of newcomer students by connecting directly with their identities, cultural commitments, and struggles/dreams. Through his modeling of culturally responsive pedagogical practices such as the *Meaning of Names* assignment, Chheub demonstrated that what is taught and learned in culturally responsive courses can have long-term, cross-generational impact—creating ripples that extend far beyond the short-term effects of courses described in student evaluations or reflection memos at the end of a semester.[2]

CONCLUSION

Research and pedagogical practice show that if teachers are disconnected from the home-family-community identities and contexts of our students, especially those who are immigrants, then we can neither reach them in meaningful ways nor tap their rich, sociocultural knowledge to share with others in the classroom (Sleeter, 2001; C.

---

[2]Chheub's example also reinforces findings from our Alumni Research Project that highlight the particular, positive long-term impact of Asian American Studies courses for those who have become teachers themselves (Kiang, 2000).

Suárez-Orozco & M. M. Suárez-Orozco, 2001; E. T. Trueba & Bartolomé, 2000; H. T. Trueba, Rodriguez, Zou, & Cintrón, 1993). Yet, most educators in the United States have had little exposure to authentic Asian and Asian American perspectives through our own formal education and professional development. Without opportunities for focused study, our awareness and knowledge base in these areas are typically constrained by media images and personal experience. This is a serious limitation, given the power and pervasiveness of stereotypes of Asians and Asian Americans in mass media as well as in school textbooks and children's literature produced in the United States.

In other writings, I have highlighted the necessity to transform curricular content in both K–12 and higher education to respond to the dramatic growth of Asian immigrant populations in U.S. schools and communities (Kiang, 1997, 2002a, 2002c). In this essay, though, I am arguing primarily for the need to enhance our pedagogical commitments and skills in order to create and sustain spaces within which we are able to share and learn together successfully with our students. One particular pedagogical strategy used to great effect in my Asian American Studies courses involves recognizing the significance of students' names.

This seemingly simple classroom commitment of voicing names and naming voices has transformative pedagogical power precisely because students' name stories so often intersect with important reference points in their lives such as experiences of discrimination as well as meaningful relationships to family, community, and homeland. These stories and reference points are, in turn, validated both academically and socially within the Asian American Studies classroom, and thereby facilitate students' integration and persistence within the university. Though by no means the only pedagogical strategy at work in Asian American Studies classrooms, assignments such as this do represent specific, high-impact interventions that teachers/practitioners can readily adapt to their own teaching/learning contexts in universities, K–12 schools, and community-based settings.[3]

Finally, given the severe rise in hate crimes and discrimination targeting Arab Americans, Moslem Americans, and South Asian Americans in

---

[3]Sample resources relevant to teaching/learning and the power of names include: Wilma Mankiller's autobiography, coauthored with M. Wallis, *Mankiller; A Chief And Her People,* New York: St. Martin's Press, 1993; Linda Sue Park's novel, *When My Name Was Keoko,* Clarion Books 2002; Richard Kim's novel, *Lost Names,* Berkeley: University of California Press, 1998; and Rashmi Sharma's poem, "What's in a Name?" from the anthology, *Living in America: Poetry and Fiction by South Asian American Writers,* edited by Roshni Rustomji-Kerns, Boulder: Westview Press 1995, 67–68. In her article, "What's in a Name?" from *Teaching Tolerance* (Fall 1998: 11–14), Diane Shearer, a high school English teacher, also suggests using Ralph Ellison's essay, "Hidden Name and Complex Fate" from *Shadow and Act,* "My Name" from *The House on Mango Street* by Sandra Cisneros, and "My Name Is Sometimes an Ancestor Saying Hi, I'm With You" from *Living By the Word* by Alice Walker. A useful reference about the significance of names, though without attention to dynamics of race and power, is *The Language of Names* by Justin Kaplan and Anne Bernays, New York: Simon & Schuster, 1997.

the United States since September 11, 2001 (Gordon, 2002; National Asian Pacific American Legal Consortium, 2002), the meaning and urgency associated with name stories, particularly for those populations, demand attention. News reports have described the case, for example, of Tariq Hasan who filed papers to change his legal name to "Terry" in order to "minimize ethnic and religious discrimination in professional life" and of parents who changed the legal name of their 3-year-old Osama to Samir (Associated Press, 2002, p. A10). Thus, the power of names refers not only to effective pedagogical practices in the classroom but reveals one point of intense contact and conflict between that which is most deeply personal and most highly political within the contested domains of civic participation and democratic life in post-9/11 U.S. society.

ACKNOWLEDGMENTS

I thank Vivian Zamel, Ruth Spack, Emi Emura, Mitch Chang, Khyati Joshi, Shirley Tang, Indrani Ray, Chin-Lan Chen, Series Fung, Colleen Fong, the Institute for Asian American Studies, and many other students and colleagues in Asian American Studies at UMass Boston who have contributed to my research, teaching, and advocacy work related to the "meaning of names." I also proudly acknowledge the intention represented by my own Chinese given name, *Nien-chu,* which means *Honor your ancestors.*

REFERENCES

Associated Press (2002, March 4). Arab-Americans opting to change Muslim names. *Boston Globe,* p. A10.

Flores, W. V., & Benmayor, R. (1997). *Latino cultural citizenship: Claiming identity, space, and rights.* Boston: Beacon Press.

Gordon, R. (2002, January 11). Victims of hate crimes recount horror stories: Outpouring of post-September 11 traumas in S.F. *SF GateNews.com.*

Kiang, P. N. (1996). Persistence stories and survival strategies of Cambodian Americans in college. *Journal of Narrative and Life History, 6*(1), 39–64.

Kiang, P. N. (1997). Pedagogies of life and death: Transforming immigrant/refugee students and Asian American Studies. *Positions, 5*(2), 529–555.

Kiang, P. N. (2000). Long-term effects of diversity in the curriculum: Analyzing the impact of Asian American studies in the lives of alumni from an urban commuter university. In *Diversity on campus: Reports from the field* (pp. 23–25). Washington, DC: National Association of Student Personnel Administrators.

Kiang, P. N. (2002a). K–12 education and Asian Pacific American youth development. *Asian American Policy Review, 10,* 31–47.

Kiang, P. N. (2002b). Stories and structures of persistence: Ethnographic learning through research and practice in Asian American Studies. In Y. Zou & H. T. Trueba (Eds.), *Ethnography and schools: Qualitative approaches to the study of education* (pp. 223–255). Lanham, MD: Rowman & Littlefield.

Kiang, P. N. (2002c). Transnational linkages in Asian American Studies as sources and strategies for teaching and curricular change. In L. Jacobs, J. Cintrón, & C. Canton, *The politics of survival in academy: Narratives of inequity, resilience, and success* (pp. 141–153, 161–162). Lanham, MD: Rowman & Littlefield.

Kiang, P. N. (2003). Pedagogies of PTSD: Circles of healing with refugees and veterans in Asian American Studies. In Lin Zhan (Ed.), *Asian Americans: Vulnerable populations, model interventions, clarifying agendas* (pp. 197–222). Sudbury, MA: Jones & Bartlett.

Krueger, A. (2002, December 12). What's in a name? Perhaps plenty if you're a job seeker. *New York Times,* www.nytimes.com/2002/12/12/business/12SCEN.html

National Asian Pacific American Legal Consortium. (2002). *Backlash: When America turned on its own.* Washington, DC.

Sleeter, C. E. (2001). Preparing teachers for culturally diverse schools: Research and the overwhelming presence of Whiteness. *Journal of Teacher Education, 52*(2), 94–106.

Suárez-Orozco, C., & Suárez-Orozco, M. M. (2001). *Children of immigration.* Cambridge, MA: Harvard University Press.

Tinto, V. (1993). *Leaving college: Rethinking the causes and cures of student attrition.* Chicago: University of Chicago Press.

Trueba, E. T., & Bartolomé, L. I. (2000). *Immigrant voices: In search of educational equity.* Lanham, MD: Rowman & Littlefield.

Trueba, H. T., Rodriguez, C., Zou, Y., & Cintrón, J. (1993). *Healing multicultural America.* London: Falmer Press.

ABOUT THE
CONTRIBUTORS

Kristine Beyerman Alster is Associate Professor and Interim Dean of the College of Nursing, University of Massachusetts Boston.

Estelle Disch is Professor of Sociology, University of Massachusetts Boston.

Stephen M. Fishman is Professor of Philosophy, University of North Carolina Charlotte.

Motoko Kainose is a graduate of the University of Massachusetts Boston who went on to complete a Master's Degree in American Studies at the same institution.

Peter Nien-chu Kiang is Professor of Education and Director of the Asian American Studies Program, University of Massachusetts Boston.

Eleanor Kutz is Professor of English, University of Massachusetts Boston.

Lucille McCarthy is Professor of English, University of Maryland Baltimore County.

Martha Muñoz is a graduate of the University of Massachusetts Boston who is currently completing a graduate degree at the National College of Naturopathic Medicine.

Tim Sieber is Professor of Anthropology, University of Massachusetts Boston.

Trudy Smoke is Professor of English, Hunter College of The City University of New York.

Ruth Spack is Associate Professor of English and Director of the ESOL Program, Bentley College.

Rajini Srikanth is Associate Professor of English, University of Massachusetts Boston.

Marilyn S. Sternglass is Professor Emeritus of English, City College of the City University of New York.

Vivian Zamel is Professor of English and Director of the ESL Program, University of Massachusetts Boston.

Author Index

223

Subject Index

A

Academic discourse, 12, 27, 37, 38, 62, 64, 69, 87, 90
Academic discourse communities, 75–93
Academic support services, students' experiences with, 22, 44, 50, 118
"The Adventures of Huckleberry Finn," 184
Alienation, of students, 4, 9, 95, 100–102, 132, 158, 211
Alumni Research Project (University of Massachusetts Boston), 215–217
American Studies, student experience in, 124–125
Anthropology
  analyses of student texts in, 136–140
  multilingual students' contributions to, 132–133, 136–140
  teaching of, 129–144
Art Education
  analyses of student texts in, 65–69
  responses to student texts in, 66, 67, 70, 71
  student experience in, 65–68
Art History, faculty expectations in, 6
Asian American Studies
  analyses of student texts in, 209–217
  teaching of, 207–220

B

Background knowledge
  faculty perspective on, 146
  role of, x, 32, 87, 90, 132–133, 158
  student perspective on, 22, 29, 30, 42–43
Basic Writing, analysis of a student text in, 49–50
Biology, student experience in, 106–108
Blackboard, use of, 8, 98–99, 101–102, 104–105, 107, 108, 114

C

Chemistry, student experience in, 100–102
Chinese Literature, student experience in, 121–123
Class discussion and participation
  as a personality issue, 43
  barriers to, 9, 10, 11, 87, 107, 197
  engaging students in, 10, 90
  in Anthropology, 135
  in Chinese Literature, student perspective on, 122–123
  in Freshman Studies, 84, 98
  in Hispanic Studies, 86
  in Immunology, 109
  in International Relations, 22
  in Literature, 103–105, 185, 186
  in Philosophy, student perspective on, 114–116, 118, 156, 158–159

227